A Bear's Guide To The Tarot

Revised Edition

HARRY VEDERCHI

Illustrated by

John Mangiapane

DEDICATION

To all the Bears I have met and read cards for
And also to
The Bear Community at large

CONTENTS

ACKNOWLEDGMENTS

I am indebted to John Mangiapane who practically pioneered the concept
that there was a need for a male-centric Tarot deck, and for his work in
adapting his fantastic 'The Everyman Tarot' deck into a 'Bear Edition';
also for his input in helping me to re-shape this book from
his original concepts

BIG BEAR HUGS

FORWARD

You may ask "A <u>BEAR</u> Tarot – why?", and my response is "Why *NOT?*" You may also be asking yourself if there is a *need* for such a thing – and in my thinking it is never so much a question as a 'need' for something as much as it is a 'desire for self-validation' that causes men to seek out and create new things. The need is there for those seeking validation; if something doesn't apply to you then perhaps you do not need to seek it.

If you bought this book – and any of the Everyman Tarot Decks – you already know what a Bear is so I don't feel a need to explain it here. As a man who identifies as a Bear you may have heard yourself described by others as (I love this one) 'A subset of gay male subculture' – can we say 'marginalization'?

When I first met John Mangiapane and I discussed my idea with him, he revealed that when he was developing what would become his book 'Every Man's Tarot: Tarot and the Male Experience' that he faced a lot of negativity about the idea of it – even from the publisher of his first book. "It's TOO niche a market" they told him of his idea to create a Tarot book that was male-centric. This did not stop John from writing his book or designing and publishing his own decks.

So, have I tried to tap into a 'niche market within a niche market'? Only time will tell if my 'need for validation' was right; in the meantime I hope it brings a smile to those hairy faces I enjoy seeing so much.
HUGS!
Author Harry Vederchi

~~~

When Harry approached me with his 'Bear version' of something I had previously spent a lot of effort developing – I was flattered that I had finally 'hit a mark' for someone and agreed to alter my original card designs to fulfill his Bear vision. Although my original book and deck is 'neither totally straight nor totally gay' Harry's concept is totally gay-oriented – and I think that's great! BTW – all my decks and both our books are completely compatible with each other no matter which deck or book you chose to buy.

Enjoy!

Illustrator John Mangiapane

INTRODUCTION

There comes a time in every man's life (usually with the onset of middle age) when one day he wakes up and asks the face in the mirror just what the hell is going on. "How did I ever get here?" he asks, usually followed by "And how do I get out of this mess?" Both are tough questions without easy answers. I am not here to tell you that Tarot is the easy answer that you seek, far from it. Tarot is a tool to find the answer that you seek, not an all-knowing, all-seeing, correct answer-each-and-every-time oracle where you shuffle and flip some cards and suddenly are given the answers to the great mysteries of life. Tarot works in many different ways on many different levels - sometimes simultaneously - and no card reading will ever give the same answer to two different people. Although badly mis-paraphrased by many, Doreen Valiente wrote ' If that which you seek you find not within you, you shall never find it without,'* and encapsulated the concept of seeking, asking, searching, and knowing that characterizes Tarot. Carl Jung once said, "Who looks outside, dreams. Who looks inside, awakens. Your vision will only become clear when you look inside your heart." Your answers are deep within you, and you can tap into them using Tarot. Accept it or not, you are the master of your own destiny. Although Tarot is sometimes referred to or lumped in with 'fortune telling,' Tarot does not predict a single, unchangeable future outcome. What Tarot can do is show you the most likely outcome based on your current actions. If you like your future, continue walking down that street. If you see troubles ahead, adjust your actions accordingly and use the Tarot to monitor your progress. The problem is that most men have a difficulty with divination of any kind. Convinced by culture that such practices are anti-religion, dangerous, veiled in stuff you don't want to know, or just plain crap someone makes up off the cuff after they have gotten your twenty bucks moves Tarot into the realm of the bogey man. The funny thing is that throughout history every culture has developed some system of divination from patterns of birds in flight, interpreting dreams, examining the shapes of animal entrails, to shaking and throwing chicken bones. All of these practices developed over time and someone became adept at interpreting them so sooner or later even the most skeptical man (usually a King) arrived at the soothsayer's door hoping to get the answer they needed, not having gotten it from other 'regular' sources. We don't have to be so dramatic. Tarot is not going to tell you today's winning lottery numbers, which iceberg will hit the Titanic, or where you grandfather is going to hide the family fortune. Tarot will tell you that you have to work on strengthening your family relationships, to stop stealing from work to cover your monetary losses, and indicate this might not be a good time to take a trip. It can do this overtly at times, slapping you in the face with startling images to get your attention; other times it can happen more subtly. Science has determined that men are visual learners, so looking at and deciphering symbols and how they pertain to you should be right up your alley and a good place to start. If you like mysteries and whodunits, then Tarot will fill your bill. This is not to say the Tarot is encrusted with loopholes, red herrings, and other such literary gimmicks; sometimes all it takes is the turn of a single card for everything to fall into place.

1 - THE MAJOR ARCANA

Tarot decks are divided into two distinct parts (three if you separate out the Court Cards). These are known as the Major Arcana and the Minor Arcana, *arcana* being Latin for 'secrets.' Many people feel the two halves of the deck were once separate entities to begin with and somewhere in history they were combined creating what we see as a standard deck of 22 Major and 56 Minor Arcana cards.

The twenty-two cards (numbered zero through twenty-one) of the Majors deal with things of importance on a grand scale. These are dealings that cannot be brushed aside lightly, and even though I have stated that 'nothing is written in stone' the far-reaching effects of these cards cannot be ignored nor easily turned aside. "Karmic" describes their natures very well. It is felt that many Majors in any spread is a 'strong' reading and that no Majors appearing in a spread is neutral to weak, even though the odds of getting three or more Majors in a ten-card spread is low but not unheard of. It is the placement of the Majors - such as being the final outcome card - which is of true importance.

Some readers only read with the Majors, ignoring the Minors entirely; there are many decks out there that contain only the Major Arcana cards and nothing else. Do yourself a favor: buy a complete deck and become familiar with all the cards before you decide to ditch any of them.

0 - The Fool

The Fool is always considered a callow youth, wet behind the ears, with his head in the clouds. How do you, now in your late 30s, trying to live up to middle class American values read this card?

For one thing, this card is about individuality and being an individual. Those of us born in the 1950s post-WW2 era were told 'boys do this -*girls* do that'. Even if your father fixed truck engines he went to work in a shirt and tie -- and God forbid you should not wear a hat to church even though you had to take it off when you got there! This card is telling you it is time to explore what makes you an individual and to seek it out, without worrying whether it conforms to some ingrained standard that no one can explain to you but you were expected to follow blindly. Perhaps you wanted to work with your hands, but your family thought that was too 'lower class' and channeled you towards a desk-bound, office cubicle job you never wanted. This card says "Explore - even if what attracts you is a role not traditionally performed by men."

Another thing this card is telling you is perhaps that you take yourself much too seriously, whether you are the fundamental workaholic ("I gotta do! I gotta do! I gotta do!), or someone who just cannot laugh at himself. A closer look at the Fool reveals he is about to step off the edge of the cliff because he is not looking down. Oops! Danger, Will Robinson! I once worked for a man that was probably five years younger than I. He was trying hard to get to the top and be the youngest person in the department to get there. He could not take a joke. The other engineers in the department would set him up to knock the wind out of his sails, usually something insignificant in the whole scheme of things. In his stupidity, he would try to set me up to deflate his frustration. Unfortunately for him (and lucky for me) I was able to laugh at myself - loud and long. He never understood that as long as I could laugh at myself I was in control of the situation. Are you setting yourself up for the fall? Take a good look around you and laugh at yourself for being a jerk.

Lastly, this card is about starting over. *Change careers at 43? Are you crazy?* As men approach middle age, they tend to act more like teenagers, or as it was once put -"You are young <u>once</u>; you can be immature *forever*." However, running out and buying red convertible sports cars is only a superficial bandage. Perhaps you are being told to go out and find the real you. You have finally realized that society's general consensus about what constitutes success and security does not necessarily bring fulfillment. As long as you are open and willing to accept whatever the future may bring, you should have little time for worry about concerns of fear. It is the feeling that everything will work out that allows you to enter into this unknown quantity with a light heart.

<u>Reversed:</u>

When the Fool is reversed, it may indicate that you are afraid to be an individual – and that you are conforming to roles and role expectations.

This is not to say that being reliable or trustworthy is a bad thing; it may indicate that you are sacrificing everything to be what everyone wants you to be without regards for yourself. (Here is yet another message of the post-WW2 era -meeting the expectations of others.)

Perhaps this shows that you are afraid to make an error- no matter how small or insignificant or the fact that five minutes from now (much less five hundred years from now) no one will know, or for that matter *care*. Like police inspector _Monk_, television's obsessive/compulsive character whose handles of the three umbrellas hanging in his hallway all have to face in the same direction, you cannot do anything that is spontaneous - for fear of doing something incorrectly. When your friend beckons you to go for a moonlight swim, chilled champagne in hand, this is not the time to worry that your Speedo is up in your hotel room. Get naked - *now*, buddy!

No commitments for you! You are being so footloose and fancy free that your relationship is suffering. This could be unintentional because you suffer from acute attacks of wanderlust, or plain lust in general. It can also be deliberate on your part if you are searching for some way to get out of your present relationship.

Worst Case Scenario: no matter what you did or carefully planned, you ended up on your head. Remember, it is one thing to be a Fool; it is quite another to be stupid. While you're resting down there, remember that the only place you can look is up. It is important to accept this reversed card as a time for rethinking, not a time of defeat. When you get to the Hanged Man card (Major Arcana #12) you will understand that sometimes having your world turned upside down is a necessary thing in the long run.

1 – Magician

THE MAGICIAN

This is a card about achieving and utilizing your potential. We all take pride in a task well done particularly when we initiated it to begin with. We are not talking wasting time by mere daydreaming here; we are talking planning, using processes of deduction and even creating alternative plans that might become necessary. We can dream about what can happen, but that's the Two of Wands card. This is a card about 'going for it'. Two words associated with this card are 'manifestation,' and 'transformation.' Open yourself up to your own powers of creativity and draw the possibilities towards you.

For most of us, what we achieve as a result of our career is the 'defining moment'. How you achieve it is within your control. For a somewhat circuitous example: for some reason it seemed that in Ernest Hemingway's era the way you were taken seriously as a writer was to go on an African safari and be photographed with a dead animal. This was some macho head-trip. The fact that 'For Whom the Bell Tolls' was written from his experiences in actual war was far less important to his readers than shooting a lion. What did one have to do with the other? Absolutely nothing - but writers did it anyway. The Magician tells us that you have before you everything within your power to achieve the end you want. You have only to discover what the best way to make it work is. Ernest Hemingway's works are well written; bagging a lion was his only way of assuring you of his masculinity. The Magician says you don't have to go to those extremes to achieve your ends. They are within your grasp.

The Magician goes one step farther and speaks about our daily creativity, too. It's part of that 'Life is a journey, not a Destination' mentality. Do we squander our potentials, disregarding things that we feel are 'unnecessary' for us? The Magician says grab your wand and get moving! You cannot fail in that which you do not try, but why *stop* trying? FDR said the only thing we have to fear is fear itself. By combining the power of your will and desire *with* those of your significant other, you can accomplish things that you once believed were out of the realm of possibilities. Unions and relationships associated with this card must be equal in nature; if one partner takes a controlling upper hand the emphasis can shift from joyous sharing to narrow self-interest very quickly.

We also have a potential for *spiritual* growth. When we are in control, as opposed to 'being controlling', our minds are free to concentrate on higher things. By combining earthly wisdom with the hints gleaned from listening to your inner voice, you can develop the power to change your life and the lives of those around you for the better. What will bring you to your highest potential? What can you do to achieve your highest potential? For one man it will be climbing every mountain; for another it will be the day he and his lover get to have a mortgage-burning party. They are both achievable, and both men could even reach the other's goals. How they see those goals and achieve them will be very different.

Reversed:

When the Magician's table is overturned it speaks of loss of potential, either through interference by another party or a lack of suitable planning on our part. The card is telling us this ahead of time to let us know it is time to make alternative plans should this situation appear. The mere appearance of this card in no way guarantees that such an event *will* occur; it is merely a warning shot across our bow. This is one of the points people miss about Tarot- many of the situations that appear in the cards will NEVER happen. They are strictly a 'heads up' warning so that you can take the steps to counteract them. They reflect what can happen if the path you are taking is unchanged.

Rather than becoming the potential user, you have become the potential abuser, making plans that only benefit one person - yourself. You are possibly asking 'I thought this card was about my making myself into what I need to become?' In this reversed state you have become the trickster, the user, and the calculating manipulator. You can charm and bamboozle people with that silver tongue of yours, but you will be running out of space for burying the bodies really soon.

Perhaps the card speaks of limitations looming that may interfere with your carefully considered plans. The Magician says to accept the limitations as a temporary occurrence and utilize your potentials to find a better situation or at least deal with the present one. Remember that the power to achieve your ends is within you.

Worst Case Scenario: This card says you have lost your focus or are focusing on the wrong thing. Once again, this could merely be a warning to get your attention because you are moving down the wrong path. If you find your world has turned upside down, pull yourself by your jockstrap and start over.

2 - High Priestess

This is a card about that much-maligned word *sensitivity*. Since this book is aimed at those with male chromosomes and this card is one of those undeniably 'female' cards, how do I keep your male attention? (There are no lions to hunt *anywhere* around here...)

This is a card about becoming a counselor of sorts and using that role to expand our sensitivity. We all remember one male high school teacher that we all thought of as a friend. He could teach his subject for sure, but was always able to break it down and explain it in different ways to help you learn it. We also remember those teachers who could only teach but could never instruct us; they forgot that students are human beings and have not seen the material every day for their past 35 years of teaching. This card says you have the knowledge, you have the experience, you know the drill - but you need to listen to the needs of others. O.K., so there are 25 of you doing the exact same job in your department, but why do all the new people get trained by only a small handful of the same people every time? It may be because those people have developed interpersonal skills that you have forgotten or ignored over time. If you have all the right answers, why doesn't anyone ask *you* for help? Maybe it's because you treat everyone as though they are incompetent, and *that*, dear boy, is where sensitivity plays a big role.

The High Priestess talks about touching nature and getting to know the world around us. 'Nature' also deals with personality and character. Do you know who your next-door neighbors are? Do you know the name of the cafeteria lady or your shuttle bus driver? Do you ever hold the door open for someone? Have you ever helped the person in a wheelchair cart put their groceries on the checkout conveyor? All of these deal with sensitivity to our surroundings. You will benefit from opening up and paying attention to the sensitive side of your nature - the feeling that you are being guided (somehow) from up above. This used to be referred to as 'courting the Muse.' Artists and writers developed the best ways to 'court their Muse' to help them overcome writer's or creativity blocks, claiming that when this happened their work seemed to flow from them as though it came from outside their bodies. Today we call it the rising of the Kundalini.

Perhaps one of the harder things to deal with in the High Priestess is the fact that She knows the secrets, but you have to ask Her, and men have this incredible defense mechanism against expressing their fears (much less asking for directions). Men are told to 'tough it out', 'act tough', or the worst one of all - 'boys *don't* cry.' To express one's fear is to appear emasculated. The HP sits before a curtain that represents 'hidden knowledge' (behind the veil). If you can learn to express your needs, and that includes fears, you can gain the knowledge being withheld from you. Do not try to force this to happen! Cultivate some patience and then proceed with caution, letting things develop naturally.

Reversed:

When the HP is reversed, she represents a hardened person who has become insensitive or desensitized to those around them. Perhaps it started off as a defense mechanism, but now it is a way of life: pay no attention to anyone and they cannot hurt you. You meet all requests for aid or assistance with harsh words, and if you don't the seeker is left with the strong idea that they should never have bothered you, that they need to find someone else and leave you alone.

The alternative response is to become non-communicative. I remember an incident where a friend came over to my house and while parking her car saw my landlady coming up the sidewalk. Since they were not at all strangers, my friend tried to start a conversation with her and got no responses until they had reached the porch (30 steps in from the street) when my landlady turned and harshly intoned "I DON'T TALK TO PEOPLE ON THE STREET." {Hello? This is someone you know and you won't talk to him or her because they are standing 'on the street'?} Is this because you are not listening, or because you just do not hear?

Worst Case Scenario: You treat everyone with indifference; it makes no matter to you what anyone does or says or needs -you could care less about them. The HP represents the crossing over of ideas from the unconscious to the conscious mind. In reversal, you are closed to this receptiveness. All your interactions are flat and harsh. Mistakenly, you believe that this is 'just the way you want it.' If this card represents you - there is a lot of work that needs to be done.

{At this point I am going to get into a little discussion of the repetitious symbolism. The High Priestess, Hierophant, Justice, Moon, and sometimes the Magician sit between two columns, trees, or candles. [The Charioteer rides between two animals.] Sometimes one of them is black, the other white. The two columns represent polarity of right and wrong; you are being asked to walk between them and choose which is correct for you. If there is a veil/drape suspended between them, it usually represents some hidden knowledge that you have to discover before making a decision.}

3 - Empress

"O.K. - what's this pregnant lady have to do with us guys?" Actually, quite a lot. The Empress is about nurturing - sustaining, maintaining, and providing for. Most gender-based (or biased) societies have been ingraining this concept into men since their appearance on the planet: Men are supposed to go out and provide everything for their families by working their butts off. Not only are you expected to cut down all the trees to build your own log cabin, but you also have to clear the stones from the field you have to plow, and find time to go out and kill all your own food, too. This would later be supplanted by working 18 hours a day in factories with bad lighting and no safety features, and still later be transformed into office cubicles. The only thing that interrupted this process was the occasional war that sent you off to defend your family. If you accomplished this, you were considered 'The Good Man.' Many people still believe this is man's only role in society. My point in discussing this is that men were *expected* to do this and their satisfaction was that they *did* do this, but never were they expected to *enjoy* doing any part of this.

Nurturing implies a sense of being aware of other's needs. To provide shelter/protection means more than being able to nail roofing shingles down. Did your father work hard to pay the mortgage and maintain the yard, but your mother chose the color of the rugs, walls, and the ruffled curtains in every room? Your father provided but did not participate; it was not expected of him.

Nurturing is a part of parenting. You father may have helped you learn to shoot the hoop or catch the ball (or dig the stones or gut the deer), but once you learned to shoot that hoop, did he ever play one-on-one with you, or were you expected to go out and find your own playmates. Did you ever hear the phrase 'Raising the kids is my wife's job' from an adult male? The Empress is about bringing things to fruition by following them through the process and then enjoying the result of the labors needed to get them there. {That is why she is usually pictured as an expectant woman.} Other definitions of 'nurture' include 'promote, encourage, and strengthen.' You are being asked to promote, encourage, and strengthen the bonds between you and others.

Self-nurturing is implied, too. Some men, particularly workaholics, work to achieve an end and have no life in the process; they don't know how to fit it into their schedules. Everything is geared for 'the end result' and nothing is geared for the present. Maybe your old man could have been a decent drummer or trumpet player, but his old man was not about to waste <u>his</u> hard-earned money on music lessons. That fact that your father could still have sweated his balls off working in a warehouse by day and blowing his horn to earn some money and relax at the same time on weekends never occurred to Grandpa. He would have expected your father to take three lessons and blow a horn like Harry James.

Reversed:

When the Empress is off her throne there is a strong sense of detachment present in your life. You have broken life up into little pigeonholes or parcels and you only deal with them one at a time (never three or four at once) and only on your terms. When you wrap that little parcel up, even if it needs attention, it is 'out of sight - out of mind' while you go on to the next. Maybe you're one of those people whose idea of straightening things up is to put everything away behind cabinet doors; the room looks good, but dare to open one of those doors and a pile of debris hit the floor. All you'll do then is put it behind another door.

There is no sense of life, only living. The counterpart is that you are not living, but merely surviving, and that does not mean it is due to extenuating circumstances such as your ideal company had downsized you. It says you have put yourself into one of your pigeonholes and contact with those around you, even those with whom contact could be good for you, is minimal. Living in that world of the undead, your focus is only upon yourself and your list of wants: I want to be a junior partner by age 22. I want to be a full partner before age 30. I want my own office with a staff of four by age 36. I want….

Worst Case Scenario: You are unaware of the needs of yourself **or** others. You scour the countryside looking for free firewood (chainsaw always at the ready) but you never offer some to an elderly neighbor. In a parking lot, you and the guy across from you both back out and hit each other - your concern is in laying blame. You really need to see a doctor about that ingrown toenail, but you don't want it to interfere with your golfing schedule because you are in a lifetime grudge match against your brother-in-law who is a total waste of brain cells in your opinion. Have you missed important family milestones because they focused on someone other than yourself, so they were not important to you?

4 - Emperor

Of all the 'masculine' cards in the deck - which includes the Knights and Kings - the Emperor is the card that screams <u>masculinity</u>. He is the man with the biggest brass pair, prominently displayed through his business suit (as though you could miss them) yet protecting them with a hockey goalie's hard cup. You wonder how he rides a bicycle.

The Emperor is the symbol of dominant male authority. His appearance usually indicates a superior of some type, either a judge in a court of law, the CEO of a company, or simply 'the Boss.' He sits on his stone throne surrounded by rams' heads and wears full armor under his robes - indicating both a warlike attitude and an air of constant defense. He may have fought his way to the top, and now that he is there he is in a constant state of alert, ensuring his dominance by always being prepared. For the Emperor, the price of getting there has not been forgotten. The gray hair and beard may be prematurely begun, brought on by his stresses.

Alongside these qualities (in fact - hand in hand with them) is the Emperor's ability to organize both himself and others. He is the general who makes all the tactical decisions and his orders are always carried out to the letter. The safety of others is his responsibility, and he bears it with great pride. General George Patton is the embodiment of the Emperor card.

"O.K." you're saying, "He's a hard-assed bastard. Now what?"

The Emperor deals with the material world and material things, in counterpoint to the Empress card. His world is a world of practicality. He makes the plans, thinks them through then makes a decision. Unlike the Magician who manipulates his world for his own ends, the Emperor manipulates others (in good and bad ways) to achieve an end that will be good for all involved. His decisions are based on years of work, sweat, and heeding the counsel of others in whom he has placed his trust. It is now his turn to give counsel.

The Emperor's work is 'meaningful' work. Although he may have a great understanding and appreciation for the finer things in life, he appreciates other's ability to create music or art, but he himself does not create or participate in them. He may be moved by music played by a fine musician, but does not consider 'playing music' to be a 'real job.' Meaningful work must be practical; practical work brings you financial rewards. Money (and the possessions that money can acquire) is the bottom line. Even if he realizes he cannot take it with him when he dies, he knows those he leaves behind will be well provided for in his absence.

In his defense, he is a warm human being under it all; the masculine trappings obscure him from view. He knows he can motivate people with a harsh, cold exterior, but also knows obedience is mechanical and wants you to be motivated by trust, not hatred. As far as a relationship goes, one partner may dominate the union in a rigid or authoritative manner. However, as rigidly conservative or stuffy as these relationships appear, they are solid as rock and will far outlast many others. Cultivate fairness, objectivity and be flexible in your judgements.

Reversed:

The reversed Emperor speaks of unrewarded efforts - that is - you are working and working and pushing and doing and you are getting nowhere. Perhaps you never leave work on time (intentionally or unintentionally) and do all sorts of additional work that gets you nowhere you want or need to be. Under whose design are you working this way? The problem with working on salary is you only get paid your salary and all that overtime is really 'free' work. Are you working 'for free?' Is a canned ham or a free turkey your company's idea of a holiday bonus?

In reversal, perhaps rewards have no value to you unless they are monetary. Sometimes the rewards of a job can only be seen in minor steps or small ways, such as so-so pay but great benefits and all you are looking for is that 5% a year, which everyone gets no matter how hard they work. Perhaps your company hands out monthly attendance or 'variance free' awards (yeah, I know- paper is cheap by the box) and you put yours through the shredder at break time. For you it isn't an accomplishment unless it's a BIG accomplishment, that it's only a Human Resources gimmick.

Worst Case Scenario: Workaholism. The Emperor sits at the top of the heap, surrounded by challenges, yet deals with them all. He can even relax as long as he knows things are being taken care of. However, in his reversed state nothing matters. It is work-work-work do-do-do work-work-work some more and keeps going on top of that. There is no enjoyment to anything at all connected with the job, and away from the job he only can think about the job. The concept 'it's lonely at the top' rings all too true, for the reversed Emperor is out of control, treats coworkers badly, and treats people farther down the corporate ladder with distain and distrust. The power behind the Emperor is maintained by balance, and until balance can be restored, this reversed Emperor is a miserable sonofabitch to work with, much less for. Pity his family, if he actually has one.

5 - Hierophant

THE HIEROPHANT

Yes, another bastion of male power- the church. However, this card is not about religion but rather about structure, roles in structure, and functioning within structure. I should probably add 'constricted structure' or 'confining structure.' I'll concentrate on the more 'positive' aspects first.

Most large and long-standing corporations (yes, the Church can be considered a corporation) are based on structure and hierarchy. Early in their formation, they discovered what worked and what didn't, and what didn't was discarded immediately. Who is in charge of what is quickly and clearly defined; there is no question of what must be where at what time. This is accomplished through defining who has the authority, and who doesn't, and what roles come into play. Longevity is acquired by organization that is better than your rivals' system of organization. The fact that institutions such as Yale, Harvard, the Catholic Church, or even Microsoft are still around and functioning bespeaks of structure, hierarchy, and organization. Knowing what works and doesn't work is a good thing. {Thank God for Pope John or we'd be in the twenty-first century listening to Latin mass.}

The problem with Mr. Pope in the Hierophant card (probably due to the weight of the oversized drag queen Madame Butterfly headdress he's wearing) is that he is afraid *of* change, or afraid *to* change. Any long-standing institution will do nothing that will jeopardize itself. Their mentality is "It has <u>always</u> worked this way; to consider changing it is not an option," or "If it ain't broke, don't fix it." What happens next is that they refuse to look at anything, even if it may improve the situation because that may 'change' things. {They think shaving your face with a sharpened clam shell *great!*} "This is the way it is; this is the way it works; this is the way it shall stay." If echoes of *Fiddler on the Roof* have suddenly sprung to mind, you are grasping the idea that this card is about conventional mores, conventional belief systems, the establishment, and tradition.

In general terms, the appearance of this card in a spread usually refers to a person the Querent respects and seeks/will seek out for guidance. They are kind and very fair, but will be conservative in their advice. The card can also refer to an institution such as a church, college, the court system, or a corporate body. If this card has appeared in a spread concerning a question about sexual issues or problems, it tells that you and your partner might both benefit from doctor's visit or may need to seek some counseling.

Reversed:

It's the SDS, Kent State, and the Attica prison riots all over again. Rebelliousness is the word of the day, and you are doing everything within your power to make sure that nothing survives. What is old is 'bad,' what is new is 'good', and even if it isn't - 'new' is the new name of the game. All the rules, lessons, and mores of your parents make no sense to you - so out the window they go, the faster the better. It doesn't even have to make sense; it only has to be the total opposite of what has gone before. Whatever something stood for, you're against it. Other people try to extend their influence by trying to tell you how things must be; if you are not careful you might start believing in them.

The 'positive' note of reversal (yes, there can be such a thing) is that you may be *unable* to conform. When the Pol Pot regime created the killing fields, they destroyed anyone who would not conform to 'their' norm. This card says you have found yourself in a situation where you cannot conform to someone else's demands. Perhaps it is time to seek the new job, get the divorce, get out and get out from under what you see as oppression. The *structure* is failing you.

Worst Case Scenario: those around you see you as 'argumentative'. Always contrary to what others are doing, always acting in antisocial ways, you delight (if I can use that term) is going out of your way to do the total opposite of what is expected for no other reason than that is what you always do. Anyone who brings a shortcoming of yours to your attention is confronted or attacked, even if they are your superiors. I once worked with someone who deliberately put on his 'act' whenever he felt a need to shake things up, intimidate new hires, or because he was bored. His ritual of histrionics was amazing. One day he was trying to berate me for something very minor and he carried on in front of his supervisor about it, doing this 'mad scientist' routine, including the BWAHAHAH laugh. I looked him in the eye and said 'You know, they have better medications for that now,' and walked away from him and his supervisor. He was fired not too long after that. For people like him Life is one big confrontation.

6- Lovers

The Lovers card is about balance (<u>no</u>, the Temperance card is about finding the middle of the road). Whenever this card appears in a spread, the Querent's general response is that it refers to them and their significant other. Although it can (and does, on occasion), it is about interpersonal relationships, and not necessarily sexual ones. The Lovers card deals with partnerships, work and social; it deals with compatibility of personalities and styles. It is the dynamic of the two people involved that creates the success or demise of the partnership.

The balance also implies integration - of male and female roles or expression. ("Oh, no - I HATE pink!" you're thinking). Let's look beyond the superficial. In the late 1970s I worked with a man who had a wife and two small daughters who would buy him shirts for Father's Day and such, usually flowered. He flatly refused them, saying that he would wear just about anything, but <u>no</u> flowers! They relented, and bought him a shirt of a vibrant, disgusting blue, so bad that several of us suggested it have a short encounter with a bottle of cheap bleach. My roommate had a hard time accepting a flowered couch. I told him that he'd better be careful or he'd come home to a living room with ruffled Priscillas (those are curtains like your grandmother had.) Anyway -

No discussions of finding your 'inner child', or 'inner woman' here. By integration, I mean integration of sexual expression. At the beginning of the twentieth century, sex was a procreative act. Couples did not 'feel' anything; anyone who professed otherwise to their doctor was considered strange or deviate. Women who did 'feel' something during sex were subjected to (or asked for) a clitoridectomy. About the time of World War One, the concept that sex could be recreational AND accepted was beginning to emerge. However, 'good sex' was the 'man's job' to achieve. Well into the 1950s and later, women did not initiate sex, and many will tell you that they didn't enjoy it, anyway. Moral and religious prejudices had a lot to do with it. In the 1980s, older men (men in their 50s and 60s) ran into The Liberated Woman who actually told their man 'what' they wanted and 'where' to do it! These men were amazed! 'Finally' the burden to have good sex - which up to that point meant guessing what they were supposed to do - was a mutual thing!

So - what does this have to do with integration or expression or compatibility? Here at the start of the twenty first century, more and more men and women in their 30s are buying houses alone, and living alone, even if they are 'in a relationship'. My grandmother would have wondered why a single woman would buy a house - and why she wasn't married by 22 years of age in the first place. Do you remember all those jokes about the young man & woman getting married and what a disaster her first attempt at cooking was supposed to be? After all, she had always lived with Mom who was supposed to show her how to cook! {As Phyllis Diller once said, 'The only thing I learned at my Mother's knee was what a skinny knee looked like.'} I remember some straight married friends having a discussion where he asked her when she was going to do the laundry. Her reply was along the lines of: "You have two masters' degrees; I'm sure you can figure out how to work a washing machine." Integration.

As more and more same-sex couples appear, the same process happens. Is our only icon of a same-sex couple Felix Unger and Oscar Madison? Kate & Allie? As I said earlier, this card is about partnerships, work and social; also the compatibility of personalities and styles. It is the dynamic of the two people involved that creates the success or demise of the partnership. We are aiming for success.

Reversed:

When the Lovers card is reversed we speak about unbalanced roles and unequal expectations. The hardest lesson about being male to unlearn is the idea that some ONE (singular) has to be in charge, has to make every decision, has to have the final say in absolutely everything. Sometimes some ONE does have to be in charge; my company has over 9,000 employees - someone has to run controls over the 9,000 different points of view on how things should be done. But - in a partnership?

The truth is, your parents probably did not have the smoothest relationship, either. However, somewhere along the line (hopefully discretely and not in front of their children) they locked horns and battle lines were drawn and terms were accepted on both sides. Many a blind eye was turned on many things. Some of these things might not be accepted as being 'healthy' today. This card says that things are being turned on their heads. It may be good; it may be bad.

Worst Case Scenario- Imbalance turns into dominance. Someone in this relationship sets themselves up as a majority of one and no one else, including their partner, has any say in the matter. Only total control will be their accepted outcome, and they will mastermind everything to gain and keep control. It can begin very subtly, such as asking where you were and with whom and escalate into blaming you for the way they feel or act. Hand-in-hand with this is Total Avoidance - the abused spouse that is afraid to leave an abusive relationship for fear of what their partner will do to them in retaliation. They are always making excuses for their spouse's behavior, or feel that no matter what they do, their partner will always be angry with them.

7 - Chariot

The Chariot is a card about moving forwards, although some feel the card is about transportation. ("Yeah! A card about a new car!" some guys are shouting.) No, the Chariot is about daring to take the initiative. Skip the two sphinxes, horses, unicorns, or whatever your deck has pulling the Chariot - they are always one black and one white and represent opposing forces. This card is about making a decision and being in control. There are one-legged skiers out there, survivors with bionic limbs entering and winning athletic competitions, and men in wheelchairs playing basketball. They are doing things no one thought were possible, much less that these particular men could accomplish them, and yet these men are. They said: "I want to do this and will not accept the limitations you are forcing upon me." Quite truthfully - they all were afraid of failure, and did fail along their way, not once, but many times. However, due to luck, sheer determination, or just plain pride, they did what they set out to do. Competitive aspects aside, they set out to do what they decided they would do. The Chariot they ride has to do with self-control, ambition, and success. This card represents the power of your own will. Stay centered and stay in control.

Inherent in this process is the idea of *recovery.* All the doctors, hospitals, and physical therapy can only do so much. The medical world can heal or correct the physical, but they can't make you *whole*. This is where moving forward can come in. I am not talking 'miracles' here - I am talking the determination that makes you stand up and demand a recount or demands that your performance review itself be reviewed. Recovery from the loss of a loved one that brought the world as you knew it to an unexpected end. When my roommate died, I attended a 'memorial' at the hospital where he'd died - held every three months - for the families of the deceased. When his name was read, I felt nauseous and started crying since being there brought back all the unhappy remembrances of his death. When the memorial was over there was no coffee and cake or reception of any kind. The effect was to make me relive a state of horrid despair and then strand me there without any way to release the emotions that were unleashed. I left wishing I had never attended. It took years to work that trauma out.

The Charioteer has a strong sense of adventure; however, unlike The Fool who is mindlessly out for a walk, the Charioteer is going places. The early Mercury Space Project astronauts were all Charioteers, boldly going...nah, that phrase is over-used. But you get the idea. People who start their own companies, look for a better way, a faster way, or seek to make improvements in their world are all Charioteers. Perhaps their sense for adventure is also a release, releasing themselves from ways that held them back or from stagnant ways of thinking or being. They are releasing themselves to move forward.

No one says any of this is going to be easy. The Charioteer looks like he is calm and cool and in control. In reality, he makes it look very easy when underneath it all he is sweating like hell. You may never know of his innermost struggles; you only see his smile as he flips you the bird when he skis past you on one ski while you extricate yourself from the snow pile you inadvertently plowed into trying to show off.

Make it look easy, and never let them see you sweat. Smile all the way to the bank, but don't drop the reins.

Reversed:

The Chariot has overturned and dumped the Charioteer on his ass or his head, both parts being interchangeable. This may have been caused by hesitation, something that stalls you out while you try to move forward. It can be from an outside source or of your own making. Everyone has a desire to exercise caution, particularly if they are unsure of what they are getting into. In reversal, this card is telling you "He who hesitates is lost" in eight-foot high letters.

In reversal, you can also be being warned of high anxiety or stress that will eventually derail your carefully laid plans. Remember - Tarot can be warning you not of what will happen but what *can* happen, and here you are being warned that an upset is coming your way, so heads up dude! It may be warning you that you are not in as much control as you believe you have, so be careful.

Worst Case Scenario-The reversed Chariot is not warning you about stock market crashes, major catastrophe, or a philandering lover with a STD. It is about being highly cautious to overly cautious, so much so that you paralyze yourself with fear before you even take the first steps. In this instance you derail yourself through your own actions, causing your own downfall by tripping over your own feet.

8 - Strength

Hmmm - a card that some men can relate to; after all - brute strength is the final answer, isn't it? That mentality helped Attila the Hun, Alexander the Great, and Caesar's legions dominate their known worlds. If they don't like your way of thinking - just beat the crap out of 'em until they come around to seeing your viewpoint. In older editions of Tarot decks the Strength card is exactly that; usually it's Hercules ripping apart the jaws of a lion. (Is that masculine enough for you?) Old Italian decks call the card 'Sforza', which translates out to 'force' or 'fortitude.' {Interesting side note: the oldest surviving Tarot deck was created in the Fifteenth Century for the Sforza family.}

Perhaps this card could have better been called 'Using Strength,' or 'Wisely Using Strength.'

If you look at The Rider deck you will notice that the figure in the deck is <u>not </u>ripping the lions' jaws apart - it is CLOSING them. In fact, the lion has its tail between its legs. Overhead floats the lemniscate (the figure '8' on its side) which is the universal symbol for 'Infinity' {And if you're old enough you may remember it from the opening of the old 'Ben Casey, M.D.' TV shows.} Not only does this card hint that the character has infinite powers, it also indicates that his strength comes not only from within but from a higher source. Will you use brute strength to rip the lion's jaws apart and kill it? Or will you close the lion's jaws and subdue it?

Face it: we all have a coworker who cannot seem to do more than five minutes worth of anything. They are popping their head over your cubicle wall to ask you how to do something or just to shoot the breeze considering you cannot find the top of your desk from all your work. You work with your right hand ready to fold into a fist. The next time his silly mug appears - WHAMMO! A right hook to the jaw! HR will probably write you up for 'creating a hostile work environment.' The Strength called for here is more of a 'kind understanding.'

Another type of Strength is 'controlled power.' Imagine if you will, two men - one in his 30s, the other in his 60s. Mr. 30s does weight training and works out. His muscles ripple, the 'six-pack abs' are there, and he bench-presses enough iron to make a new Volkswagen Beetle ®. His theory is: 'If you're not here to sweat - get lost!' Mr. 60s practices Tai Chi. His workout consists of a series of predetermined movements done in a ritualized order; his workout is almost ballet-like in execution. His strength comes from within. His theory is: 'Anger is like a cracked cup; it will never be contained and never be filled." {I know - sounds like an old 'Kung Fu' episode}. Each of these men do what they have determined is correct for them: Mr. 30s can punch his way through a cinderblock wall; Mr. 60s will assume the correct mind frame and *walk* through it.

'Strength of Character' or determination. The Strength to carry on in spite of all odds. When I wrote my first book, there was almost two years between its completion and being accepted by a publisher; another year before it hit the shelves. It was three and a half years between the first word being written and walking into a bookstore and finding my book for sale. I greased all the right gears; I did everything I had to promote myself. I did not give in to a publisher who wanted me to pay them $11,000 for the privilege of printing my book! The book was within me; I merely had to find the right avenue to get it out. You achieve your goals when you look to those areas of your life where you find your true strength.

Reversed:

When Strength is reversed the lion gets the upper hand and attacks. In this position is says you are someone who uses force first, reason later. And not just any force: we are talking anything and everything gets an unmediated reaction, i.e. sending a B-52 to take care of a mosquito. There is no forethought - only reaction and it is always an aggressive reaction. This works well in the final quarter of the Superbowl where fortunes and history can be made ... but you are only playing 'shirts and skins' with some friends.

This aggression rolls itself over into road rage where someone tries to legitimately pass you and you cut him or her off so that they can't get to the stop sign before you do. This is rival gangs who only exist to antagonize other gangs. It spills over into racial tensions, gay bashing, and ends in anarchy.

Worst Case Scenario: Loss of control, loss of will. Think 'Mad Max' movies where the last man standing wins, no matter whom is right or wrong to begin with. Think hatred fueled by bias. If you cannot confront your own inner demons and release the pent-up energies that you are holding back and/or are being held back by, you can never achieve release or peace.

9 - Hermit

The Hermit is seen as the male version of "Calgon! Take me away!" The Hermit probably at one time said "I'm as mad as hell, and I'm not going to take it anymore!" Whichever version echoes your sentiments, the Hermit chucked it all, shucked everything he knew and decided the only one he could depend on was himself. Separated from the madding crowd he is reborn, dependent on no one - searching for the answer to the Great Mystery of Life. In losing everything, he has gained everything. He stands on top of a mountain, lantern in hand, lighting the way for the ones who come after him. In our version it appears to be a younger version of himself.

Cut to the real world - The Hermit sounds so noble - is he for real? Are we supposed to hike into the woods on an eternal camping trip, live off roots and berries, wash our clothes on a rock? Live without cell phones, email, polar fleece ®, or deodorant? This will make me a better person?

The Hermit is about living your own life, or better still, learning about living your own life and not trying to keep up with the Jones. Do you have one of those neighbors who has to have a bigger <u>(fill in the blank)</u> than anyone else on your block? Did he measure your new deck so that he could be sure to remind you that his new deck is two feet longer? Do the guys at the gym discuss who has the biggest this, the newest that, and the most expensive other thing? Do you get tired of comparing your own happiness with other people's success? You are a prime candidate for learning to live your own life.

Perhaps you are middle-aged or retired and find you have a lot of time on your hands. Becoming the Hermit means that instead of shutting yourself up, you should be seeking daily fulfillment or providing meaningful actions. Perhaps you have always wanted to try your hand at oil painting. Maybe you have an eye for color or picture composition but you were concerned on how to get started. Sometimes jumping in and doing is best; perhaps taking a painting class at a museum or crafts center can provide you with the basis and springboard to contentment for the rest of your life. You enjoy the ocean, you learn to paint - you paint the ocean! Maybe no ultra-chic New York gallery is going to come knocking on your door, but you will paint for the satisfaction of it.

Perhaps your role as the Hermit will involve the teaching of others, for this card can also indicate others look to you for strength and encouragement. {In this version of the card, the Hermit is lighting the way for a man who bears a resemblance to his younger self.} Rather than casting yourself into the role, you have had it thrust upon you. In this day of computer-aided just about everything, you still remember how to do mechanical drafting. In one of the Adult Education centers I taught at there was an older woman who taught an old-fashioned dictation class. People wanted to learn shorthand - not for dictation - but for taking lecture notes! Imagine - doing something with a paper and pencil in the twenty-first century! Passing that skill on, as dated as it is, was a sense of fulfillment for her. The Hermit is not about retreat as much as it may be about 'recharging.'

In a strict sense, this card represents celibacy or a temporary withdrawal from sex or sexual activity! By the same token, its appearance can also signal the end of abstinence. The Hermit can be telling you that your loneliness is about to end.

Reversed:

The Hermit slips from his lofty peak; his lantern goes out, his old walking stick snaps in two and he lands completely flat on his ass. Discontentment is rife in his life; nothing is right, nothing goes right. Gone is civility and reason. They are replaced by distrust brought on by disillusionment. The first thing a reversed Hermit might be telling you is that you are/were seeking the wrong goal, or seeking a goal in the wrong way. Your lantern did not blow out- it was put out by refusing to see, as though you had blinders on.

You may also be being told that you have unexamined goals- that you once had and discarded, either by yourself, due to circumstances, or by the intervention of others. You are being told to pick up the lantern, re-light it, and see what is standing in your way. You feel alone and dejected and are wasting energy feeling sorry for yourself. Take advantage of this time to go on retreat, get back in touch with your deity, or seek out spiritual teachers.

Worst Case Scenario: You may also be being told you are lost in roles that you cannot fulfill or should not have taken on. In error there can be wisdom, but only when you see that you have been making a mistake. Perhaps you are following the lead of another, and they are leading you astray or do not have your best intentions at heart. You are being warned that someone is out to do you no good.

{PS – 'Calgon' was a popular bubble bath in the 1960s & 70s.}

10 - Wheel (of Fortune)

THE WHEEL

Just like on the TV game show or on a roulette table, the Wheel spins around and around and where the ball stops will be anyone's guess. If we look at the old decks which have four figures on the wheel and translate the banners they hold, they would read: 'I *shall* reign,' ' *I* reign,' ' I *have* reigned,' and 'I am *without* reign.' It all depended on which side of the card was upright when the cards were dealt as to how it should interpreted **, for the Wheel deals with opportunities, changes, and risk.

You are walking by the company bulletin board when a sign catches your eye: the Company has immediate openings in ... Malaysia. "*Malaysia*?" you ask, "Who wants to move to *Malaysia*? Where the hell IS Malaysia?" You walk away scratching your head. If you had the upright Wheel in your reading ("I reign") you might be the first one in the office, inquiring about the positions. Samuel Clemens (Mark Twain) is quoted as saying "An opportunity seldom looked as good approaching as it did after it had passed." The Wheel deals in opportunity and what may seem confusing on the surface could be the opportunity of a lifetime. However, until you walk in that office and ask, it is another opportunity passing you by. This is where the risk is involved. The card merely being upright does not guarantee success any more than the reversed card guarantees failure. The opportunity is there; is it the opportunity that you need? A favorite saying of card readers is 'Tarot is not written in stone.' In the 1960s, Jerry Herman and several others created the very successful musical 'Mame' from the writings of Patrick Dennis. Buoyed by their unparalleled success, the same creative team created the musical 'Dear World' based on Giraudoux's 'The Madwoman of Chaillot', and even got two of the 'Mame' stars to be in it. It was a turkey that barely lasted a month before closing. How could one show be so right and the other so wrong? Risk. {Note: Angela Lansbury starred in both and won a Best Actress Tony Award for both shows, so being in 'Turkey of the Year' didn't hurt her a bit. Remember that.) Risks have to be taken, changes have to be made. Chances come and go. The cards can only tell you of the looming possibilities; the final choice is yours. I remember (in my youth) a story where in a small town one summer, not one, but three circuses were coming to town. The family was poor, so they asked the child which circus they wanted to see. The answer came back 'I'll take the first circus.' As the summer progressed, the family found the money not only to go to the second, but to all three circuses. 'I'll take the first circus' became their family motto - taking the first opportunity when it comes, but not cutting off future possibilities by being short sighted.

Reversed:

A reversal of Fortune can mean many things. In the old Wheel card mentioned above, the figure at the bottom (usually being crushed under the Wheel) is 'without reign,' meaning, rather painfully, 'I never had it and I never will.' Perhaps you receive no 'good' changes because you are stuck in your routines and never <u>allow</u> changes to happen, or resist them mightily when they do. You are being told you miss opportunities because you are resistant to change. Take the Wheel out for a 'spin' instead of just spinning your wheels.

A reversed Wheel can indicate boredom or stress. Boredom in that we will not inquire into the job in Malaysia, even as an intellectual exercise. What was it Goldie Hawn said in the movie 'Private Benjamin' - "Guam? I can't go to Guam - my hair will frizz!" Make all the excuses you want and you will stay in your boring little rut forever. Stress- or rather the ability to try to alleviate any more stress from happening by not changing anything will get you just as far, too.

Worst Case Scenario: You avoid changes to avoid risks. In avoiding either or both, you deny yourself opportunities, and like the spinning of the wheel, you will be literally 'spinning your wheels' and get nowhere. You feel that you are at the mercy of Fate- without rhyme or reason. Remember that 'what goes around comes around' and that a cycle is about to start and about to propel you in another direction.

**{Side note: The only time you would see a card on its 'side' is the second card dealt in a Celtic Cross spread which is called the 'cross card.' This card influences the effect of the first card (which is upright or reversed) and lays across it, so either its left side figure ("I *shall* reign') or its right side figure ("I *have* reigned") would then be 'upright.' This adds to the possibilities for interpretation of the spread. Most modern card readers will tell you the second card influences the first, but in being 'sideways' - it is neither positive nor negative. The old four-figure card has definite polarity! The closest this comes in a modern deck is in the Robin Wood Tarot where the Wheel has eight figure/faces on it, emoting from sheer joy to utter devastation, and back.}

11 - Justice

Without a blindfold, the all-seeing Justice sits with scales and sword in hand. What does 'justice' mean, anyway? The definition varies from simple 'honesty' to 'vindictive retribution' - YIKES! Where do you fit into this vast desert between two poles? [Slight detour: there is a difference between #11 Justice and #20 Judgement: Justice has to do with fairness, neutrality, and tolerance; Judgement has to do with decision, obligation, and resolution.] The gut reaction to this card is the legal system or a court judge handing out a verdict or at the very least the Querent's lawyers. So to some degree Justice and Judgement overlap and the upright appearance of this card traditionally 'indicates' a judgement in the Querent's favor.

The Justice card is about having compassion and exercising compassion. In the callous world of the twenty-first century, the reporters doing the 'story' bring world events into our living rooms, receiving instantaneous analysis, commentary, and judgement. You set yourself up as judge and jury, make a decision, and go on to the next story. This attitude of judgement carries through into everything you do; you apply it to the people on the bus, your coworkers, and your family. Soon, as actor Robert Blake used to do in the talk show days of his early career, you start to pass judgements and talk like your opinion is golden and, because if *you* said it, it has to be right. ("Dat's de name of dat tune.")

But this card is NOT about judging. It is about trying to understand the needs, and also understanding the why and the 'how come?' Sometimes the results are not pleasant; sometimes there is no correction for the situation. Sometimes NOT judging is the answer. A friend of mine is a soft touch for a stray cat; she daily feeds a bunch of them in a deserted lot. You can't feed every stray cat in the world, right? Wouldn't it be better to 'let nature take its course'? She also traps the strays and the feral cats and at her own expense has them spayed or neutered. In this way she is helping to control the spare cat population and still indulging her love of cats. She is making a tiny dent in a large world.

There is no one in these United States that has not been panhandled at one time or another. Face it- you don't know if these people have concealed weapons, are on drugs, or will use any money you give them to buy food and not buy drugs. It's very easy to stereotype the homeless and the needy. Once, I was hired to play Santa to a soup kitchen, and found myself surrounded by the expected low-income people. I also found a family of people whom were dressed much better than the rest and wondered what they were doing there. It turns out the night before their entire house burned to the ground, destroying all their possessions, including the family car. Stereotypes flew out the window! Santa Claus being the ultimate philanthropist, treated everyone they with equanimity. An outsider to the situation may not have been so nonjudgmental. You should practice Justice by understanding the needs of others. Making your donations to a trustworthy charitable organization may not save the whole world, only a little portion of it.

Justice tells you that you may find yourself in a situation where you may have to give encouragement or guidance to someone. Guidance is not judgement. Did you have a guidance counselor in high school that pushed everyone to go to his former college? Were you ever asked, "Why do you want to go THERE?" Guidance means giving someone the opportunity to see or find all of the options and that helps them to make their own decision. The sword is there to help remove the bad or wrong choices, and the scales to help them achieve balance. Their balance may not be your balance.

Justice says you have to have an unselfish concern in your dealings, being as altruistic as possible. Just because you do not like a particular person does not mean you cannot be fair in your dealings with them. Part of justice is being impartial and as objective as possible, not how large is your piece of the pie.

Reversed:

Reversed Justice says that you treat everyone and everything with suspicions, the sword swings widely and wildly. Cut it off! Cut it out! No reasons for long thought processes or understanding- just stab that sword and make them bleed! You are an island unto yourself and need on one coming up to you with pleas because you have already made the decision. Strangers beware!

On its head Justice's scales cannot function. You may be dealing with feelings of prejudice towards others for personal reasons or for slights real or imagined. Right or wrong, give or take does not matter as long as you are right and get to take. In the 1960s musical 'The Roar of the Greasepaint" the game of Life is played out between the 'Haves' and the 'Have-nots.' The first rule of the game is that the rules must be changed so that the 'Haves' will always win. {And who says musicals aren't realistic?}

Pride - one of the Seven Deadly Sins - an exaggerated sense of one's ability and worth is also indicated by the upset scales. It may imply that you feel you are beyond judgement by others.

Worst Case Scenario: You are an unaccepting individual who makes no difference between friend and foe since in your eyes everyone is a foe. You are without equal and in your eyes the right way means it is done your way. There are no opinions other than yours. The egoistic side of you blinds you to everything that makes someone an individual. If someone should have the audacity to disagree with you, your ego will never allow you to consider that they could be right. [Think: last reel of *Citizen Kane*]

12 - Hanged Man

"Yeah, that's exactly how I feel - getting nowhere fast!"

There comes a time in every man's life when he realizes that it's 'one step forward and two steps back- or worse.' The Hanged Man is a card of transitions and changes. "WHAT CHANGE? He's hanging there, doin' nothing!" Precisely - for a reason. There are many cards of change in a Tarot deck; some are dramatic, like the Death or Tower card. Their changes are fast, abrupt, and usually more than disconcerting. The Hanged Man is in a period of stasis. Suspended like a bungee jumper waiting to be rescued, he has the time to look around and think, but his point of view is decidedly different. This change of perspective is the reason for the stasis - to make him take a good look around and even give him some opportunity to affect that change, something the Tower card would never let you do.

Suspended between Earth and Sky with no rescuer in sight, the

Hanged Man has no choice left but to accept his momentary predicament. Accepting the change is part of the change. You are being told not to make a gut reaction - do first, think later - but to work this out in your head (whether the Man's hands are tied behind his back is a subject of debate).

This is a card of new beginnings, sometimes even a spiritual one. The Hanged Man's head is surrounded by a halo, indicative of a connection with a higher source. The fact that the image bears close resemblance to the legend of Odin, who hung upside down for nine days and discovered Runes, is also there. {This is considered one of the cards of 'the psychic.'}

Perhaps your transition is not so profound. Perhaps you've decided to accept the fact that you're 47, that 50 is starting to loom on your horizon and you've just started or finished your 'mid-life crisis.' Aging, one of men's greatest fears ('aging <u>sucks</u>!') is one of our hardest transitions. We've spent our whole male lives being programmed that we had to work to be able to provide. Suddenly we discover our children are adults and are not dependent upon us. Worse than that, the new employees, the younger men coming into the company are making more than we do! {We won't even discuss erectile dysfunction!}

Perhaps you're at (as the French say) 'a certain age' when it's time to think of the future as 'what do I want to do when I am retired X number of years from now?' Right after high school, the father of a friend of mine died. He had worked hard and long his whole life, doing overtime driving trucks and snowplows for the Street Department. When it finally became time to retire, he had no clues about what or how or where he wanted to do or go. Rushed to the hospital for an emergency appendectomy, he died on the operating table, three days before his retirement was to take place. He never took a break, and death robbed him of enjoying his retirement. Who knows -if he had lived, he might have been able to enjoy drag racing with his grandchild, both of them rushing down the sidewalk on their separate three-wheeled bicycles.

A change is there, a change is a' coming. Look at it with new eyes.

Reversed:

Based on everything you've read so far, you are probably thinking that when the Hanged Man is reversed, his feet touch the ground and the change has taken place. He is now off and running again. That is only _one_ of the interpretations, albeit a positive one based on the theory that his stasis is somehow a negative experience. The cards in the spread that follow this card would determine what really happened or happens.

The other school of thought looks at the (card upright) Hanged Man suspended in the spiritual plane, and when his feet touch the earth in reversal, not only is he 'grounded', but also the problems and temptations of the material plane overtake him. In this position (again-dependent on the other cards in the spread) the Querent could be afraid or fearful of changes. His thoughts are unfocused and scattered and rather than looking ahead he only moves without direction.

On his feet, the Hanged Man becomes preoccupied with concerns for self and self-preservation, based on his perception that the people around him are trying to control him, and rather than hear their words as wisdom, he runs from them, afraid of their 'influence.'

Worst Case Scenario: Not only do you fear change, but also you shun change. Your perception is that the status quo must never be changed; nothing must upset the balance so carefully maintained and the mere thought of even the minutest detail being altered sends your mind reeling. Suspended in space you at least have some movement; with your feet planted firmly on the ground you are paralyzed.

13 - Death

I've said this before and I'll say it again - THE DEATH CARD IS NOT A CARD ABOUT PHYSICAL DEATH; IT DOES NOT IMPLY DEATH FOR YOU, YOUR QUERENT, NOR ANYONE THAT YOU KNOW OR ARE RELATED TO.

That aside - in the mid-1970s there were several good books written by Elisabeth Kubler-Ross, a psychiatrist who studied death and dying. One of her books was titled "Death - the Final Stage of Growth." It is appropriate that I mention it here for the Death card is about growth and transformations.

The Death card is yet another card of change, of permanent, lasting change. It is not stagnant like the Hanged Man hanging or overpowering like the Tower card - it's only requirement is that it IS going to happen, like it or not, and you will never be able to return to your previous state. Of course, that statement is enough to strike terror into anyone, but the card's point is that 'death' is needed for you to move on.

We are creatures of habit; whatever little rituals you have made for yourself to get you through your day, much less your life make for a great deal of security. You've figured out the fastest way to cut your lawn once a week, how to be three minutes late for work and not get your pay docked, and how to convince your lover that the two of you would be better off going to a restaurant even though it's your night to cook. The Death card is popping up to tell you that something is going to change or have to be changed.

Being complacent is stagnation, and the possibility for your developing potential becomes zero. I can hear you saying "But there is no NEED to change at this time. Everything is fine!" By now you must be aware that the cards do not care about your opinion; your belief or disbelief makes as little difference to the cards as it does to the weather. This potential can take various guises. Some could be very complicated, such as learning an entirely new computer system that your company is installing even though you feel there is nothing wrong with the old one. Perhaps it is as non-life threatening as learning to speak Spanish, something you did for two years in high school and never pursued thereafter. Death is a card for continued growth.

The Death card - for obvious reasons - has always gotten a bad rap. It is not to say that these changes will not come without trials or without challenges. Growth can be a very frightening thing! Growth and death is a cyclical thing (also hammered home by Dr. Kubler-Ross). I think the thing that frightens most men, myself included, is that the very idea of change has a negative connotation. Growth is not self-defeating! This change and growth may be problematic but what I see is that most people look at the face image of the cards and never look at the fact that possibly, just possibly the 'way of life' being overrun by Death is holding them back. It could even be bad for them, and once they pass through this period of 'death' what will come after will be so much better than what has gone before.

There is sometimes five-petal white rose on Death cards that signifies the Life Force. In this card of cycles, Death carries the Life Force in its (skeletal) grasp. This card is telling us to keep moving forward, ever onward, and put whatever held us back behind us, once and for all.

Reversed:

Complacency is a stagnant condition, and in this position the Death card says you are refusing to move or progress. You are under the delusion that you have somehow stopped Death in a safe spot and that you will be safe and warm in your snug little world. Even if you were able to achieve this, it will of short duration.

This card reversed also can indicate someone who is comfort-dependent. You have someone to do this; you pay someone to do that. They do what you tell them and it gives you a false sense of accomplishment. By expecting others to do everything for you, your false sense of security says, "This is the Life!" You don't have to do anything you don't want to. Even in reversal, this card is moving forward and although you might delay that change, it is still going to creep up and bite you in the ass. You can only hope it's just a flesh wound. Remember: the only sure things are taxes *and* death.

Worst Case Scenario: You refuse to do anything that involves risk of any kind. You flatly and completely block anything coming into your life without bothering to see if perhaps there could be some good attached to it.

You are unmotivated - at work, at play, in all aspects of your life. You have probably lost friends because you have stopped accepting social invitations, even ones your partner might have wished to partake in. You may perform your job well, but you are an automaton, cranking out the same old contracts in the same old way. You almost never leave your cubicle and take no interest in those coworkers who seem to be enjoying their jobs.

You are boring. You are so bored with life that even if an opportunity popped up, your disinterest would cloud your vision and the opportunity would pass you by or die on the vine. This card is a bugle call to get off your ass.

NOTE: 'Vivere senza rimpianti per ieri' Google-translates *roughly* out of Italian as "Live (today) without regret for yesterday."

14 - Temperance

Temperance is a card about finding the middle of the road. How do we achieve this? We do it by applying *reason* - the ability to think cohesively and logically. Also by using *moderation* - avoiding extremes, freedom from excess, and applying restraint.

The angelic persona [the Archangel Michael - if you're interested] on the Temperance card is in *balance*; he has one foot in water, one on earth. He stands pouring fluid from one chalice into another (In some decks he is juggling spheres), mixing the different contents of the two together to form one homogenized whole. Other than looking like your favorite bartender and maybe the title having some connection to the Temperance Movement of the 1920s, what is this card telling you to do?

There is a Pennsylvania Dutch saying that goes "We grow too soon old and too late smart." Neither of these has to apply to you. The

Biblical concept of Sages having long life spans, grays hair and long beards is a dated one. As a child you may have run to Grandpa when something went wrong; he's gone now, and suddenly the younger members of your family are asking you questions and looking for you to make things fair, and ... you don't know what to do. For one thing - children don't think like adults.

Knowledge and wisdom - two elements of higher thinking - have been lost in the twenty-first century. Someone just handed you a paper cup of black coffee straight out of the coffeepot - shouldn't it be HOT? If you spill it in your lap, will you somehow NOT burn your jewels? Did you never hear of "Murphy's Laws?" Wisdom - making the best use of your experience - is the first step of Temperance.

However, the very concept of the word 'experience' somehow carries a 'been there, done that' aspect to it. How do you 'apply' an experience you've never had? By going to step #2- trying to be or stay rational, which means you will have to do some reasoning, particularly if you are not mediating for yourself but trying to mediate between two others. The Temperance card says you will have to see what is good about within the arguments, what is wrong about both arguments, and how to settle the difference with a few scars as possible. Being rational means keeping your head while others lose theirs.

A directed focus can also help you see your way through the mire. The Temperance angel follows that last drop of fluid every step of the way. There is no chance for spilling or losing any. So, too, should you leave nothing to chance nor allow yourself to be distracted. This may not be easy. Finding the middle of your road is one thing and taking it is quite another. See that (in some decks) triangle in the square on his chest? It represents the Spirit embodied in flesh. Think adaptation, self-control, impartiality, compromise, patience, and modification. Tempered and refined by the raging problems of your life, you realize that you have to learn to adapt your behavior to fit into changing circumstances. If you find your relationship is a little shaky, the two of you will have to find the comfortable midpoint on give and take without sacrificing or compromising your individuality.

Reversed:

When Temperance is reversed and spills its cups it can mean you are prone to emotional reactions. {Any pools or streams in Tarot usually apply to the emotional state of someone- from calm, quiet streams to churning oceans} Anyone who gets taken by surprise- whether it be a shutoff notice or a court summons cannot be expected to instantly act quietly or calmly, but in reversal this card says you are likely to become upset first, think later.

No attempts to remain impartial for you! You tend to get overly involved in situations, taking one side over another without thinking the situation through, and either siding for the person you expect will win or that you want to have win the disagreement.

Worst Case Scenario: See the background mountain in the sun's rays? It represents the crowning glory of mastery. In reversal it says you act only on impulse, never stopping long enough to take consideration into consideration. It can go in two directions, and both say you care nothing about the outcome. In the first case, you say that you will win at all costs, making phone calls to your doctor, lawyer, butcher, baker to get them all on your side. You care nothing for how the other person is left, as long as you come out on top.

In the second instance, you plead ignorance, wash your hands like Pilate, and dismiss the whole thing from your consciousness. A friend once revealed that when he and his brother would get into childhood disputes, his parents *locked* the two of them in a room together and would not let them out until they settled the dispute, which usually means they got tired of arguing. Their parents never settled their disputes, so who knows what unholy alliances were to be made? Arbitration is not a part of the deal here. The Reversed Temperance says you show a lack of good judgement.

15 - Devil

We now come to one of the more misunderstood cards in the deck "Ye Olde Devil." Traditionally, (and in brief) its symbolism is about chaining oneself to the wrong ideals, of greed, corruption, lack of knowledge, and half-truths. If someone is attempting to seduce you into an unhealthy situation (money, drugs, power) by appealing to your darker side or nature you had better think twice before complying with them. The Devil deals with your darker side because he knows your secret desires, deep secrets, and all about those kinky taboo fantasies you are having.

In my childhood of the late 1960s, there was an overused phrase popularized by television where a character was asked why they had done something and the response was "The *Devil* made me do it!" This spread like media wildfire and soon everything from soda glasses to bikini underwear sported the phrase "The Devil made me do it!" It was always meant as a joke, yes, but it does underscore the intent of this card - a lack of courage, or the need to blame someone else for our shortcomings.

This is a card about 'giving in'. If you look closely, the couple in the card is chained to the Devil by their necks. But take a closer look - those chains are quite loose, and the casual stance of the couple does not hint at brimstone and hellfire. [If you are really paying attention, they are the same couple from the Lovers card and Devil #15 = 1 + 5 = #6 the Lovers - for the numerologists out there] They are bound, yes, but only themselves are holding them there. For some of us, the 'Devil we know' is better than facing an uncertainty we are unsure of, and it binds us to patterns of thinking and doing that are wrong to unhealthy for us. We still give in anyway, for it is the easier thing to do. Addictions are a part of 'giving in,' or following the paths of least resistance.

The Devil speaks of a lack of courage or of a 'withholding.' After all, why go bravely where no man has gone before when it will be easier to lift the footrest on your recliner and pop the lid off another pint of Ben & Jerry's ®? A lack of courage to do ... what? Anything from mowing the lawn to installing a ceiling fan, from losing your gut gained from lack of exercise to taking up a new hobby, from realizing you need someone in your life to making a commitment.

The 1980s gave birth to the 'Me!' generation, an isolationist group that said 'Numero Uno' deserved all their attention. Everything they did, bought, felt, or thought was geared to make 'Numero Uno' stay on top by showing other 'Numero Uno wannabes' that they were actually number Two. The dawning of the Age of Aquarius meant nothing to them; they are too self-centered to realize there is anyone else there. Once again, the Devil holds his torch upside down, so rather than giving forth enlightenment it merely consumes itself.

Worst Case Scenario: You are emotionally distant to others, even those you say you are 'close' to. The fact is that you have closed yourself to others and although the 'chains that bind' may be strong, the chains of your own making (think of Jacob Marley) are much stronger. Once again, the case you make for yourself is stronger than your involvement with others, so perhaps the phase 'The Devil made me do it' is not that far off track.

Reversed:

{-Wait a minute- I put the 'worst case scenario' section with the *upright* card!} Well, my friend, not all cards are negative in reversal.

When the Devil card is reversed, those loose chains slide off from around the couples' necks. Free at last- unfettered by demands of a lifestyle or history that held you back, you are now free to move forward, rather than be stagnant, chained in one spot. Break those bonds and change those behavior patterns any time by altering your thoughts and actions.

One of the first gifts of a reversed Devil is a feeling of shared optimism. If you were prone to obsessive behaviors, this says you are willing to fight to regain your life back. This might entail classes in better living or listening to cassettes of 12-step programs. The important thing to remember is that what was holding you back was You, and you will never become the 'old you' again. Accepting encouragement and giving encouragement to others will only help you succeed.

The Devil can be reversed through selfless giving, something the introvert or addicted personality cannot do. Giving of self, financial help, or even community service are all ways of giving back to the community. Reaching out to others is one way to break the chains that are holding you back. This liberation can bring forth a new inner courage, something that being chained to an addiction can never accomplish. Having strength and inner courage will ensure the Devil cannot tempt you again.

Best Case Scenario: being released from chains means you are a fighter and a survivor, something the winner of no 'Reality TV show' can ever be. The combination of giving, optimism, courage, and surviving help you to say 'I was wrong. I have overcome. I will survive.'

16 - Tower

BAM! Let's kick it up a little! One of Tarot's most definitive images comes leaping out of your spread at you! The dreaded Tower card - far worse than the nastiest Devil - rears its head and the top of the Tower comes crashing down at your feet. Your hopes are completely overthrown, dashed to pieces before your eyes by a thunderbolt from out of the blue! Is it Divine retribution? Personal negligence? Or a warning shot over your bow?

Three of the last four cards have dealt with a personal Hell of some sort. Here, you are shaken to the very foundations of just about everything you stand or strive for. Your Ivory Tower is flawed; if you don't destroy it first, it may destroy you. The universe delivers a giant 'bitch slap' in your direction. What could you possibly have done to deserve this?

Similar to the Devil, you have built your tower on uncertain ground.

Perhaps here, too, you are clinging to some outmoded way to thinking that either does not suit the situation, or is totally erroneous. Unlike the Devil where you made a bad decision and can still alter the outcome, the bolt tells you that a change is needed- so quickly that you do not have time to think it over or try to influence its outcome. Not only that, but you won't see it coming or be able to prepare for it, either. **BAM!**

Perhaps you are clinging to the concept that you can do it all alone - **BAM!** Perhaps you are dealing in less than savory business practices - **BAM!** Maybe you believe no one knows about your deep dark secret - **BAM!** Perhaps you are possessive about people and treat them as if they were things - **BAM!** Maybe even it's your guilt for doing all these things, but never trying to get help for it, or trying to stop it -**double BAM!** Whatever those carefully guarded secrets you have, they are about to be exposed to the world in living color on CNN. You come home unexpectedly and discover your significant other in bed with your best friend - **KABOOM!**

Does it have to be something so dramatic? Your action may not be dramatic, but the events surrounding their exposure or expulsion will be quick, unforgettable, and maybe even surgical. A lack of maturity on your part, such a being spiteful, wicked, or greedy shares equal footing on the bill with deception, injustice, or writing bad checks. A lack of humanity on your part, such as being prejudiced or biased needs a permanent correction. Your floundering relationship comes to an end when you come home and find they've moved out without so much as a good-bye.

Worst Case Scenario: Not only do you acknowledge you have done wrong, made poor decisions, or hurt other people, but you don't even care *and* you do not expect punishment for it - ***BAM!***

Reversed:

If the upright tower is being destroyed, then is the reversed Tower being rebuilt? Once the Tower had been destroyed, the base upon which it was built can be re-examined. Perhaps you were an 'activist' in the 1960s or 70s who said 'Never trust anyone over thirty!' or held demonstrations against the Viet Nam war, pouring red ink on files in the campus ROTC office. Perhaps you even caused a tower or two to fall. Now you look at those fading pictures taken with a Polaroid Swinger ® and wonder how you ever did it. Evolving maturity is one of the reasons. You still believe Einstein's statement that ' You cannot simultaneously prevent and prepare for war', but now you write letters to your congressman instead of taking over the Dean's office.

If your current structure is breaking down, remind yourself that it could be the best thing for all concerned parties. Reversed is a time for examining attitudes, or re-examining attitudes. Maybe in your haste, you did the first thing that sprang to mind, never thinking of its impact, never thinking of the consequences. Are you clinging to old hurts and old resentments? Are you still lying to yourself? I work with someone who thinks that they are 'perfect' and believe they never make mistakes, and will never *admit* they made a mistake if it killed them. One day they made a real boner on paper and signed it, a sure guarantee of guilt, and still would not admit to it! I said 'Just admit you made a mistake! 500 years from now NO ONE is going to care!' They could not.

In reversal, the Tower says it is a time for the moment of truth by letting go. People change, times change, attitudes change. Be part of the change.

Besides - the Major Arcana improves *drastically* after this point!

60

17 - Star

In the Star card, as in Temperance, we find another 'balanced being' standing on both land and in water, but the Star is pouring one pitcher on the earth and the other into the water, instead of blending the two together. The one poured on the earth splits into five rivulets, signifying man's five senses. This is a card of hope, inspiration, and good health. In general, the Star is one of those eternally upbeat cards that usually say 'everything is going to be all right.'

This balance can take the form of alliances of value. The calm waters of the pool signify emotional stability, so one thing that is possible for all is the development or furthering of supportive relationships. There are seedlings growing in what otherwise looks like a desert, suggesting that new growth is possible with a little encouragement.

The eight-pointed stars that represent radiant (or cosmic) energies flowing down onto the Querent indicate inspiration that can lead to cooperation. Cosmic energies, new growth, and emotional balance - all indicate a sense of well-being that comes from this cooperation. Perhaps the two of you have not been slashing the cubicle walls, sticking pins in voodoo dolls, or sending fish wrapped in newspaper to each other, but things have been a bit strained. The appearance of the Star says that being a little more rational will be able to get the two of you through the difficulty. The Star card inspires and guides you into 'getting the job done.'

In its most definitive state the Star suggests the joining together of two forces. Although the pitchers' contents are not being mixed, if you pay attention to the five rivulets, you will see that one of them looks as though it is flowing back to the pond of calm emotions. This can indicate the end of warring factions, or the coming together of minds. It can also indicate a deepening of emotions of a love interest. Whatever has played itself out beforehand now is smoothing it out and the most positive quality of the Star (hope) is being given a chance. Think of it this way: the energy of the universe pours inspiration into all lives. Some falls on fertile ground and is cherished; some gets wasted but goes back to the source to get recycled and later poured out again.

In a physical sense, the Star tells of good health or the return to good health after a period of illness.

Reversed:

The Star is such a positive card that it is difficult to see negativity in it, even when it is reversed. Some writers get nebulous and say things such as "Its positive qualities are diminished or lessened," which means - what- a 'lesser degree of good?' Your new car will be a Volkswagen and not a Volvo? Your bowling team only gets new sweat socks, not new balls?

When the Star reverses, the waters pour back into their separate pitchers, and stay that way. It indicates feelings of or desires to be separate, of wanting to be separated from people or things, maybe for good reasons, maybe not. It indicates a desire for withdrawal.

If this condition has already begun, it indicates the Querent feels himself alone or isolated from the world around him. This may be a deliberate condition where he has actively chosen to withdraw, or possibly indicates his recent emotional state has caused others to shy away from him. Perhaps you find yourself taking nice long walks in the park...with your dog. Couples pass you by, and you wonder why you are not one of them. This turns to doubt, to stubbornness, and finally into pessimism. Although isolationism can have its good qualities (see the Hermit) this can indicate antisocial behaviors, and possibly hint at mental illness. [BIG NOTE: You are not a doctor. Do not attempt to get your psychology degree vicariously through a deck of Tarot cards.] The reversed Star can also indicate a general period of feeling unwell.

Worst Case Scenario: You are totally uninvolved with the world around you. You have rejected the company of others, even though you may speak rather coolly to them if you absolutely have to. You are devoid of emotion, seek inspiration from nothing and you do not hope … for anything. The positive energies of this card drain past you but not through you.

18 - Moon

The Moon is an odd card. Its interpretation has varied on how the Moon was viewed in history. You may think of romantic naked moonlight swims but historically the Moon was seen as evil or dangerous. During the American Civil War period, it was even considered dangerous to hang children's clothing to dry in moonlight lest its evil influences overtake them! I suppose that the Sun was seen as courage and strength, so something had to be thought its philosophical opposite. You will see references to 'deceitful moons' in Shakespeare, and many older books say the Moon card appearing denotes the presence of a strong enemy, and the possibility of being caught in a web of deceit at the very least!

Looming in the card are (again) two objects with a road between them, signifying polarity and choices. This time, however, there are two characters placed between them: a domesticated dog and a wolf both baying at the full moon - or is it? Here again we have another repeated

Tarot symbol l- a moon that is both full <u>and</u> in first quarter. This usually signifies a passage or delay of time roughly two weeks in length. The wild and domestic dogs represent the dual nature of man, and the crab/crayfish/lobster (in some decks) in the pool of the unconscious signifies the pull of the moon on the tides, emotions and (still being debated) the fluids of the brain. The Moon rules the zodiacal sign of Cancer (crab).

So, what does this card of bad friends, temporary lunacy, shyster lawyers, or turning into a werewolf have to do with you? The Moon is a card about withdrawing away from others or withdrawing into yourself. In the musical "The Fanstasticks" - Act One of which takes place in moonlight - Matt, the juvenile asks the old actor about something that is happening. The famous reply to him is 'Try to see it under *light*,' hinting at the blinding difference between moonlight, which is merely reflected sunlight, and the direct rays of ol' Sol himself. Things can look very different under moonlight, and perhaps you are deceiving yourself into believing that what you see is correct and true. Is the moon pulling on your brain and the dimmer, reflected light not strong enough for you to take a clear look around? Perhaps in two weeks' time (bet you were wondering how I was going to work <u>that</u> in there) you should take another look. In fact, if you are doing a Tarot reading, you should always check and see what phase the moon is currently in. A full moon must go through its dark phase before you will have light, and a new moon must get to Full Moon in order to have its brightest light.

Playing into an older theme, the wild/domestic dogs hint at a dysfunctional relationship or an impasse. Both are dogs, and came from the same species origin; however they took two different roads in evolution. Perhaps you both really do agree on something, but the practical parts of how to implement it are being disagreed on. Perhaps at this point it does not matter who is wrong or who is right, but it is unacceptable to both or you. Possibly it goes even deeper than that - maybe instead of being deceived, you try to deceive others to achieve your ends.

Worst Case Scenario: You are afraid of losing your independence. Due to circumstances beyond your control (medical condition, effects of aging, loss of personal affects) you find that others are making decisions for you, with or without your consent or approval. Perhaps you feel others are forcing you to accept their decisions for you. The Moon says others are asserting their influence or power. Instead of fearing dependency - stand up and be counted!

Reversed:

When the Moon is 'Down', so to speak, what's the next thing to happen? The Sun will rise, of course! (The fact that the Sun card is the next card in the sequence is not accidental). When the Moon is below the horizon it cannot extend its influence. Once deceitful people are dispelled, it hints of support from true friends; friendship is the opposite of deceit. ("Once these fears can be counted and compelled, they can quickly be dispelled" - part of a poem recited by Zero Mostel).

The reversed moon speaks of accepting weakness if you are in a position of support, and also accepting support if you are in a position of weakness. One reason that the people that use wheelchairs get adamant against people who are mobile helping them is that the mobile people treat them as though they are helpless, which is usually far from the truth. Mobile people will do things the Chair people would rather do without asking first. People in wheelchairs will ask for help *when they need it*. Learn to be respectful of that. On the other hand, if someday you find yourself on the ground looking up, accepting the help of others is not a sign of weakness. Although I am mobile, I cannot kneel down without great pain; most coworkers know this and will pick up things I happen to drop. I always thank them: thanking them is easier than taking chemical medications (and cheaper, too!)

The reversal of the deceitful Moon indicates a restored faith in others ("I have always relied upon the kindness of strangers." -*Blanche DuBois*). It can also indicate a period of distrust is coming to a close.

In my card interpretation, the wild dog stands with the wild, older man; the domesticated dog stands with the younger, modern man. I found that a better visual than just dogs baying at the Moon (and I dropped that lobster/crawfish out of the image).

19 - Sun

The Sun is one of the few cards that depict children. I have seen readings where this card did represent the Querent's *son*. It can represent your children or your younger siblings in a reading concerning them.

The Sun is a vibrant card. The majesty and energies of the Sun benignly smile down on a naked child gleefully riding a horse out of a walled garden. The red banner he holds signifies his conquest of Life over the cultivated garden of Man that he is leaving behind. The four sunflowers behind him turn their faces from the Sun to the child, looking to him for their nourishment. In the great scheme of things, the Sun appearing in your spread is a guarantee of success so strong that it overpowers any negative cards that may surround it. Naked you go forth because there is nothing holding you back, and nothing that you have to hide. When you draw this card a ray of sunshine enters your life, making you strong, confident, and ready to rise to any challenge.

The Sun deals with activity, including creative activity. There are men you know of whom you say they 'have a lust for living' or 'have a love of Life.' These are the men whom may have drudge jobs, but channel their energy outlet into having magnificent lawns or gardens. They spend hours after work tending plants and pruning shrubs. These are the Old Italian men you see who always plant too many tomato plants because they know Heaven on Earth is walking into their garden with a salt shaker and eating a fresh tomato off the vine. They give their surplus to you with no strings attached.

Vitality is another consideration. When you immerse yourself in living your life, as opposed to merely surviving your life, you learn to draw strength from the world around you the way the sunflowers face the child. The sunflowers, which represent the five elements (Fifth being Spirit), indicate diverse pursuits. Perhaps you like canoeing and white water rafting, that are highly active, yet balance it with fresh water fishing which is quiet and contemplative. You actually bought an 'off-road' vehicle to go 'off-road.' Maybe you like backpacking with a friend because you love to have company, yet at the end of the trail you both can enjoy the fact that civilization and the madding crowd are far away. Don't you hate people who say they go camping to 'rough it' and bring a battery-powered television and their electronic gizmos with them?

Your sunny personality shows you to be a fun-loving person whom everyone is comfortable to be with. Fun, activity, and recreation are a part of you. No sitting, waiting for the next pension check to get delivered, wondering what boring thing you have to do today; you're too busy to sit and rust. Think of Anthony Quinn as *Zorba the Greek* dancing on the beach; and in the words of Zorba: 'Life is a pain in the ass, so pull down your pants and enjoy it!'

You can stop worrying; the news you will receive will be good. Whatever your goal is/was you have reached it, so enjoy your success.

Reversal:

Some people feel that there can be no such thing as a reversed Sun card since the excellent qualities of the card can never be diminished, even if reversed. They compensate for this by saying that 'your happiness with only be delayed a short time' or 'the happy ending you seek will come through a different or unexpected route.' As a reader I learned a long time ago that it is one thing to temper unpleasant news and quite another to become a Pollyanna because you don't wish to be the harbinger of bad news.

When the Sun is down the vitality and juices of life drain out of you, leaving a dry, empty shell. There is no 'go forth and conquer'; it is more like "If I don't get out of bed today, I won't have to make it after I get up." 'Activity' consists of hitting the speed dial button for Chinese take-out. We won't even mention you have more dirty clothes sitting in a pile next to the washer than you have clean ones in your dresser.

Perhaps the reversed Sun presents itself in other ways. Are you unenthusiastic about just about everything? Do you shy away from trying new restaurants? Do you wait for a movie to come out on DVD before you rent it cheaper than seeing it in the theatre? Are you bored easily? Do you 'channel-surf' even if you are watching a favorite show? Do you have a short attention span? Have you not read a book in years, because even though you have turned into a couch potato, sitting too long in one place doing one thing holds no interest?

When the Sun goes down, the heads of the sunflowers droop until the next morning. Possibly you are feeling excluded by others; perhaps it is you yourself who is doing the excluding. There is no interpersonal dynamic here that holds your head up or keeps your interest. Links to others are not severed - they merely dry up or whither on their vines.

Worst Case Scenario: Like Count Dracula shunning the brilliance of the dawn you have put yourself in total seclusion. Listen to a very young Paul Simon singing the words to "I Am a Rock; I Am an Island."

20 - Judgement

When I started writing this book I knew the Judgement and Justice cards would present a small problem since in most people's minds they overlap or are interchangeable. They both also carry some distinctive images, and Judgement with the Archangel Gabriel blowing his trumpet to raise the dead for their final judgement does not set well with many people. This judgement finds you lacking and brings damnation. How does this image come between the wonderful Sun card and the even better World card? Why isn't this card farther back in 'the Fool goes to hell' section? If you remember correctly, in the midst of those hellish cards the Temperance angel appears to say that choices must be made. Here in the midst of the final cards of the Major Arcana yet another angel appears to ask if those choices were for the best. Justice is the quality for being correct or right; Judgement is the process to ascertain truth from agreement and disagreement.

Traditionally, the Judgement card is about a sense of renewing or renewal. This renewal comes from a period of reflections on the past that brings forth an awakening. Perhaps you will receive an opportunity for reassessing what has gone before, or are about to enter a time of testing. One has to discern if this judgement is external - received from others - such as a job review or a legal judgement, or if this judgement is internal - how the Querents evaluate themselves. But where does all this celebrated 'determination, decision, resolution, and outcome' (Webster's Universal Dictionary) lead us or leave us?

Forget about the dead rising from their coffins floating on the sea of the subconscious. {How many naked people get buried at sea, anyway?} Forget about *destiny.* Gabriel's blasts are to awaken Man from his limitations, to show you that limitation is holding you back or making you 'dead.' This card is about learning about **uniqueness** - learning what makes you unique, developing ways to express that uniqueness, and learning to accept that uniqueness in others. Yes, Mr. "I went to Berkeley to study the effects of gamma rays on man-in-the-moon marigolds", your father is still a Hassidic Jew still wondering 'where you went wrong.' You are worlds apart in your theologies - but Father's Day is still coming; you can still send him a card. He's still going to ask when you're going to get a haircut and when you are going to get married. Accept that as *his* uniqueness.

A tolerance of others is part of judgement. By definition, unique means there are no duplications or imitations, so it goes to say that everyone's uniqueness may not necessarily be simpatico with yours. Look at your personal history; everyone's life has a few 'I can't believe I did *THAT!*' statements in it. These actions moved you in or out of harmony with others, possibly even alienated a few, too. You discovered that even if you botched a few things up royally that a certain few friends were still there, even if they thought you were a complete jerk at the time. Unless you live in a plastic bubble you are going to find people who do things that revolt you, eat foods that would make you vomit, have ideas that are strictly Martian, or otherwise have lifestyles that are incompatible with yours. Gabriel's blast tells you to broaden your viewpoint. It's like the 'Serenity Prayer' that states: 'God, grant me the patience to change the things I can change, accept the things I cannot change, and the wisdom to know the difference.'

Reversed:

In reversal, Gabriel flies away, finding no one for which to blow his horn, and therefore leaves man encumbered by his limitations. The concept of the uniqueness of every individual collapses, and those powerful personalities who know how to dominate others take over, forcing everyone else to accommodate their wishes while the wishes of the dominated are forgotten or ignored. In this way, not only are you making judgements, but you are jury and executioner, too. There is no aesthetic discernment here; it's strictly 'No, no, no, yes, no, no way in hell!' Not only to the meek not inherit the earth, they don't even get a say in it.

Rather than understanding or accepting people, you hand them a list of expectations that they are required to meet, regardless of how realistic or unrealistic they are. There is no decision making or conclusions to be drawn from the process; there is only a bottom line with a date and a time it must be completed, printed in red. There is no consideration of being 'fair.'

Worst Case Scenario: You have such a fear of others judging you that you are immobilized when anyone asks you for an opinion, fearing that you will disclose something that will ultimately be used against you. You hide your uniqueness and try to blend into the office water cooler. You are the boss's 'yes man'. As long as you don't make waves you will have no problems. Making no problems means you will keep your employment, comparable to the character Mr. Twimble (how's *that* for an appropriately pathetic name?) who sings "The Company Way" in Frank Loesser's *How to Succeed in Business Without Really Trying.* He says that when he joined his firm as a brash young man he said to himself not to 'get any ideas.' He stuck to it - hadn't had one in years!

21 - World

We have been through the Sun, the Moon, the Star, and now we get to the final card of the Major Arcana - the World (sometimes known as the Universe.) This is the absolute unparalleled card of success, the one that says no matter how hard, unusual, or weird your dreams may be that they will come to a happy and successful end. And who knows what dreams may come?

Repeating the same corner symbols of the Wheel card, the four figures represent the four fixed signs of the Zodiac and the symbols of the four gospels. Sometimes she is encircled with a laurel wreath of success, its crossed ribbon ties making double lemniscuses of infinity. In all of them the Cosmic Dancer dances her dance of life, freed from earthly cares. Her nudity signifies a lack of the trappings that could hold her back.

It is a time to value your goals for those goals are about to be achieved. We speak here of our worldly or societal goals - the bigger, better paycheck, the bigger, better car than Dad had, the burning of the mortgage that says 'I own this, not someone else.' Many men may aspire to these goals and never achieve them, due to circumstances beyond their control, or by lack of trying.

It is also a time of pursuing personal successes - things that may appear minor to the outsider but represent something to ourselves just as satisfying as a major societal goal is for someone else. When a cancer survivor wins a sporting event multiple times and you can't ride once around the block without wheezing it says something about personal goals. These goals are not ended with champagne toasts, silver trophy cups or a barrage of press cameras flashing. These are those goals that never make it to CNN - losing twenty-five pounds and keeping it off, coming in last on an amateur running marathon knowing that you competed in it and did not drop out. When I wrote my first book there was almost two years between crossing the final 't' and getting it on a shelf with many rejections and publishers in between. The day the contract arrived in the mail I actually sat there and stared at it for several minutes, not believing it actually existed. But when that first book advance check crossed my palm, buddy boy, even Cole Porter's song *"Ridin' High"* didn't come close to touching what I was feeling at that moment.

It is a time for considering spiritual pursuits, looking for the bigger and better things that Life has to offer you, not merely the most costly. Like the dancer you, too, should think and consider what is holding you back in your life, what 'trappings' are holding you down. Freed from those trappings you don't look back except to say 'That was holding me back - no longer!'

Perhaps like the laurel wreath you go full circle; once you are freed from worldly cares you actually take a better look at the world around you and it heightens your concerns about the environment, world peace, or even loving your neighbor. Perhaps that concern points you in another direction and that is good, too.

Reversal:

There are many readers who feel that the World is such an excellent card that even in reversal it is almost impossible to read negativity in it. If you want to be a Pollyanna your whole life, don't let me stop you from the wealth of my experiences. After all, Tarot is mostly subjective.

The World on its head says you are a victim of misdirection either from shortsightedness on your part, or from your blind pursuit of someone else's goals. It pops up in reversal to give you a little 'heads-up' warning that the 'Beware the Dog' sign is only the tip of the iceberg that you cannot see, that it is Cujo in that doghouse and not Lassie. It asks you to take your head from the clouds and ground yourself thoroughly and see where you are. Even in misdirection, you may still think you are gaining ground and achieving your goal, and possibly even *are,* but like so many others when they think they see the goal in sight they forget everything else and never look side-to-side as though they have blinders on. What will you do when you get to the top of that mountain and find out Everest was the next mountain over?

Perhaps you don't have any goals at all, possibly out of boredom. Perhaps your Cosmic Dancer is the cosmic couch potato, not even oven-baked, merely microwaved. It is truly hard to fail if you don't try, but harder to achieve a goal if you don't have one.

Worst Case Scenario: What could be worse than having no path (boredom) or being on the wrong path (misdirection)? Picking a meaningless path. In Boredom you waste no time or energy to get you nowhere; in Misdirection you may achieve your goal, even if it was the wrong one to begin with. But to be on a meaningless path wandering in circles that grow ever larger the ending gets farther and farther out of your sight, like being in a dream where point A and B are close but getting from one to the other never happens. The Cosmic Dancer is waving those wands at you like the guy who guides the airplanes into the gate. Are you paying attention?

2 - THE MINOR ARCANA

The fifty-six cards that comprise the Minor Arcana have been compared to or labeled as the precursor to the modern playing card deck. Both have Pip cards numbered Ace to Ten, and have face cards labeled Page (or Jack), Knight, Queen, and King. There are versions of the deck that add to or eliminate what will comprise the Court cards for that particular deck. The standard suits are Wands, Cups, Swords, and Pentacles or Coins, but modern deck creators substitute anything they feels works for them, and I have seen the Cups become soda bottles, and the Pentacles become television sets! I chose to retain the traditional Suit designations, but decided to give each suit its own distinct male personality to walk us through.

The Minor Arcana deal with the problems of everyday living and existing, the things that get in our way or go bump in the night. Broken down into four suits they cover every range of human emotion and experience yet still deal with the mundane parts of your daily living. There are beautiful and drastic cards contained in the Minors, but these problems are still something that can be dealt with by showing you where your errors are, or how to deal with the problems that pop up when you least want them. I feel you need to use both halves of the deck in order to get a balanced reading. If you were to only use the Major Arcana and were given a reading that warned you to '*run for the hills*' you still might want more information concerning what you are running from or what you are running towards.

I have ordered this section by number instead of by suit. In this way you can compare all the Aces or all the Fives instead of trying to learn ten cards of a particular suit. Experience has shown me it is easier to deal with learning the cards if you can see what similarities the cards have before you learn the specific differences.

THE ACES OR ONES

Traditionally, Aces deal with fresh starts, things starting anew, or a cycle having ended brings us to the new beginning of the next cycle.

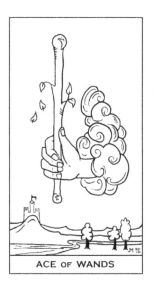

ACE OF WANDS

ACE OF CUPS

ACE OF SWORDS

ACE OF PENTACLES

Ace of Wands

ACE OF WANDS

The Ace of Wands deals with exploration. You should think of the hand being that of a wizard holding his 'magic wand', about to swing it over his head and make something happen. Perhaps you look at the hand giving you a big 'thumbs up' - the symbol that everything is set for you to keep going forward. This is a time to discover not only your abilities, but also your capabilities. Once again, the wand has growing leaves sprouting from it- old wood having new life in it. This should be your clue to not be stagnant or complacent. It is telling you that although you feel limited, there is a world of untapped potential if you would only seek it out.

Maybe it is time for you to go on a journey of creative discovery. Although Wands are generally considered a 'work card', they deal in 'that which you do' and are not limited to your work inside your cubicle. Perhaps it is time for you to say: "I have been doing this for X number of years; although I cannot go out and learn a new job, I can expand my focus into other job-related places and see what I can do." My father was a mechanical draftsman/toolmaker his whole life. Everything was drawn with a pencil, by hand; he retired long before CAD was in its infancy. He even worked with the artist Alexander Calder on a couple of Calder's sculptures, designing the base for one of them. With his ability to think in three dimensions and to draw it out, my father could easily have moved into drawing, watercolors, or oils. Drawing is drawing, whether it's a plate to patch the side of an airplane (my father was an airplane mechanic in WW2) or the symmetry of drawing a cityscape. It will only take the heart of an artist to make the transition from a blueprint to a canvas.

Inherent in this process is a sense for adventure and the willingness to take a risk. In fact, many men may look at the risk as being the more interesting part. Maybe you are tired of working for someone else, but cannot start your own business. This is when you become 'the Consultant'! You work for yourself, helping people by showing them where their weakness and strengths are. Perhaps it is time to look into starting your own business.

This sense of exploration may also bring with it a time of introspection; after all, who knows you better than yourself? Who wants you to succeed more than yourself? Who knows you haven't moved your fat butt in years better than yourself? Doreen Valiente once said 'If that which you seek you find not within, you will not find without.' In other words, until you know what you want or what you need, no one can help you find it- the answer must come from within. If you need to exercise and know you cannot pump iron like the 20 year-old next door, you can still take a low-impact aerobics class, or take up swimming. What this card is telling you is not to substitute one drudge with another drudge. It says figure it out, make a plan, and then hop on it!

The phallic symbolism of this card is rarely lost on any male over the age of nine, particularly in the Robin Wood Tarot with its crystal-tipped wand upright between two sunflowers bursting with seeds - *go*,

Robin! Your approach to sex is lusty and impulsive, and you may be inclined to take risks, losing sight of their possible consequences. For those who can keep up with you, this Ace corresponds to making of an attachment that goes far beyond the physical act of sex.

Reversed:

When that wand points down, burying the growing leaves into the dirt, it is like the proverbial ostrich burying its head in the sand. 'If I ignore the problems, dilemmas, (fill in the blank), even if they don't go away, I still won't have to contend with them.' The reversed wand says you are avoiding a challenge - one that brings opportunity with it. Although it can indicate a now-lost opportunity, *you* are the active principle in this action, and it says you are doing some serious sidestepping to *ensure* that this will not work. You are guaranteeing failure through neglect.

Not rising to the challenge indicates that you are involved in some addictive routines or behaviors, some manmade, some self-made. Are you a gambler? Do you drink to forget and forget why you're drinking? Perhaps they are not as dramatic. Perhaps you always wait to pay the bills until the day before they are due, even though you have the money in the bank. How many times will you call and try to get the late fees removed, blaming it on the mail delivery? How can you move forward when your own actions are holding you back? It's one thing to botch or lose an opportunity; it's another thing to destroy one.

Worst Case Scenario: You deny or deflect challenges because you are comfort-dependent. Everything is in its little niche, behind its little door, and on the surface everything is fine in the Universe. You avoid all challenges and ignore all opportunities they might bring because you don't want to be disturbed, don't want to be 'put out', and have no desire to expend any energy. The world has already been explored, so there is no need for you pack your bag and run up the gangplank. Just like the hand in the card, you have 'thumbs down' on everything and anything.

Ace of Cups

ACE OF CUPS

The Ace of Cups deals with open affections and open expressions of emotion. The tag line to the old song 'The Red, Red Robin' ends with "Live, Laugh, Love, and Be Happy." The five streams of water over the edge of the cup indicate your 'cup overflows' meaning you are filled with and share your feelings, emotions, and affections with others. The therapeutic aspects of experiencing laughter have long been recognized in cancer wards. Patients watch comedy shows and other upbeat programming, not to deny their pain or their diagnoses, but because it is found that a good belly laugh a day is good for you! Sharing your daily healing has a profound effect on others.

Spontaneity has all but gone out of modern life. We are programmed from the minute our eyes open in the morning until the minute they close at night. We have a doctor's appointment here, a board meeting there, soccer practice over there. And you want to have sex TONIGHT, too? Even on vacation ("If it's Tuesday, this must be

Belgium") the trip director runs you from one museum to the next, expecting that everyone can see the *entire* Metropolitan Museum of Art in forty-five minutes. Being open with your inner emotions makes you stop and say: 'This restaurant looks interesting; I'm skipping the next two museums and having a good meal.' Since your cup is overflowing, why not enjoy the good things that seem to be coming your way? If this Ace has popped up in a card reading concerning love, romance, or sex, something brand new and emotionally satisfying is about to begin or is starting to develop. Tonight you're only planning a seduction; tomorrow you could be planning a wedding.

Spontaneity and humor make all things palatable. A good humorist finds the humor in everyday situations and plays them back at you in a way that makes you laugh. Samuel Clemens (Mark Twain) died over one hundred years ago and we still read his quips and fall over laughing at their originality and universality. Clemens often made himself the butt of his own jokes, but in laughing at them we realize ourselves within them. Can you do the same? You've just rushed up to the closing elevator door too late to trigger the sensor. The doors slide shut with the hem of your jacket caught between them. Do you stand there cursing a blue streak that cannot be printed in family magazines, or do you bang your head against the door and laugh enthusiastically? This brings up to another aspect of being open and sharing - keeping perspective. Everything we do tends to be 'of the moment.' We make millions of decisions every day without realizing most of them, many so trivial that they don't even register as having made a decision in the first place. We cannot account for every action, nor can we be held accountable for every action. Do the people on the next floor know that your office buddies are 'razzing' you for having your jacket caught in the elevator door? Of course not. Five hundred years from now, will it matter to anyone? Of course not. Five minutes from now no one will even remember it happened. Keeping perspective on the situation will be much better than cursing, tearing your jacket out of the doors, or punching the nearest sonofabitch in the nose for laughing at you. Drink from the cup of your emotions and keep a sense of humor and perspective around you. A new beginning is about to start.

Reversed:

In general, when any of the Cups in the deck are overturned their contents spill out and cannot be retrieved, or the Cup cannot be refilled until it is turned upright.

Do you know a coworker, friend, or family member for whom everything is a mountain, not a molehill, who magnifies everything to such titanic proportions that you wonder how anyone's life could be filled with such dramas and traumas? This is the reversed Cup, whose content splashes against the ground with hurricane force winds rather than trickling slowly into the sands. Being open with your emotions is one thing; being flagrant with them is something else. Perhaps it is only an attention-getting device. But it truly indicates you tend to overturn everything and throw things out of balance, sometimes without regard for yourself or others.

These outbursts tend to be extremely emotional and very theatrical. Have you ever seen Fay Wray 'act' in the original 1933 "King Kong"? Everything is a big pose, toss the head back, put a hand to the brow, and then cry, shout, or scream? I don't think people way back then acted that way in real life, but this is what the movies show us. Sharing your affections or emotions does not mean you have to get emotional about it, but then, the card is reversed, so all sense of proportion and perspective are lost, too.

Worst Case Scenario: A sense of non-reality settles in, probably due to the extreme lack of perspective. All struggles become unhealthy ones fed by paranoia. There is no 'Oh, just snap out of it,' here, like telling an addict 'Just say no to drugs.' A person who is showing signs of this deep emotional state needs to find help from a professional.

Ace of Swords

ACE OF SWORDS

The Ace of Swords is traditionally considered a card of victory, usually over an adversary or life obstacle. Since Aces indicate a new cycle, the Ace of Swords signified your defeat of those opposing you, a few heads getting whacked off in the process, and now life begins from your victorious point of view. It does not have to be so violent. This Ace relates to the power (and force) of the mind, the place where ideas begin to take their shapes. Under the mind's guidance, you use your courage, intelligence, and willpower to cut away the obstacles that keep you from reaching your goals. One fine day ideas start coming to you in waves and you feel energized to begin new projects galore. You should be careful not to overdo things, for the power and energies connected to this card can be destructive as well as constructive. Swords are cards traditionally associated with stress, strife, and things that 'go bump' in the night. You should aim at relieving stress, not hoarding it. Remember that the Swords depicted are all double-edged or two-sided, so you must combine intellect and intuition to get to the heart of a situation.

There are many times you may have to 'take up a sword' for your cause, but this indicates the broad use of force will bring you to victory. Many men overreact to things in their lifetime believing that 'search and destroy' is the way to go. These are the men who use an entire can of bug spray to kill the mosquitoes at their cookouts; they waste a lot of energy to accomplish something that could have been done much more simply. Victory for them is 'victory at all costs.'

The Ace of Swords is telling you to use your imagination when dealing with your problems and to use creativity when faced with a new challenge. Perhaps your current cycle is ending, but things seem to be dragging along; in such an instance a bit of imagination may help stimulate the situation (or others) to pick up the ball and keep moving. This could be as simple as showing up early with pizza and beers to show your appreciation before they haul your boxes down three flights of stairs, not after. Your new beginnings may have some uncertain aspects in them, or perhaps your partner is not in the same cycle as you. Innovation may be the word of the day. Sometimes your partner feels alienated or does not share the same level of enthusiasm as you do. As you two walk through the park trying to sort things out, perhaps you should try a new approach and stick an 'I need you' message in a bottle and float it down the stream to them. Don't allow difficulties to fester or a problem could erupt into a serious disagreement.

At the very least, the appearance of the Ace of Swords (which does indicate victory, after all) is daring you to *try.* Inertia will get you nowhere - take the chance! If you have asked if the timing is right or if a certain project will ever get off the ground, the answer you are being given is a resounding *yes.*

Reversed:

The Ace of Swords with its tip pointing down says you are stabbing yourself in the foot - or higher up. It indicates a returning cycle of problems in your life, some of which are a real pain in the balls. Victory at this time is uncertain. When you get this card in your reading, the most important thing you should consider is the probable cause of these problems. Do others put them into motion (such as your creditors) or do you yourself cause them? This card may serve as a warning that it is time to look for a new or better solution than you have utilized in the past to deal with these problems.

In reversal (which also ties in with the previous paragraph), you may be bogged down in familiar patterns of behaviors or actions that no longer suit the given situation; but you continue to use them anyway. This is why innovation is such an important concept. This reversed Ace may be telling you it is time to *end* the cycle for once and for all. It is not telling you to risk everything to win or die in the trying; it is saying you have to initiate the change for yourself and possibly by yourself.

Teamwork may not be your strongest suit. You prefer and do your best work alone. If you have to team up with others, resist the impulse to grab control of the situation and run it yourself.

Worst Case Scenario: At the first sign of challenge, strife, or disharmony your path to victory is to accept defeat as quickly as possible to 'get it over with.' You are easily deterred by the most minor inconveniences and 'wimp out' at the earliest possible moment. People know they cannot rely on you in a jam.

Ace of Pentacles

ACE OF PENTACLES

The Ace of Pentacles deals with the material or tangible things in your life but it deals with how those experiences with them develop or form your perspective - and your beliefs. Like it or not, we are all products of our environment, but we are not born and die in a box that someone else decided on and chose for us. In the Middle Ages if your father was a peasant farmer, chances were so was his great grandfather, and so would your great grandchildren be, too. The chances of a dirt farmer being apprenticed to become a maker of fine furniture were non-existent.

This Pentacle being handed to you represents a golden opportunity that you should be accepting of and run with, even if it is not completely understood at the moment. This tangible opportunity asks you to further develop yourself. Mom and Dad still own and work the family farm, but fewer farmers are producing more and more product. If being a member of the Future Farmers of America did not appeal to you, you knew you had to find something else and prove to your parents that you had found something else to be, and have to prove to them that you can be successful at it. The arrival of this Pentacle signals the beginning of independent thought.

This extended hand represents your inner nature, too. Not only can it represent something coming to you, but it also can represent your giving of something to others, such as your generous nature. The buddy, who is always there to lend a helping hand, covers your ass when it needs covering, or helps you out of a jam. Many people view Pentacles as something always coming *to* them, but few view Pentacles as a distribution of part of themselves. Perhaps this new cycle of opportunity for is has to do with forgiveness - extending your hand to others, showing them that you have progressed beyond what divided you two and you are making the first gesture of reconciliation - another chance in the development of your beliefs.

Perhaps this opportunity will come in the form of a lesson to be learned. The start of this new cycle may follow a conclusion that was not expected or was not anticipated, leaving you dazed and confused instead of happy or complacent. That old cliché about making lemonade from lemons may come to mind. Many men are programmed to believe that you receive a challenge, you work it out, and eventually you get rewarded for it - end of sentence. They look on the 'conclusion' as final, written in stone, no need to go back to review it. What they fail to see is that sometimes a challenge is a series of lessons like the labors of Hercules, and not a one-time one-answer-fits-all questionnaire like taking your SATs. This lesson is being revealed to you; learn it well.

Reversed:

When the hand is covering the Pentacle - or in some cases dropping the Pentacle- it indicates being closed or closed off from the rest of the world. If your roots are very, very strong (which is not a negative thing in itself) it could indicate a narrow series of beliefs that you follow blindly. Perhaps your parents ingrained in you that certain kinds of people were evil, or that people who did not worship as your family did were to be avoided at all costs. Growth that would come from lessons to be learned, i.e. finding out that differences between people is what makes them interesting - is being covered by the hand. This says you do not look past what you were told instead of finding an answer for yourself. The top point of the star that represents man's head is being buried in the sand.

Perhaps you are successful, but feel embarrassed by your sudden achievement, or even feel guilty for being successful. Many boys are taught that you can enjoy success, such as tossing the winning basket or making the winning touchdown, but to be boastful or prideful about it is unmanly. In my earlier years when I was dabbling in textile art, I made a quilt that was appraised for $1,000 and when I opened the appraisal and saw the amount, I was dancing around excitedly. My father's response, disgusted, was 'What are you so *excited* about?' My sewing talents - not manly enough - did not impress my father. Was I supposed to have opened the letter, said in a deadpan voice 'Oh, my last quilt is valued at one thousand dollars,' then go out and do something more masculine, like paint the house?

Worst Case Scenario: You tend to deny opportunities exist when they are in plain sight. Through some methodical system of denial, you size up every opportunity and ignore them if they are not 'big enough' for your estimations or will not produce the exact outcome that you have predetermined. Possibly you are under some dogmatic delusion that you must deny anything that is given to you; the only things worth having are things that you yourself produce. There is no development of the psyche here, only existence.

THE TWOS

Twos indicate the involvement of another person; the situation cannot be handled or cannot develop while the Querent is alone. Twos indicate a period of waiting with more to be revealed later. Although Twos indicate stability, they also indicate duality, the pairing of opposites, and creativity not yet fulfilled.

Two of Wands

The Two of Wands is a card about risk taking, or potential that has not been fulfilled. In general terms the man on the card is some kind of merchant who although patiently staring over the horizon for 'his ships to come in' still has a slight air of concern about him. His wands are also sprouting new growth, signifying new possibilities. The globe in his right hand suggests that he has only to reach out and snag them for the world is in his grasp. During this time of transition, you might feel trapped, uncertain, and definitely restless. It is an important time to be patient for everything will work out to its best advantage. Use this 'down time' to clarify your position.

Twos in general also signify that there is another person involved in this risk process, sometimes more directly as in finding backers to assist your project, and sometimes subtly as in having a good cheering section. This card highlights relationships based on joint creativity and common interests. Your relationship will prosper when you and your partner share the workload and ideas. If your business negotiations are stalled, take care to *listen* to those across from you at the bargaining table. Since this is a card of success through collaboration, mutually agreed-upon arrangements will bring the increase in sales and profits.

Why should you want to take risks? We all have needs that stretch our boundaries at times and this card says you are in the position to do so -with some help. Perhaps you have always wanted a cabin in the woods or mountains; perhaps you even wish to build this yourself. Perhaps you see this as a long-time project taking two or three years to complete. Once the foundations are laid, you know it may be a challenge but you know you will see this project through to its conclusion.

Maybe it's not a physical but rather a mental challenge. Possibly you really want to do something daring but short term such as bungee jumping off a bridge or taking a white-water rafting trip through the Grand Canyon. All the above will take extensive planning, they will involve the input of others, and also require some examination of financial output.

Stretching our boundaries involves a degree of self-examination, also. What are our real limitations? What is purely fantasy? Which risks are worth taking? This card says be sure to 'dare to dream.' At the end of the nineteenth century, an actor named William Gillette decided that in truth 'a man's home is his castle' and built at three-story stone castle overlooking the Connecticut River. He had an extensive and successful career in theatre (he created the stage character of Sherlock Holmes for his friend Arthur Conan Doyle), saw the property, loved the view, and was eccentric and rich enough to build it - and he did. Did people think Gillette was a crackpot for wanting to build a private castle in the Connecticut countryside? I'm sure of it. But he had vision, sized up the risks, and now has immortality in the form of the State Park his property has become. Does building that log cabin sound good to you now?

Although this card does tell you that you must be patient for the plans have been made but they will happen in their own time, look to the globe. In it are endless possibilities for change, advancement, and enrichment. Take the chance, dare the dare, plan carefully and then set the wheels in motion and await your outcome.

Reversed:

Rather than make plans for the future that might involve some risk, you spin your wheels in the pretense of going somewhere while in actuality you are getting nowhere. Is this due to the involvement of others (those who promised to help roof the cabin never show up - and it's going to rain) or were you unrealistic in the planning stages (you build a four-bedroom house with one bathroom)? As much a warning as a prediction, the Two of Wands says possibly your plans are not as well thought out as you think and some reworking or revising is necessary. Perhaps this is where you will need the advice/input of another to help you see the flaws in your thinking. Being put on your head is a temporary situation.

In reversal there is a sense of being 'stuck in a rut.' Those glittering possibilities seem father distant that you thought they were. Maybe you are just experiencing cold feet. Whatever the case, take those two wands and use them like crutches if necessary to turn yourself around and get upright again. It may seem like a defeat, but it can only be one as long as you are flat on your back and not taking the initiative to get up.

Worst Case Scenario: Perhaps this reversed state is *not* an accident. Perhaps you are deliberately avoiding a risk - any risk - and are planning to 'wimp out' at the next available opportunity, effectively undermining any possibility of success. The going got tough and you got going ... in the opposite direction. This card says you do not face challenges well - or at all.

Two of Cups

Way back in the Lovers Card (Major Arcana #6) there was a man and a woman and the card was about balance and harmony; even though the Lovers are naked there was no focus on the sexual aspects since it could represent a business partnership.

Here in the Two of Cups card we deal with sensuality - our own and that which we see in others. [Incidentally, there are decks that portray same-sex couples, so this discussion is not limited to heterosexuals.] Since Twos represent the involvement of another individual perhaps we should add 'sensitivity to others.' Cups deal with emotions. The couple portrayed is exchanging vows; and in most religious contexts this includes a phrase similar to 'and two shall become one.' Gone are those aspects of 'me me me,' replaced by 'us us us.' The way to achieve this is to become responsive to your partner's needs.

The easy and enjoyable partnership that is indicated in this card often leads the way to financial success. You and your other may work together, or you offer each other unlimited support in your separate endeavors. There is an element of luck connected with this Two that helps you attract the aid of others.

I had two married friends, now deceased, who were only children who married an only child. Although they did have mutual friends, their house was clearly divided into 'his stuff,' 'her stuff,' 'his interests,' and 'her interests.' Sometimes they even went to the same place in separate transportation, leaving and arriving at different times. Having themselves as their only focus as a child did not change when they reached adulthood and married. Appropriately, they are buried in separate cemeteries! Sometimes life (and death) works out that way. This was their arrangement, and evidently it worked for them.

How does one become (more) responsive to another's needs? Without trying to act like a marriage counselor here, from experience I will say that the best way to have something done *for* you is to *do* it for your partner, also. Face it - anyone who stands at their job all day could probably use a nice foot massage when they get home. If you are expecting your partner to cook dinner tonight, you can hardly expect them to drop everything to massage your feet, no matter how much they love you. You could both prepare dinner and then share a nice glass of wine while you massage each other's feet...yes? Sensuality includes developing our senses about the other person. One friend of mine is big on textures; loves to have different textures piled on top of each other for the differences in tactile sensory experiences. You don't buy him a sweatshirt with a beer logo on it; for Christmas you buy him a sweater with some fantastic combination of wool or weaves. They will both keep him warm, but the textures appeal to his sensual side.

Sensuality and sexuality are connected but different things. Sensitivity to others in relation to sex can be harder than it sounds. In a physical world based on 'me Me ME- if it feels good I want to do it right *now*,' the idea of sex being mutual and mutually satisfying doesn't seem to come up often. In a world of STDs, AIDS, and whatever else is lurking out there, one wishes it would.

Reversed:

When any Cups card is upside down, you should think about the contents of those cups draining away, being lost, or being abused. In this card of sensitivity to others, the reversed cups signify that the mutual aspects of emotional stability are gone. There is no mutual trust, no more 'we' or 'us', but a return to that annoying 'ME only' routine. The focus becomes an internal one instead of external. Perhaps this is only a temporary situation - the card indicating that your partner or you have done something that makes the other feel very let down. Possibly a lack of sensitivity was involved.

Of course, the opposite is also possible- the reversal indicating that you/they has become *over sensitive.* Maybe you have created such a lofty ideal for someone that there is no possible way they can live up to your expectations for them. Possibly you are taking offence at something they did or didn't do because they have no idea of what you want, or you have never explained to them. Many couples living together for a period of time somehow believe that their partner is somehow 'supposed' to have magically figured out how they feel about an issue that has never even been discussed. This reversed card indicates a need to keep lines of communication open.

Worst Case Scenario: Control issues. Someone believes that they alone have the knowledge, training, brains, or whatever to make all the decisions for the couple and that they must have the final word in all the decision making processes...provided that they even allow their partner to have a voice to begin with. Being mutual here is actually being exclusive - "I know what's best for us." Although there is no true utopia where both partners sit and discuss everything that affects them as a couple, this reversal is the card of The Control Freak.

Two of Swords

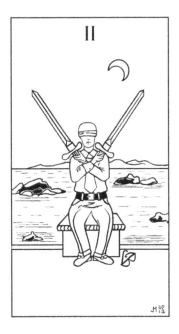

Uh-oh! 'Midlife Crisis' time! In various versions of this card the background differs from a calm sea to a raging tempest but the central figure remains the same: a blindfolded person caught between the rock and the hard place. The condition of the sea is supposed to give us some insight into the emotional state of the question or of the Querent but the ugly truth is that they are hopelessly stuck and cannot see their way out of the situation. Most books, including my first one, discuss the fact that waiting out the situation might be better than proceeding blindly into one far worse; for the men reading this book I feel the need to discuss the feelings of 'rusting out.'

There will come a time, if it hasn't happened already, when the plans have been made and put in motion and it seems as though things are going to work out pretty much as planned or hit their mark close enough to make you happy. This is all part and parcel of The American Dream. For those lucky enough to have gotten that far without too many scars the next big step (planning their retirement) will probably work out along those same lines. After all, success *should* breed success.

However, left to their own devices, men can be pretty lazy, especially if they are unchallenged in what they do.

If the sea in your card is calm it possibly indicates you are ensconced in a boring routine in everyday living: wake up, grab a cup of coffee, run to the can, get dressed, and go to work. There are some men who thrive on this - in fact they expect it. Once they get out of the can and get dressed, they immediately grab those blinders and put them on, blocking out their peripheral vision for the rest of the day. They take the same route to work, occupy their little cubicle, eat the same lunches with the same people, nuke something for supper, and then become a couch potato for the rest of the night. Repeat the next day. You blind yourself to other possibilities and remain unchallenged. You also blind yourself to other problems, too, expecting that if you ignore them long enough they will go away of their own accord. Sit still and stay calm and you'll always be safe.

If the sea in your card is churning or turbulent you are afraid of challenge or change. Blind to the storm brewing around you, you claim ignorance when the lightening starts crashing all about you - after all, you *'didn't know this was going to happen.'* This ploy sometimes works out when someone else steps in to rescue you, but you cannot rely on him or her to do it a second time. When I worked at the casino I sometimes ended up doing training for new employees, and with that position I have learned to size up potential problems in people. My job gets incredibly intricate at times and teaching it overwhelms some; others think the million little steps are something they don't have to learn since there is always a supervisor or master banker close by to pull their ass out of the fire. By experience (and design) when management knows someone is struggling but trying, they allow them to learn at their own pace. Anyone who is indifferent, or shows no interest in the job, or acts like they know everything when demonstrating the opposite is given "the bombshell." One night at the start of shift, the manager

100

walks in and announces to the trainee and banker that the trainee is to balance the bank ~ alone and unassisted! I suppose you thought people rending the hair and gnashing their teeth only happens in the Bible....

Worst Case Scenario: You are neglecting your own skills. By shutting yourself off to the input of others, you have also shut yourself off to the possibility for growth or expansion. The skills you finely honed to get you there achieved their purpose and are going rusty. Whether the seas are calm or turbulent does not matter for you will not move to help others or help yourself.

Reversed:

Although reversal tumbles you off your seat, the blindfold slips off, so even though you might temporarily find yourself in an uncomfortable position at least you can see what happened and what you should do. After the experience of being contained, the freedom now afforded you can be very enlightening. Possibly those churning seas washed away your doubts and fears, or has carried them away the way flood waters move a house off its foundations. Only when everything holding you back has been removed can the fulfillment take place.

Possibly, you will meet challenges head-on, or even incur those challenges for you have no fear of putting yourself on the line. Rather than neglecting your skills, you combine them for best advantage. Jim Henson was painfully shy about speaking in front of an audience but had a great sense of humor that could not be fulfilled. With a puppet stuck on his hand, 'he' was no longer speaking: his original 'Kermit' is somewhere in the Smithsonian Museum and his creations for 'Sesame Street' will probably be in permanent syndication. By challenging one's own abilities there is only one way you can move - forward.

Two of Pentacles

Life has its ups and downs and the ships in the background of this card ride the crest from one high to the next low (yes, water symbolism is not limited to just the suit of Cups) telling the hapless character in the card to cope by ... *staying focused*. He carries - and juggles - two Pentacles whose path forms another lemniscate, the symbol for infinity. Since all things in our life form a spiral and 'what comes around' is sure to make an appearance, how do we stay focused? We do so by learning to ground ourselves.

Grounding and centering - the two buzzwords of the 1980s New Age Movement - were an attempt to explain to people how to turn off the external Life noise and take themselves far from the madding crowd. When your life is bouncing you around so badly that you feel like a cork stuck in a washing machine's wash cycle how are you supposed to ground and center? One of those ways is to determine exactly what your *needs* are. If you don't know what your needs are, how can you tell when they are lacking? In some Hindu fable, the Great Master tells the student to write down a list of his problems and also a list of his solutions. The Student is then instructed to return with the list of solutions because these are what the Great Master wishes to discuss with him. Sometimes you really do have to sit down and make a list and then prioritize them. Often many people can make a list of their own or another's faults but cannot think of anything positive to say. Once you have a list of needs, you can define their *purpose* because needs and purpose have a direct relation to each other. Once you are *aware* of your needs and the purpose for their existence you can then work on the *practical.*

For instance: You know that your workplace is loud, noisy, and intrusive. Although you may like a high-energy atmosphere at times you may find that sometimes if feels as though the atmosphere is feeding off *you* and not vice versa. Sometimes you feel energized but many times you feel drained. How do you ward off those psychic energy vampires? The first thing which many people have not learned to do is learn how to leave 'work' at work and not bring it home with them. At work (I worked in a casino for five years) I was surrounded by electricity and electronics - computers, machines, music, neon lights, bombarded all around by noise, power fields, and sounds - and then had the human element added on top of that. I can control none of it, but I have learned how to tune it out. Driving home late at night I listen to classical or jazz music. When I get home I arrive and live in silence. As I sit here banging out his manuscript there is no TV or radio blasting in the background (I don't have a TV in this apartment to begin with) and usually there is no CD playing either. The only sound that interrupts me is the soft whistling of the boiling teakettle. I focus by removing all noise and electronic distractions; I can't control what affects me at work, but I can control what affects me at home. I need peace and quiet; it allows me to reflect on the more important things such as my relationship, my family, or my next book.

Once you can focus your attention you can focus your energies, which will help bring you into balance which is the second aspect of this card. The man is actually supposed to be dancing some kind of jig; in another deck he is walking a literal tight rope. Your ability at maintaining that delicate balance may sometimes be easy and most times be a lot of work. Learning to juggle as you dance through this life may be one of its most important lessons. Walking that tightrope from Point A to Point B requires real determination, energy, stamina, and focus. The appearance of this card says you have a ways to go but you've got a good start.

Reversed:

Dropped your balls again, huh? Are you one of those over-programmed men who just does not know enough to stop? Is your idea of relaxation doing something that is less frenetic but still high energy such as Extreme skateboarding - claiming 'But this is *fun*!' Do you run from work to the gym to home to only go out again that night and do something else? This reversed card is about scattering of the energies, dropping of the ball or balls, overextending and overreaching. It says you have fumbled and the result is a complete crash of the system.

In your defense, the cause of this may not entirely be your own doing, but the effect (not seeing the consequences) most definitely is. Perhaps you seek more to avoid unhappy situations than try to create pleasant ones. In seeking to avoid - boink! - stepped off the tightrope. Perhaps you went for the easy way out, the quickest buck, or 'the sure thing' without pausing to take a solid look around -boink! - whacked your nuts on the rope on the way down. Being focused will help you to create 'Plan B' even when Plan A seems foolproof. There is no way to entirely avoid or avert everything life throws at you, but having ways to deal with your problems helps keep them from becoming bigger problems.

Worst Case Scenario: Not only do you lack focus but you function without purpose. You have no sense of belonging, and no sense of accomplishment because of it. Everything is 'Get in, get it over with as quickly as possible, and then get the hell out.' There is nothing contemplative in your life, only action and reaction. The father of a friend suffered a heart attack at age 52 that left one side paralyzed for a week. His words of wisdom: "When you cannot move it leaves you with a lot of time to wonder about what you will do if you *can* ever move again." The early heart attack was the warning shot he needed to focus more on his family and less on his job. Twenty-plus years later he enjoys his retirement, playing in a jazz band, watching birds, and enjoying his family and grandchildren.

THE THREES

Threes usually indicate group activities or the involvement of more than one person. They can indicate delay, but with a fair promise of future success.

Three of Wands

Remember in the Two of Wands the man was waiting for his ships to come in? In this card he receives his answer. It is generally accepted that when this card is upright that his ships are full of precious cargoes and success is guaranteed. That is what this card is all about - *positioning oneself* - success giving power to your voice. How can anyone argue with success?

No one will doubt that the man in the card did not take a few chances. However, he did have a vision, worked to get support, tried to discover all the possible problems ahead of time and make plans for them, then put his plan into action. In that waiting period that led to his success there is no doubt that possibly he wondered deeply if he had made the correct plans or had all his bases covered. With his success no one is questioning his abilities. And so should it be with you: do not let successes (of all things) hold you back. There are times to make your voice heard and this is one of them.

This is the time to assert your beliefs and what you stand for. In a small company this is easier to do when everyone knows everyone else, but what happens when you work for faceless Megacorporation Incorporated? It is time for you to stand up and be counted, time to go down to Human Resources and speak to someone about having this success noted in your file. It is time to ask for recognition it more material ways and the best one is some form of career advancement.

You may be thinking, "Yeah, *this* time is worked out well but the last three times it blew up in my face." Now is the time to discover what made your success and what made your failures happen. No one is going to walk up to you and say 'Terrific Job! Here's a bigger cubicle!' What will have to happen is that you will have to point out the flaws in your failures and contrast them to the reasons for your most recent success. Assert yourself, position yourself, and make your own voice heard. In my job as a banker, there are three different types of banks, each decidedly different from each other yet connected by a paper trail. According to the casino job description a banker must learn to function in all three types of banks. In theory, anyone can learn to run all three banks, but in truth just because you are great in one bank does not guarantee you have the ability to make all three banks work. One bank is very easy to learn and run; another is easy to learn but a total bitch to make run correctly. Not everyone will have this ability although that is generally recognized. The best move a trainee can do is to say to management 'I feel very comfortable in this bank. When do I start training in the *next* bank?' The faster you can absorb the process and show the leadership ability is your best move. [Unfortunately, if bankers were receiving the raise only *after* they've learned all three banks it would probably speed up the training process; the 'bankers raise' is given as soon as someone decides to move into the banks. Management has not figured that out yet.]

Do not let your success go unnoticed!

<u>Reversed:</u>

The immediate response to this reversed card is that the venture was not a success; the ships have capsized and all is lost. There is some truth to this interpretation. It indicates some kind of major oversight in the planning stages, a 'wild card' coming into play in an unexpected way, or perhaps you misjudged the strength of the opposition or competitor. It may indicate you threw all caution to the winds and now having seeded the winds you reap the whirlwind.

It may indicate that you undercut yourself, unconsciously or deliberately. Sometimes men say 'Oh- what have I got to lose?' and the answer comes back; 'everything.' This card may serve as a warning to rethink, recall, or regroup rather than reflect the actual failure. You may question 'Can one really bounce back from such a predicted failure?' The answer is if you are being given adequate warning of impending failure, wouldn't you try to take every possible step to change that outcome?

<u>Worst Case Scenario</u>: You have a fear of success. Like the character Eeyore in *Winnie the Pooh* you walk around moaning how everything is not going to work, that everything is doomed from the start, that no one pays attention to you. In a child's book this may be cute; in an office setting there is nothing more unnerving than negativity because it breeds. You guarantee failure by influencing other's minds; that way when it does fail you can say 'See? I told you so!'

Then, too, there are those who shun success, who work behind the scenes and never wish to be in the limelight. How can you contribute to the success of something and not want to be part of the success team? There are true philanthropists out there who work and donate sizable amounts for charitable causes but never want their names used. They are the real heroes. Are you a hero or just a schmuck?

Three of Cups

Three figures, one bearing a large bunch of grapes, dance in a circle, raising their glasses in honor of someone. Is it a celebration over a victory, a toast to 'Auld Lang Syne,' the three Fates, or the three witches in *Macbeth*? Or is it something simpler - a coming together for a common good? Where the Twos general mean only you and one other person the Threes involve two or more others, and sometimes it turns into a party scene. One of the more interesting archaic meanings assigned to this card is 'a healing,' so perhaps the concept 'to your health' is not so far off target. What do these three maidens and you share in common? Compassion - sympathy for other's situations and understanding other's needs.

Anyone can sound sympathetic or empathetic on cue -'Have a Nice Day!' is tacked onto the ends of sentences everywhere you go, and can imply anything from 'Have a Nice Day!' to "Why the *$#&! don't you stay out of my face?" The true compassionate understands where you are coming from and how you got into this predicament. Although they may not be able to remove the obstacles that brought you to this point they will try to help you overcome them, or at least give you the confidence that you will. Those of us over a certain age actually remember when doctors made house calls - right to your bedside at home! Good Ol' Doc was physician, healer, therapist, psychologist, and social worker all rolled into one. My late uncle was a GP; his 'office hours' did not start until late afternoon because he had morning rounds at the hospital followed by patient visits at home. Imagine a doctor who came out to see you even if the weather was bad! A compassionate person is characterized by selflessness. Brian Piccolo is quoted as saying 'God is first, my family is second; I am third.' Many people have come to realize that the universe, indeed, does not circle around them only. Another tarot author once confided that when she was a child she always felt as though she was the only *real* person and everyone else was a cardboard cut-out, not real or part of the story, merely there to make the picture look better. An accident on a playground made her realize that *everyone* gets hurt when the fall, even though we do not directly feel their pain. Because we cannot feel their pain does not mean it doesn't exist.

Being compassionate does not mean that we give away our car, hand our fortune over to a charity, and walk around in sackcloth with our feet wrapped in rags. It deals with a sense of *accommodation* - extending parts of us to help others in need. In a couple of European countries, houses have an additional toilet near their front entrances so that if a stranger 'in need' might come to the door there will be a facility for their comfort. How's *that* for accommodation? It must keep the plumber's union happy!

Others ask most people who are compassionate usually why they can be so selfless or giving to others and never expect to see a reward when they themselves could use a hand or two. The answer deals with the future - or the betterment of the future. When we can lift a glass 'to your health' and truly mean it, when we give of ourselves whether it be staffing or stocking a free clinic, giving our time through a child/adult program, collecting donations for a food bank, or merely soothing a child who has skinned his knee - we have learned the meaning of compassion.

Reversed:

The dancing people stumble and fall, spilling their wine and losing their gaiety. Although his can be indicative of overindulgence in food & drink, it can also be an overindulgence of *self*. You are pretty involved with yourself at the moment, busy replacing the spotlight over that "Numero Uno" plaque. The concept of giving something to others does not make any impression, particularly if they have nothing to offer (or repay) you in return. Nothing is lost; all is for gain.

Tooting your horn in one thing but the self-promotion deal you have schemed up for yourself makes the beer ads for the Superbowl look like first-grader stuff. There is no way you could deal with another's emotional needs or physical requirements because everything is sought after and rated against the bottom line: how good will it make you look? If you see compassion as weakness of character you probably believe that life should be treated as 'Every Man for Himself.'

Worst Case Scenario: Your egoistic extremes border on fanatical. In *A Christmas Carol*, when Scrooge is asked about making a donation to the poor, he responds by asking if there are enough (debtors') prisons and workhouses. He implies that the poor should be out of sight and therefore would be out of mind and should not deserve a handout at Christmas. {Historical note: at the time of Dickens writing neither America nor England recognized Christmas as a work holiday. Unless Christmas fell on a Sunday you were expected to be at work.} If they did their workhouse work they would be compensated or vindicated, and therefore did not need Scrooge's time or money. Have you removed yourself so much from mankind that you will need three spirits to come visit you to help change your mind?

Three of Swords

Some Tarot images bring an immediate visceral reaction - and this is one of them. Have you been stabbed through the heart or in the back - by someone you thought better of? If this explanation works for you - then run with it. It implies that you are a victim of other's actions; let us look at the possibilities of it being the result of your own.

There is nothing wrong in being conservative - at times. There are reasons not to bid the family farm or damage the family jewels. Daily we make many decisions based on gain & loss and some things we would chose to retain at all costs, even if the chance for loss is slight. It is a great thing to be prepared the way a squirrel gathers nuts for the coming winter- gather it in and hope it's enough to tide you over but expect you will make do. In a popular TV commercial in the late 1990s, a squirrel used yellow office notes to remind him where all his nuts were hidden. Have you become like this squirrel building defenses against an unknown or imagined problem because you have already planned 'just how' others are going to try to hurt you and how you will counterattack? Have you thoroughly figured out how you will deflect every foreseen problem and built up a defense that will protect you that you have lost track of who the enemy really is? Perhaps those swords have *your* fingerprints on the handles. In keeping yourself safe from others you have inflicted the deepest wounds.

One incorrect assumption people make in reading Tarot is that they always consider that the action of the card is happening *to* them, and not that they are 'doing it' to someone else. This card can very easily indicate the opportunistic personality, the parasitic endeavors, or the person who gains from other's misfortunes. Have you ever seen a coworker get fired, and they haven't even cleared out their cubicle before someone is already sucking up to the boss to get their job - before that person has left the office? I have seen it. Some people don't even have respect for the dead. Let's stab that sword in and twist it a little.

Worst Case Scenario: Egoism - the tendency to consider only oneself and one's own interests. Although being self-centered sounds like a rather easy thing to be, an egoist spends a lot of time and wastes an incredible amount of energy analyzing what is best for them, and then deciding what the best way to achieve their self-centered goals is. These goals rarely deal in merely going to a particular college or getting this or that degree. Although the education part of it is deemed a necessary evil, it is the carefully considered 'who do I eliminate first' that pervades their thinking and ultimately guides their next actions. Remember - those are not lithe fencing foils - those are two-sided battle swords that can cut in any direction they are swung or stabbed in, and it is no polite fencing match in which they are used. Even though this card is upright, it indicates a need to destroy.

Reversed:

I always take the time to explain to my students that when the Three of Swords is reversed, the swords fall out and healing can begin, even though scar tissue may remain. When we can control the egoistic and egotistic desires of ourselves we can move towards *altruism* – the 'becoming unselfish', or developing an unselfish concern for the welfare of others. We recognize the need for others to have healing or even to help them to heal - this card (reversed) can also represent spiritual counsel or a counselor. It can indicate a need to move on or move forward or a desire to be helped to do so.

Different people have different ways of expressing themselves. Sometimes we may have difficulty in recognizing the needs of another person. Just because the person sitting next to you at lunch seems like a bright conversationalist, you may never guess they are medicated daily for bipolar syndrome or clinical depression. They may never tell you, either. Sometimes all you have to do is 'be friendly.' There is a *rather* strange woman where I work; many people would avoid her because she mutters to herself constantly, no matter where she is. Most of her mutters are seemingly incoherent. One day, for inexplicable reasons, somehow I 'tuned in' to what she was muttering about and responded. She looked at me, and smiled. Now, whenever she passes me, she says 'hi', calls me by name, and wishes me a good day or a safe trip home. I am still at a loss to explain exactly what happened. Does it matter?

We are not all cut out to be psychologists, ministers, or social workers. Some people try to help the world by creating meaningful works, such as oil painting, sculpting, or writing about their world. In this way the viewer is made to think, to reflect on what the object presented meant to the artist, reflect on what it means to *them*, and then move on to absorb the experience. The sculptor doesn't care if you like his twelve-foot bronze tchotchke or not, it is there for you to absorb; if viewing that bronze brings meaning, healing, joy, or sorrow - or a combination of all at once - it affected a change in you. Being able to affect others without bludgeoning them is a true and unselfish act.

Three of Pentacles

The illustration on the Rider-Waite-Smith deck of the Three of Pentacles card has been enigmatic at best; the stone cutter - the important figure in that card - is turned away from you and what exactly he is doing (in case you didn't know what he is) is obscured. What is the hooded figure with the polka dot robe? Some say it's a *nun*. What religious order is *that*? The Three of Pentacles is the card of the Master Builder (the Eight of Pentacles is the card of the Apprentice) which implies several important things. They include being at the height of one's talents, having the experience of time behind them to support them, and being at the height of their earning potential. The appearance of this card usually signifies "You're the Man." This card says that you've been there, done that, and reaped the experience from it. People respect you and your abilities because, after all is said and done you can apply them so easily and yet completely that you are the person people bring their problems to. You make the difficult appear easy. It is as though you are creating energy and passing that energy onto others. In this card interpretation, the Master Builder sees a plain drawing of three Pentacles, and in his mind they become more elaborate the longer he thinks because he is capable of creating them that way.

Because of this ease with which you can accomplish things, you tend to be easy-going. There is no reason to rush or play 'catch-up' because you have the situation under control. Whether you believe this or not, there is a certain charisma that you have that also puts the distressed at ease, so the combination of the two works well in your favor. The energy you have or created is channeled into the best form needed to complete the task. Enthusiasm and energy can be very infectious.

These qualities do not make you complacent or bored, however. The impulsive spikes in other people's problems do not waste your wealth of experience. In fact, you are very receptive to their problems. You can explain a certain procedure time and time again without tiring or showing boredom. This receptivity to others also makes you a magnet - why should they try to talk to the old fart down the hall when they can come to you and get the correct answer and a smile at the same time? "Being there" for others sits well on you. In fact, it is this desire to share yourself with others that makes you the most sought-after person in the office. Do you know the term 'busman's holiday'? It is where you perform your job on your days off, usually for a lesser or no fee, giving of your services to someone else who needs them? When you've reached those heights there is no need to milk it dry - besides - you already have the energy to spare.

Reversed:

When the Master Builder comes down from - or falls off of- his ladder, pedestal, or desk chair, there is a definite change in his personality. He is ill at ease when others come around because he feels paranoia that others are watching him to see what flaws they can discover, as though they do not believe his qualifications and feels as though he is constantly being put to the test. This feeling of distrust pervades his thinking and speech; rather than merely offering suggestions for possible solutions, *his* is the best and only way and demands that his way be done first. Instead of gently nudging someone towards the best conclusion he pushes him or her full force to accept his decisions before they can think the consequences through. After all, he's the one at the top, so his ideas should not be questioned.

Conversely, the reversed card can indicate someone at the top who should not be there- the living embodiment of what is known as 'the Peter Principle' - being promoted to the height of one's incompetence. Having barely made it to the top through no fault of their own they find they have no idea of what is going on. They do not have enough background (or balls) to make a concrete decision so everything they say becomes a gray area so vague that someone else has to come in and translate it into English. This is the boss who never comes out of his office; his supervisors run everything not because he has confidence in them or that they are following his orders to the letter but because someone has to keep the place up and running. Creatively done, people can hold a job like this for years.

<u>Worst Case Scenario</u>: Although most people at the top will tell you the frightening thing is that there is no place left to go but down, they will tell you that at the top you look at lateral movement. Maintenance is relatively easy, so you tend to look for opportunities already on your level. In this worse case that is not so. Here you resist movement of any kind creating a 'dead zone' at the top where you can stay safely forever. Howard Hughes the reclusive godzillionaire or the last reel of *Citizen Kane* should come to mind: all that money and power turned them into eccentric caricatures of someone who had absolutely everything but they isolated themselves from everyone and when they died they still could not take it with them. There they resisted movement, and stagnation equaled death.

THE FOURS

Fours indicate fruition, or the manifestation of an idea, along with a foundation or "space" where things can grow.

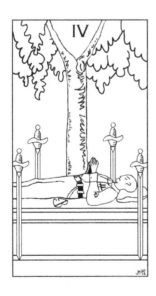

Four of Wands

The Four of Wands usually looks like a wedding reception or a big shindig of some kind. Fours deal with stability, having a solid base on which to start building, and fours also indicate some kind of a 'group' involvement. No longer single, in pairs, or a threesome - your involvement with others takes another step forward. Look at those people beckoning you to join the party - after all, it's a good time and you seem to have come along at just the right moment.

In the late Twentieth century the term *schmooze* became very popular; it's a much better sounding word than *networking*. Not all dealings in your life will require sitting in smoke-filled boardrooms of stuffy air and stuffy men in dark suits with furtive glances wondering how the person seated next to them voted. Sometimes you can actually enjoy yourself! Think of any telethon you have seen; volunteers all giving their time and energy, trying to sound as helpful as possible, cajoling as necessary to help raise funds for whatever their charity is.

They may have plastered that smile on for the cameras but they are working with others - for others - all trying to achieve that same goal within the designated time. The effectiveness of such a social activity cannot be denied.

O.K. - you may never be required to drum up money on cue. Working with others may require other personality makeovers such as honing your management skills. Not everyone is a leader; most employees are followers in the scheme of things. Just because you have not become a manager does mean you will not have to look like one or think or even (God forbid!) *act* like one somewhere along the line. Effective managers will tell you that being a manager entails a lot of interpersonal skills for dealing with all types of people. It involves learning how to sort out their questions and access the real problem, and learning how to keep lines of communication open when the best selection may not be what the employee is hoping for.

The best way to continue working with others is to prove your ability to be able to work with them. Where I work there are three daily shifts and the department is sub-divided into three categories. Personal tensions tend to run high at times; people's attitudes pump them up, at other times it is caused by differences in manager's styles. Sometimes one shift just likes to badmouth another shift. As you can expect, some people will not work with certain others and whine and complain to their boss the entire time about it. There is no easy solution about it because we all have to work with each other through a rotating schedule, so some of us have learned to 'just do' our jobs and do them well and leave all the petty crap behind when you go home. If you're unlucky you will end up like me- being the one person everyone wants to work with because I can get their job done. The more people you know, and the more people you can work with, the better off you'll be.

Reversed:

Rather than extend yourself, your social effectiveness, your management skills or proving your abilities, you tend to try to have as limited a contact with others as possible. Networking? Not on your life! You have worked too hard and too long to get where you are and learned what you now know to pass any tidbits along for the benefit of others. Since knowledge is power, to pass that power on to others that may be able to use it against you - isn't that their real reason for asking you to begin with? - That just isn't going to happen, baby! Stay outta my office and my files!

Perhaps it isn't quite so dramatic; perhaps you feel that you lack the proper social skills to deal effectively with others, whether it's a board meeting or Thanksgiving dinner with your entire family. Do you have a family member who sits there and eats but never talks? Their comments are confined to the weather and the weather. Perhaps you need to socialize some more, even if you feel awkward or ill at ease. Perhaps you have to become more tolerant of people who do not share your interests or vice versa (I think golf and tennis are two of the most boring sports in the world - no action). Since feigning an interest is always seen as being condescending, you might have to do some digging to find neutral ground.

Worst Case Scenario: Being resistant to the input of others or making others feel 'guilty until proven innocent.' A reversed Four can indicate being unstable, meaning you might tend to have so narrow a focus that building a strong base is nigh impossible. Like a pyramid built point down, anything minor can come along and upset the delicate balance, knocking your pyramid off its point onto its side. Maybe you tend to go off half-cocked, or never take the time to look at all the options, therefore depriving yourself of the broad base you really need to have. Whichever it is, you are defeating the purpose of having others around you, depleting the power of Four.

Four of Cups

A disconsolate young man sits dejectedly against a tree lost in thought or (as it was once explained) rendered numb by the shock of receiving of bad news. His thoughts are so focused on that news (the three cups before him) that he has 'zoned out' and is unaware of the fourth cup that has appeared from nowhere. There are two valid arguments about the Cups before him: first- that the cups are empty {"I've lost my job, the IRS is auditing me, and I need to get laid"}. The second argues that the Cups are in fact full {"I have an expensive house, I bought a new car, I just got laid"}, but that the observer feels unfulfilled. Both arguments hold that the appearance of the mysterious fourth cup is possibly the solution to their problems, if only they would look up and see it there. Regardless of the argument used, it is the mindset of the subject that we are going to explore.

If you were in a shipwreck and someone tossed you a life preserver wouldn't you grab for it? If that floatation device had been broken and was only one half its size, wouldn't you *still* grab for it? Would you be sinking and say "Oh, it's too small; it will never be able to support me, it probably doesn't float, anyway?" Of course not! At such a time the desire for self-preservation should kick in and any chance to help escape, no matter how slight, is held out for and held onto. Think of Cuban refugees floating on old doors, or the pictures of the helicopter evacuation of Saigon. The window of opportunity is small but the hope for freedom is strong.

Perhaps you are sabotaging yourself, consciously or unconsciously. Your empty cups cry out for filling, but you deny these needs {"Why should I work so hard? I'm getting nowhere fast!"}. Perhaps your full cups make you uncomfortable so you devalue yourself, believing that Pride is not acceptable or that boasting about your ability will somehow tempt Fate and then everything will be lost. [I am not talking mere humility here; I am referring to those ingrained parental admonitions from childhood about your talents coming from a higher source who will remove them if you boast about them since they are a 'gift' and don't belong to you.] There are many men out there who feel that you should not take credit for what you do; that may have worked for Albert Schweitzer but it doesn't necessarily have to apply to you.

This card can also indicate a 'willful neglect' on your part, choosing to avoid a situation or problem by not interfering with the process so that it *will* fail. Perhaps you have decided that it is a 'lost cause', so rather than seize an opportunity to correct or rectify the problem you let it die a natural death. It's like the plow horse with blinders on who keeps moving forward because there is nothing distracting them (or giving them a choice). "Oh- *that* help came too late to do any possible good." It's like the landlord who does not attend to any minor problem until it becomes something 'worth spending the money to fix'; in the meantime you have to deal with the problem that they chose not to worry about.

Worst Case Scenario: [I sincerely hope you realize by now that all upright cards are not necessarily positive nor all reversed ones negative!] Oh, you can see that fourth cup quite clearly, glowing like the Holy Grail beacon in a Monty Python movie - and it has the answer you seek! So what are you doing about it? You fold your arms across your chest and repeat "I see nothing!" like character Sergeant Schultz in *Hogan's Heroes*. The failure to take responsibility, the dropping of the ball, Pilate washing his hands to absolve himself - all these things indicate a willful choice to deny participation where your involvement could instead bring about a different outcome. What if the crew of the *Enola Gay* had decided to drop the bomb into the ocean instead? Not everyone who was involved could have agreed 100% with Truman's decision, but they followed orders. Will history remember you for what you did do - or didn't do?

Reversed:

You are probably wondering where all that stability and blahblahblah that I said the Fours represented went to. Inactivity (sitting under a tree) is *not* stability, but being self-valuing can be very stable. Being reversed dropkicks you out of your comatose state and says 'move your ass' and stop expecting that someone else must make your decisions, and says to stop over-analyzing and get doing! Sometimes men forget that they have personal needs, particularly when they have familial responsibilities. Perhaps what you always wanted is a private space where you can relax from work pressures, but don't have the space for a hot tub - the one thing you've always wanted. So, you have a whirlpool bathtub put in, get a nice sound system, wine cabinet- whatever would make you happiest, and learn to close the door and chill out completely. We sometimes deny self-care.

In reversal, we start to take responsibility and move forward into *action*. The period of seeking and weighing the pros and cons is over and now we step forth to implement those decisions, whether it's finding a better investment broker, saving for a rainy day, or starting to dig the footings for the new deck. The point is that sitting is stationary but not necessarily stable; standing and moving - that is- taking action and the responsibilities for that action, moving the plan forward will get you the fulfillment you seek.

Four of Swords

Traditionally, the Four of Swords had to do with recharging your batteries, a need to get your act together, or even convalescence. All of these possibilities indicated increasing outside pressures and a need for defenses to be strengthened. What if they worked from the other direction - totally from within? What kinds of scenarios would we have to deal with? What 'head games' are you forcing yourself to play?

"Joe's sacked out on the couch again - things must be really tough at work." Joe spends a lot more time sleeping these days, not because he is tired but because he really can't cope, so sleeping becomes his escape. At work everything appears fine on the surface but in reality Joe is facing the start of a decline in his effectiveness. People with more education, more stamina, and that dreaded word - *younger* - than he are entering the company and its leaving him feeling as though he is in the center of the void. Oh - the rest of the staff may not really be aware of it - he sails right along because he has experience behind him, but the truth is that he feels as though he is being left behind. To counter this effect and the feeling that his personal skills are decreasing along with his effectiveness Joe is desirous to do more work but with fewer people around to assist him. He isn't resting; he's passing out.

This decline in activity may also be more of 'rusting out' than passing out. Perhaps the new day has dawned and Joe finally realizes that he is lacking the real skills to get the job done effectively anymore. Once upon a time, people 'learned' the new stuff right on the job, usually from other, more experienced workers and it trickled down. New procedures were a hands-on type of learning, a memo was sent out, etc., and things just moved right along. Anyone who has entered the workforce after 1980 and The Age of Computers may wonder just how the business world *ever* ran using business typewriters and paper interoffice memos! How did you ever get your work done moving so slowly? Joe is one of those folks who remember using carbon paper and the little eraser pencil with the brush on the end -- is he now a dinosaur, or what? Learning to type - excuse me - *keyboard* was something high school girls learned to do because they wanted to become secretaries. Boys did not take typing classes at my high school in the early 1970s. Joe isn't passed out on the couch - he's comatose. You've analyzed your current professional situation and you're primed and ready to make a change ... but nothing works out the way you have been expecting it to. Everything you do leads to more disappointment or loss. You're worn out and the waiting for things to turn around is becoming frustrating and fatiguing. Remind yourself that 'this, too, shall pass.'

Sexually, this card implies a period of restraint to total celibacy. If a long-term relationship is breaking up, this is the time to remove yourself from the dating scene and the pressures of dating and intimacy.

Worst Case Scenario: You aren't under any stress or strain at all; rather than worry about anything, or become concerned, you have gone in the total opposite direction and become *complacent*. Your reaction is "So-what's the big problem?" or as it was once said to me "I hardly get paid enough to work; I don't get paid to worry about it." Like the

128

proverbial duck shedding water from its back your feathers never seem to ruffle. What others don't see is that you are not a duck (swimming smoothly but paddling like hell underneath} but an ostrich who's head is stuck in the sand (or up elsewhere) and are in total denial of the situation.

If you are uninvolved or feeling lonely or isolated at this time, this card is an indicator that this is not the best time to try to find a new love affair.

Reversed:

Having taken some necessary rest, you wake up realizing that the world has continued to move forward without you, but rather than be depressed about it, you decide to get your ass in gear and move with it. *Enrichment* - a clever term that means 'Stuff you didn't know you were lacking before' gets used a lot. You get off the couch and start to look for ways to increase your personal and/or interpersonal skills. You look for ways to combine things such as buying a stationary bike or treadmill with a bookstand so you can read (which you dearly love to do) while working out (which you dearly need to do).

There is a certain resilience within you that makes you still desire to get ahead, but now you have learned *adaptation* to changes rather than resistance to changes. You've come this far so your skills aren't wasted unless you yourself waste them. Keep moving forward.

At best you will consider Life an adventure for nothing ventured is nothing gained. Learning is a lifelong process, so why stop?

Four of Pentacles

The Miser sits huddled, clutching his material wealth tightly to himself in fear that someone will try to take it from him. Although the image varies from deck to deck, the underlying idea of "It's <u>mine</u>! *All* mine!" permeates this card. He sits with both feet planted firmly and yet for all his wealth he frowns angrily, for the desire for wealth does indeed weigh heavily on his mind. It is a very unhappy card. If money is tight you feel discouraged and depressed because life is always a struggle. Even when things are going well for you, you have a sense of foreboding for the future wrapped tightly around you like a cloak.

Like this miser, you, too, hold onto a past and will not let go. You hold onto your hurts, your hatreds, and your failures. Unable to find cleansing or release, those feelings that caused you pain maintain it in perpetuity. Like the wounded animal with its paw still caught in a trap you glare at anyone coming close. Your gain is your gain, your pain is your pain and no one should try to separate the two. You are not in the mood for platitudes, and you won't stand for anyone telling you that you are the one responsible for your present situation.

What's even worse is that once upon a time you were not like this; people remember you as an aspiring, enterprising individual who was loving and caring and even laughed occasionally. That was lost forever when you started treating those around you as though they were merely possessions, not people, trying to control them like pennies put into a piggy bank. Those who were able to leave you left long ago and those who can't leave yet already have their bags packed in anticipation. But what should you care? You don't need them! Brooding in your cave, you are full of unhappy memories and unresolved guilt. Someone hurt you and you have steeled yourself never to become hurt or close again. The best way for this to never happen again is to withdraw from those with the potential for caring or loving and thus the ability to hurt you again. And no- you don't live in miserly squalor! Why need people when costly, showy items will let people know of your success for you? Deep within your gated trophy home or behind the tinted glass of your expensive sports car you lurk unattainable and untouchable ... and alone.

<u>Worst Case Scenario</u>: You have never recovered from some profound loss. Like Rhett Butler barricading himself from the outside world with the body of his dead daughter, your sense of reason is distorted and you believe all are against you who do not share your loss. Perhaps, too, you hold onto a system that no longer works, but you refuse to see the reality which would mean losing something you cannot bear to part with. Do you hold so tightly because you are afraid of losing it, or are you afraid of losing it because *it's the only thing you've got?*

If you are not in a relationship it may be that you are having a difficult time meeting the right person; those you meet are unable to provide you with what you are looking for. If you are currently partnered, you feel deprived of the love or sex you feel you need. Either you feel you are unattractive or unlovable, or at the least feel very unlucky in love.

Reversed:

Some readers would say that this card in reversal shows the actual loss happening. No matter how hard the miser tries those coins still elude his grasp. I tend to speculate that those falling coins represent a release rather than a loss. No longer bottled up inside him, those feelings and emotions have run their course, and with their release there is a sense of letting go and moving on. If you are a parent, there is something very strange about your child leaving for school for the first time whether it's first grade or the first year of college. By letting go and moving on, both of you have the potential for further growth.

Those falling coins also speak of adaptation to new and possibly unfamiliar circumstances. Whoever really said 'The only thing constant is change' was very correct. To hover around quivering in limbo because you do not want to face a change (or a challenge) becomes an unhealthy obsession. Learning to deal with changes may take one or two tries; no one guarantees it will always be easy. But isn't getting up and out and doing something much better than sitting alone haranguing yourself over slights of the past?

Perhaps the card in this position does deal in some loss in some way; the loss of what was holding you back. Rather than mourn that loss be thankful that you have finally been unburdened of it! No matter how bad things seem, try to remember that this situation is only temporary and the potential for happiness is close at hand.

THE FIVES

Here, in the middle of the Suit cards, things take a departure from the norm. Fives indicate challenge, fluctuation, and change. "Change?" you're asking "Is it going to be a positive or negative kind of change?"

In the scheme of things, it's going to be difficult to tell, for what appears on the surface may not indicate the final outcome. In Kabbalah (or Qabala), Geburah, the fifth sphere on the Tree of Life represents the destruction of the Temporal, the breakdown of the forces of nature. These destructive forces (and the reasons behind them) can sometimes be more positive than those forces of construction. Although Geburah deals with restriction, severity and the vices of cruelty and wanton destruction, its virtues are energy, courage, and lessons that must be learned.

In my experience, these cards of change seem to have a pattern to them; upright they seem to be at their worst - the antithesis of their suit. To me it is their reversal that makes more sense or gives a better answer - or at least makes them seem more positive. If you have not yet accepted my idea that a reversed card can be positive, perhaps the study of the Fives may help change your mind. How will I make this explanation work for you? I am going to simplify the concept using the phrases **TOO MUCH, TOO LITTLE, TOO LATE,** and **TOO SOON**, and their statements about timing and perspective. My original concept was that there would be no need to include reversals for the Fives (how can TOO SOON have a reversal?), but I have amended that, too.

Another new concept begins with the Five of Swords. Up to this point most of the cards we have dealt with have one central character that is easily identifiable as the Querent. Other characters are drawn on the same plane, such as in the Two of Cups. In the Five of Swords, however, there is a large, central character looking back at two figures walking away from him. Generally speaking, most readers see the central character—the largest one--as being the Querent or the Querent's actions. In this card there are the Defeated and the Victor. Which one is the Querent? Does the Querent feel defeated by someone or something and identify with the smaller background figures while the larger central character signifies the oppressor? We will explore this concept of characters depicted on different planes representing different people as we continue through the deck.

TOO SOON

TOO LATE

TOO MUCH

TOO LITTLE

Five of Wands

Five men armed with Wands battle it out. They all have the burden of multiple sparring partners. All of them want to win, but in truth there can only be one victor in a battle, even if he only wins by being the last man standing. It is **TOO SOON** to know what can happen. Another Tarot author states that although the battle may be uphill, it will still be fair, since the Six of Wands indicates a victory, but I still feel this card and its situation are still **TOO SOON** to call.

The appearance of this card indicates that it is too early to ask even though you may have a burning desire to have an answer. Perhaps there are too many variables connected to the real question and the one simple answer you want will not cover the question. Situations are going to fluctuate rapidly and since they may be under the control of other people, it will end up being their decisions coming before yours that will cause you to have to change your plans once again.

Perhaps the situation is in the wee beginning stages and has not reached its development yet. Information is just becoming known, and it is unwise to speculate on your success or failure. Challenging others could be a bad idea. This is a card about 'spinning your wheels' - marking time to keep yourself from sinking but still getting nowhere. The time for the making alternative plans and possible escape routes is *before* the battle, not during it. Don't do anything foolish while marking time, but don't let them take an unfair advantage over you, either.

Worst Case Scenario: This card also says you might have incomplete information about the situation and it causes you to strike out at others, perhaps looking for a fight that really isn't necessary. You are only guessing what will happen and have no concrete basis for your actions. In doing so you will put others on high defense so expect them to react badly to your behavior and challenges. If you start a fight you will end up in one; it does not mean you will be the victor for catching someone else off guard. They may have a better defense strategy up their sleeve than you may.

Reversed:

How does one *reverse* **TOO SOON**? In reversal, the Wands slip from the men's grips and they are left without means of destruction and the playing field has been leveled - for the moment. There are those among you saying 'Now we can beat the crap out of each other with our bare hands!' {Sigh} Since it is too soon to effectively deal with the situation, without having any real physical means you are left to use your brain and wits and analyze the situation. Think about the unfolding events more thoroughly, make rational decisions- DO NOT just jump in and blindly start slugging it out.

On a personal observation - once you have removed the weapons, perhaps you will see that as individuals you were weak. However, by forming partnerships with each other - instead of trying to destroy each other - you can gain ground by putting the numbers to work *for* you instead of against you.

Five of Cups

A figure cloaked in an attitude of deep sorrow stands on a knoll overlooking a stream. This person is very upset by the spillage of three Cups, whose contents seep into the ground or join the moving stream of this person's emotion. The phrase I have chosen for this card is **TOO LATE**. It is much too late to ask about this situation *now* for the Cups are already spilled and try as you might there is nothing you can do about it. Whether these Cups were spilled by the actions of another (raining on your parade) or by your own neglect (swinging that vampire cape or blanket around carelessly) you failed to see or heed the warning signs that a storm was a-brewing! It is too late to ask for help or try to build a defense for this change of course is already in progress and turning its tide is going to prove a wasted effort.

The emotional upset brings a confusing mix of sorrow and loss. Whatever the contents represent for you - goals reached, financial security, a longing for someone - they are dashed on the sands and clichéd responses about 'spilt milk' do nothing to help you resolve it. Suddenly everyone else's problems pale in comparison to yours. The stream in the background is calm in contrast to the churning emotions within you, and perhaps you decide to hide all emotions from others, holding them all in. Without diagnosing (something you should never do as a reader) this card tacitly hints at mental confusion brought on by an overwhelming sense of grief. You will need to find a strong shoulder to cry on, or become that shoulder for someone else.

Worst Case Scenario: The flip side of this is that you are about to be hit squarely in the face with a harsh reality that is unexpected and for which you will be unprepared: what you are doing, wanting, working towards - is no longer relevant. You may have done the homework, made the plans and have set them on their courses, but you are about to find out that life happens while you were making those plans and your plans don't fit. {Of course - the mere appearance of this card does not *guarantee* this; it may only serve as a warning that something unpleasant to downright nasty is about to happen}. The cousin of my roommate was a happily (he thought) married man whose wife 'had met someone on the Internet' and flew across country to meet him. If this had happened to me, I would have changed the locks, called legal counsel, and started divorce proceedings for her wanton abandonment of her children. He expected her to return to him and the children. She did. She also filed for divorce and got the house and the kids and lives in it with the schmuck she met on the Internet, whom she married. He is probably still scarred from this episode. Remember that the lessons of Geburah can be very cruel.

Reversal:

In reversal **'TOO LATE'** can become 'it's NOT too late.' In this card of Five only three Cups have been spilt. The confused figure has its back turned and does not see that in spite of this upsetting tragedy, there are still two cups of possibilities within reach. Even though you have been turned completely around, this card is telling you to look around and see what there is to grab onto, to build from, or which new direction you should be considering. The event is now in the past and cannot be changed. Rather than stagnate, you should move forward.

Five of Swords

Restriction and severity - big time - raise their ugly heads in this card of **TOO MUCH**. The gray skies, the clouds and clothing of the figures being buffeted by the winds, the defiant stance of the man with the Swords- all combine and say "there is too much to deal with here! I cannot go on!" One figure is bent in sorrow; another is walking away holding onto whatever small shreds of self-dignity they can muster. Both of them have taken heavy losses. The only thing they can do is retreat in whatever way is easiest for them.

In sharp contrast the defiant man smiles as they leave. As he picks up the fallen swords one wonders how many opponents there might have been - and how he was able to subdue them all. Did they challenge him, not knowing how strong an opponent he could be? Did he rightfully challenge his opponents to protect himself, or did he challenge the weakest ones knowing that he would be successful due to their lack of skill, knowing there was no way he would lose? Was it a fair fight, or did the winner cheat them out of their victory? Did he contrive the whole thing- was there a 'real' purpose for this fight? Did he strike out saying 'Victory at all costs - I cannot be second-best!'? There is a clear division of thought here: the victor and the vanquished. Someone must win and someone must lose but was everything above board or were the extremes really in excess? Whatever happened - the winner takes it all.

This is one of those unusual cards where the outcome is clear but the protagonists are not. If you are reading for yourself, you are one or the other, but you cannot be both victor and vanquished. The appearance of this card usually brings a strong gut reaction and usually you immediately will know which one you are- if reading for someone else you may have to clarify the characters, but the Querent will usually do that before you even ask!

<u>Worst Case Scenario</u>: Dominance - short and sweet, a bully of the first order. Whether it is through the tact of a diplomat, the intellect of cunning - or the relentless push of a bulldozer - your desire is to control everything in your path. At times you can actually make it appear as though you are using your 'influence,' but in reality you keep your brass knuckles polished to a high shine.

In contrast, you are easily dominated or influenced by others. They know this and they use it against you whenever possible, and like the proverbial jellyfish, you lay there in the sand as spineless as ever. You are the first person to change your opinion in a debate or duck out of the way when the going gets tough.

<u>Reversed:</u>

In reversal **TOO MUCH** becomes *equilibrium*. As the swords elude the grasp of the dominant man the playing field becomes leveled. As in the previous card, once the many weapons and their potential are removed from the situation, a dialogue can take place. Yes, someone may still try to charm you or disarm you with his or her tongue. Remember the old nursery rhyme about 'sticks and stones' and keep a level head about yourself. Eleanor Roosevelt said 'No one can make you feel inferior without your permission.'

In reversal this card indicates that a potentially dangerous or damaging situation can be averted or that its affects will not be as far-reaching as they first appeared. There is still an 'aftermath' to get through but the rebuilding can begin.

Five of Pentacles

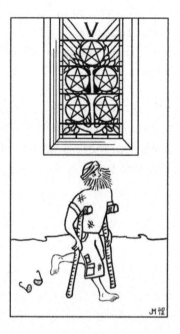

In this card not only are the forces of nature breaking down but they are out of control. One of the lessons of Geburah is courage, and it will take all your courage and energy to get through this card, often referred to as 'The Dark Night of the Soul.'

TOO LITTLE - this card of abject poverty works on several levels and with different messages. The first is material/financial poverty, which can be real or imagined. It indicates a desire for material comforts without any way of obtaining them. Perhaps you are thinking on a grandiose scale that far outstrips your abilities to pay for them. Putting yourself in the red will make you end up like these two wretched creatures tossed out in the cold without a means for warmth or comfort.

The stained glass window speaks of spiritual poverty. Why are these people outside when a warm, lighted building beckons them?

Have they turned their backs on the spiritual end of things, the concept that we are all in this thing together and we have to help each other? Perhaps they distanced themselves from others for so long that now, in their hour of need there is no one to help them? Or, as has been suggested by others, these people relied religiously on the institutional machine to help them, and in the end that machine failed them?

To say this card is about 'lacking' is an understatement, but lacking you have become. Since Tarot cards are usually warnings or indicators rather than the actual event, this action of yours that brought this card into the reading - is missing some very vital aspect and you are missing the point, chum. You are clearly being warned that the action is chancy at best and will have negative influences since it is practically guaranteed *not* to work in its present state. Perhaps, too, it is an indicator that you are placing far too much importance upon something that is of too little significance in the scheme of things, following a pipe dream, investing at a clearly inopportune time or even throwing good money after bad. This card works on shock value - it is trying to shock you to your senses.

Worst Case Scenario: Not only is the situation bad, but it is totally out of your control. Unknown influences come out of left field and devastate you, and all your preplanning could not have foreseen *this*. In the early twentieth century, the stock market crash caused people on Wall Street to commit suicide because they had lost everything. Don't put all your eggs in one basket and watch out for falling bodies.

Reversal:

The sphere of restriction carries a high price. When this card is reversed, it indicates that you will have to hit rock bottom first before you can attempt to make a recovery. As much as that means that things will indeed have to become worse than they are in order to get better, remember the virtues of energy and courage connected to the Fives. In numerological terms, think about the Fives' connection to the Temperance card (#14 = 1 + 4 = 5) and remember that you will have to find middle ground on which to stand, looking for the safest passage out of your dilemma. It will not be an easy road to find or to walk. It does, however, indicate that a long string of bad luck will come to an end, and that little black cloud following you around will finally disappear. It will be a slow recovery period since the far-reaching effects cannot be dismissed overnight. You will be required to look forward and move forward for all changes have a purpose even if they cannot be fathomed at the present time.

THE SIXES

The Sixes indicate adjustments in thoughts, attitudes, or conditions. They can also represent the ability to transcend difficulties. Sixes stand for balance and equilibrium.

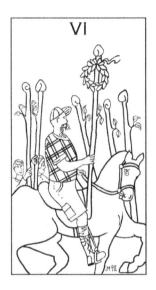

Six of Wands

A man bearing the laurel leaves of victory rides a horse through a gathered crowd of supporters. Details are unclear although it looks like a parade of some sort. Whether they are only mere bystanders, team members, platoon members or the entire office staff the one thing that seems certain is that the gathering is to honor and support the man on horseback. Sixes represent adjustments in thoughts, conditions, and attitudes, also the ability to transcend difficulty and this is exactly what this card represents - performance.

To exist in the day-to-day world men's self-evaluation deals in how they perform: at work, in sports, and in bed. Our bosses and coworkers are constantly evaluating our performance, the captain of the opposing team sizes us up, and our lovers want to feel satisfied every time. The appearance of this card shows you are successfully demonstrating your potentials and applying your skills. Perhaps you do not choose your tasks - they are thrust upon you. They may be chosen by others to test your limits. Perhaps you are allowed freedom to set your own priorities and you wisely have decided that being complacent is a bad idea promotion-wise, so you seek out tasks on an ever-increasing scale of difficulty. Whatever that may be, you are rising to the task and people notice it.

In carrying out these duties you have also or are also demonstrating a sense of responsibility that puts you a head above the rest. In any group activity there are sure to be individuals who can be classified as 'doers' or 'shirkers.' Hopefully, if some upper management has got a clue, they know who the shirkers are; also, hopefully once the shirkers understand that management does know about them that they will be motivated to transfer somewhere else. You, on the other hand, are demonstrating your abilities and responsibilities very well; perhaps even your leadership abilities and those around you have no choice but to notice. The celebratory aspect of this card indicates a *public* recognition, so this is no pat-on-the-back forget-it-later type of thing. We are talking about certificates, plaques, trophies, promotions, raises, and pictures in the newspaper kinds of stuff.

Your performance and skills have also brought two things forward for you. One is a sense of daring- the concept that you have been on an upward climb and have stayed the sure and steady course. The second is that as your abilities have grown so has your confidence. Feeling sure of yourself (whether or not it has been true at all times) has brought about a great change in the way you see yourself. There is nothing to stop you now!

If you have had some physical or emotional problems regarding your sex life the appearance of this card denotes a major breakthrough or step forward. What was once difficult or impossible becomes easy and even pleasurable. In one of my Italian decks - *I Tarocchi delle Stelle* - the six men on the card are naked, holding their ... wands high. If that does not add a new dimension to the term 'getting a woody,' I don't know what does!

Reversed:

Nothing can stop you – do you <u>really</u> think so? Having fallen (or been thrown) off your horse fills you with unnecessary caution - a sense that you will be defined by your failures, and not by triumphs. Instead of picking yourself up and trying to reseat yourself and possibly regain some control of the situation you say to the world around you "I'm down here and I'm staying here."

It may indicate that you are about to do something that - although this act may be deemed necessary by yourself or others - will prove to be very unpopular. Even if you are right in this matter it will be very difficult for you to gain the support or interest of others. They will possibly detour around you to avoid having to listen or deal with you, or you may end up avoiding them because you see their indifference as a betrayal of sorts: 'fair weather friends.' It is a time for cold shoulders and frosty environments. You will have to come to grips with the situation and learn to transcend it.

<u>Worst Case Scenario</u>: Whether or not you will fail is immaterial at this moment because it is your overwhelming *fear* of failure that will probably cause you to fail and not your actions in the matter. We are all faced with unknowns and chances. Sometimes we openly speculate on the negative – it is human nature. No one can ever be 100% sure of anything. But your fear of failure overwhelms your chances for success. It might be because you are in such need for total control and you cannot let go. Rather than bring on an 'iffy' success you cause a definite failure. I work with a young woman who is such a control freak that she has to try to control things when there is nothing to control, has to check everyone else's work, has to answer the telephone every time it rings. She has great potential but she has undermined herself on more than one occasion. No one wants to fail, but shooting yourself in the foot when you have the ability to do otherwise...?

Six of Cups

In traditional Tarot terms this card deals with nostalgic feelings and connections to the past. A young man takes or gives a flower token to a younger companion, and it is presumed he will next walk over the bridge into adolescence, taking her memory with him. In more modern terms, this is a card about acceptance - accepting the love of others, and giving of love to others in the most non-judgmental way possible, in other words unconditional loving.

It is said that you can only be truly hurt by someone you care about. After all, if you don't really care about them, how can their actions hurt or bother you? No one's family is ever quite as dysfunctional as yours is, but many families with problems try to meet their problems head-on as a unit. Sadly, individuals can put degrees and conditions on loving, as though they have a chart that says "If you do this I still love you, but do that and I don't." Can you love someone this morning, have he or she disappoint you tonight, and then not love him or her at all tomorrow morning? The point is to accept the disappointment, yet to care without judgement.

For couples, acceptance is usually a trust exercise. After all, two individuals have their own set ways of doing things and once you become two incorporated instead of two separate ones, things need 'adjusting.' My partner and I came together in our late 40s after we had both had former long-term relationships; the ghosts of the past die very hard. There were many false starts and big problems and a lot of smoothing out to do. For some couples this acceptance comes along with the sensual pleasures of life. After a lot of bad dates, one-night stands, bar scenes or whatever, trusting someone enough to love them is difficult, much less trying to be non-judgmental. As with the young man in the card, the past should stay in the past. Or as Rhett Butler said, "Tonight there will only be two of us in the bed."

One problem many people have is that they tend to be skeptical of kindness, especially from a total stranger. In the distressing daily world in which we live, when someone does something nice for us, such as holding a door while we struggle with a burden, the first thing that flashes through our minds after saying 'thank you' is "I wonder what they want from me?" Accept kindness for what it is; enjoy it and reward it somehow. Go out of your way to do something nice for someone without expecting to receive a reward, like shoveling their walk or watering their lawn. Perhaps that means not cursing at the idiot who gave you the finger in the parking lot. Do you remember when people actually respected each other and spoke civilly to each other? I do. Learn to accept others without always analyzing their motives, or as the phrase goes "perfect love and perfect trust."

This card is focused on 'things remembered.' It can manifest in collecting items such as antiques or memorabilia connected with childhood. You may find you have a talent for writing about, painting, or photographing children. It can even manifest itself with a connection to a past that wasn't yours; I have a handlebar mustache and collect antique mustache cups with matching saucers. I will never use them, but the fact is that they are 100 years old and connect me to a bygone, elegant, *slower* time that no longer is. I cherish them.

Reversed:

Civility has long been absent from daily living. In this day and age, no longer is it sufficient to disagree with someone, we have to announce it to everyone, reiterate it on an hourly basis, and let our displeasure be known at every public gathering. There is no 'live and let live' here, only a need to perpetuate hostility. It is this daily routine of judgement going on that bypasses the level of being the mere office gossipmonger. You no longer accept things at face value and those values change hourly as you make judgement after judgement - usually *against* someone or something. It is known as 'disliking with continuous judgement.'

Rather than accept people for what they are (or aren't) you believe that it is somehow under your control to make them improve, or expect them to be under your conscious control. People are not automatons or the Stepford Wives who will do everything and anything you wish the exact way you wish every time. What is worse is that these individuals might also be correct in their actions, and in your jealousy you cannot see it or steadfastly refuse to accept it.

Worst Case Scenario: The need to judge rather than accept others goes full tilt as you become over-demanding of those around you. You are constantly upping the ante of what you will accept, making those around you work harder or longer or whatever in a futile effort to insinuate themselves back in your good graces. You are the boss who never promotes anyone, the parent who demands high grades from a 'C' student, and the lover who takes without giving. Nothing will satisfy you and you let everyone know it.

Six of Swords

In some decks this is a card about wimping out, about taking the path of least resistance. There is no 'stand up and fight;' it is more along the lines of ' I can't take this anymore! Run – away!' The waters on the right side of the stairs (a rowboat in most decks, particularly the Rider-Waite-Smith) are rippled and moving; the waters on the left are calmer and smooth. But a storm is brewing! This journey suggests things have become overpowering and the best thing to do is flee as far away as you can, even if it involves risk. In the Swords Man's case, he must weigh facing a strong unseen force, or flee over the swords – risking personal injury, but evading that gathering storm. Will the avoiding one harm still put you in another harm's way?

This card suggests that you may give up too easily, that you sit there idly by while others cover your ass for things you've not accomplished. You tend to leave all the details until the last second and then are unprepared for the overwhelming burden they create. You also tend to leave many projects unfinished. Once you hit any kind of a snag in your path to completion, the project can sit unfinished until someone nags you to death about it or someone else finishes it for you. You constantly claim that you 'didn't have the time' or that great all-time male line: "I don't have the correct tools!"

Perhaps you bit off more than you could chew and this is you tucking your tail between your legs as you skulk out the door, hoping that no one will notice your departure. Mediocrity works in this manner - set everyone up for a really fantastic show and then disappoint him or her. The problem with mediocrity is that it feeds on itself. Many people take painting classes and learn to paint in oils. Everyone cannot and will not be the next Seurat or undiscovered Van Gogh. Although having mediocrity is not a bad thing in of itself {after all, mediocrity suggests ability but not talent}, some people will always be mediocre and never know they are so. This usually keeps them working toward improving. Some people pride themselves in the lack of talent. {Personally, once you've seen two of Grandma Moses' paintings of a horse pulling a sleigh in the snow, you've seen them all}. However, this card says that sometimes rather than take some constructive criticism and work to improve that you merely take your bat and ball and go home.

This card also can suggest your general ineffectiveness in the area of the question you asked. Perhaps the man is not the husband but merely the boatman doing his job - that is - to get people through their problems to the other side of the river. As the passengers in the boat did, you also engage someone to do the job for you. Your lack of authority in this matter puts you into the hands of someone who can, and you merely follow what they instruct you to do, but you perform without interest in the process. The boatman can suggest a counselor or therapist trying to steer you towards a better conclusion, but the captain of the boat you are not.

Reversed:

In reversal, you go from mere participant to captain of your destiny. You do not need (but *do* heed) the expertise of others, but you recognize their contributions accordingly. Knowledge is knowledge but knowledge is also *power* and the best thing you find to do share your expertise with others. No huddling in a corner and looking pathetic for you! You do not sit wishing for someone to help you; you pull yourself up and help yourself, or seek the best authority to get you started in the correct direction. If *you* are the best authority around, you seek to help others but do not lord your authority over them. If you are the best damn bird carver in the state, you teach classes in wood carving because although no one can reach your pinnacle of success for the moment, someday someone will - and you'd like it to be someone you nurtured. That will be your crowning success.

One of your active choices is to help others improve ... something. Rather than by being a nagging pain in the ass, you realize that everyone needs space to move and grow and that all leadership is more than telling someone what he or she has to do next. You lead by example, giving people alternate choices where appropriate and allowing them to make their own choices. You help them to see their limitations; you don't form them. You realize that everyone has some limitations and not all of them can be overcome in time. I, for one, can't type worth a damn and wrote this (and my first book) completely by looking at the keyboard, glancing up at the screen every now and them to see how many errors were underlined. Why don't I learn how to type? Wouldn't that make my writing efforts easier? Personally, I want voice recognition software and just *talk* my book. Learning keyboards - computer or piano - just doesn't work for me. Not being able to type does not stop me from writing; typing is only one step in the multi-faceted process.

<u>Best Case Scenario</u>: The contribution of knowledge, the ability to help others to achieve their potential. Sixes represent the abilities to

transcend difficulties. Perhaps you once did huddle in your cloak in the bottom of the boat nervously hoping things would just improve on their own or just go far away. Using that weakness as a starting point, you have come full circle and now stand on your own. Always move forward and help others to do the same. {PS – step on the stringer near the sword hilt – not in the middle of the flexible and sharp sword blade.}

Six of Pentacles

In this card a man distributes coins to some needy characters. The set of scales he carries signify his desire to give each their due, to distribute fairly and to give based on need. It is a card about charity, about giving of material things, but mostly a card about support and involvement in the lives of others.

If Life was fair and every family was completely functional, there would be no need for therapists, bad situation comedies about family life, or a need for charity collections. Everyone would be kind and understanding and loving and it would be Utopia for all. There would be few needy people, and those that found themselves down on their luck would know that it was only temporary and fleeting at most. We all know this is just bullshit. Life is not a situation comedy where all is well in the end. Children do get abused, people do get abandoned, and large companies just mysteriously close their doors and disappear overnight. This is where supportive commitments come in.

Everyone needs a base of support at times; sometimes that situation is codependent. When Stephen King was almost killed after being hit by a van, his wife Tabitha knew that part of the healing process would involve King continuing writing. Their children were grown and moved away and King could have lived the rest of his life on royalties and residuals. WHAM! His leg is broken in nine places. No sooner than he came home from the hospital than his wife set up a place from him to write with a broken leg in mind. Did King really need to write for the money? No, not really, but writing was a way to work through the healing process. By providing support and comfort, Tabby gave him a way to cope with the injury and a way back to wellness.

This card shows a dedication to purpose in the helping of others. Do you know people who always seem to 'be there' at the right time? Or always know what to say at the correct time? These people inevitably are good listeners first, accessing what is going on in someone's head and then saying and doing what the other person needs most. This could be loaning a quick fifty bucks, borrowing a van (in my mind a SUV is just another van) to bring a large purchase home, or just holding the sheet rock in place so it can be nailed.

Commitments - supportive commitments - the understanding of two people working together as one. Two people make a family and a community is made up of families. Sometimes it seems we have to give more in proportion to what we receive. Community is working towards the common goal, and some will always need more than others do and hopefully there will be those with plenty to give. Being an involved person is our way of giving of ourselves to both our family and community.

The alternative to this is you seeing yourself not as the man with the money, but rather one of those in need. Sometimes situations and circumstance roll over us with the subtlety of a freight train and we might find ourselves in the uncomfortable position of being dependent on others. The situation may ominously become long term. The appearance of this card says that you will reach out to others and should find solace or help, maybe some financial assistance. If you are unemployed, this can be the receiving of unemployment compensation, or even having the prospect for a new job. Perhaps it might not be what you want at the moment, but this person is giving you the opportunity to pick yourself up again. Accept this gift and remember to do likewise in the future.

Reversed:

In reversal it looks like the money is slipping from the needy to the rich man's hand. Which figure are you? Does this indicate you are paying and paying and feeling like you are receiving nothing for the money or time involved? Do you feel as though you cannot ever get ahead, that someone else is taking your money before you make it? It can indicate you have or will place too much trust in the wrong kinds of people, or believe in those phony 'get rich quick' schemes. As I have said before, many times Tarot cards are merely a warning and not the actual event.

As the central figure, you may be sucking the life out of those around you, possibly even intentionally. There are people who are energy vampires who suck everyone else's spirit and strength. Not only do they expect it they demand it. Such people 'withdraw' their affection and use it as a weapon, as in the wealthy parent who constantly threatens to cut a child off from their inheritance unless some particular act is performed or behavior is modified. Their commitment is always to themselves, not others. Instead of drawing others towards them, they seem to favor a separation except when they have wants or needs to be fulfilled.

Worst Case Scenario: A total disconnection from others. You do not want to know their problems, care to understand their needs, and definitely wish nothing to do with the solutions that you could be able to provide. You shirk from the affection of others, feeling that there must be some secret plan to undermine you and gain access to your money. You become suspicious not dedicated, become reclusive, not community-minded.

THE SEVENS

Sevens denote a period of introspection or solitude. They deal with wisdom, completeness, and perfection, and relate to the development of the soul.

Seven of Wands

A young man stands on a hilltop poised and ready to face off six unseen attackers. In some decks he shows fear; in others he is radiantly confident. However prepared he is or is not no longer relevant since a battle is about to begin. The important point is that he has an advantage of location: that is - that being higher than the rest gives him the advantage.

As we found earlier with the Strength card there are different kinds of strength. Who wouldn't, when faced with six attackers go running off as fast as possible? This man is facing the odds, relying on his own inner strength.

Perhaps your life does not have such dramatic qualities ... or maybe it does under other guises. Perhaps you are constantly feeling pressure from others around you to do things you are not of a mind to do. Perhaps your job is very polarizing and once again you have to try to get people to understand your point of views or try to rally them for support. Maybe you are running up against the office clique. Perhaps you are supporting an very unpopular candidate. Where does one gather or develop the inner strength needed to deal with the constant onslaught?

Sometimes it is best to take that mental health day, an extra weekend day, or take a day trip to get a fresh state of mind, even if only for the time that it lasts. In the 1970s 'biofeedback' (the term) was created where you took classes in how to block out the outside world and pay more attention to what was going on within you (for once). Some of it involved being connected to silly machines and some bought into this. Others sought a simpler and workable way to accomplish the same goal: regular exercise or something quite radical such as taking yoga or meditation classes. Soon, men in jackets and ties were removing their shoes and chilling out on their office floors during lunch breaks, for after all - what's easier to do than meditate?

The purpose of these forays into the self is a major teacher in how to stay calm in the face of a struggle. The man in the card may still get the crap beat out of him; who will win is up in the air. Panic is not going to help him, remaining calm and working it through will be his best ally. Although one can feel confident, it is not arrogance that will get you through this but rather humility, relying on what is within you ("Use the Force, Luke!"). Sometimes you can size up that to fight will be a total mistake; once again the humility within you will allow the situation to pass over you. Humility is not weakness; sometimes one has to realize which battles are worth losing and being respectful of other's viewpoints does not mean you have to change yours. In my high school I'm sure most of us thought that the school's dress code rules were archaic, moronic, or just downright superfluous. We had to wear jackets, ties, and shoes in class in high school; they were shucked the second we walked out the door. Our hair was not allowed to touch our collars; in this age of shaved heads our old principal would be in Heaven if he weren't there already.

The appearance of this card may indicate that you will be called on to demonstrate your abilities and that you should look on the challenge as something to overcome, not something that is meant to destroy you. Perhaps it indicates you have been chosen for a task because you have successfully met such challenges in the past. Proving your abilities is a constant thing, and the upright appearance of this card is accepted as a sign of success. Although Sevens denote a period of solitude or introspection, they also indicate unlooked-for advantages or gains through events than can come unexpectedly.

Reversed:

There are several ways to interpret this card in reversal. The first is that it indicates defeat by being overpowered by the efforts of others (be wary of those internal reviews). You may have put up a valiant struggle but misjudged the competition, misjudged your capabilities, or were fighting for the wrong cause. Your attempt to be King of the Hill will put you at the bottom of the heap.

A second interpretation is that this is only a warning to you that you are missing some important information that can give you strength, or that (even worse) someone who has been supporting you all along suddenly will change sides. You are being warned to rethink your position and question your supporter's positions and loyalties. Someone backing out now will be sure to knock the legs out from your solid platform. The situation is no longer as good as it first appeared. In some decks the man has on one boot and one shoe (Aha! Go back and look!)- an indication that things were gathered together in a hurry and perhaps he isn't as prepared as he once thought. As a warning it tells you loud and clear: don't get caught with your pants down. You may still be able to win this battle if you rethink your battle plans or provide alternative ones.

Worst Case Scenario: this whole situation you are involved in has nothing to do with who is right and who is wrong. You are grandstanding for the sake of drawing attention to yourself, using a lot of smoke and mirrors and like the Wizard of Oz are really doing it all for show. There was a certain presidential candidate who had no hope of ever winning, but he popped up every single election year and tried to draw votes away from the two serious candidates. Perhaps being able to say he was twice a presidential candidate was very important to him, for he had no party, no platform, and really had nothing to say other than 'Elect Me!' You have no plans for what you will do if you achieve your perceived victory; you are only there seeking attention for that is what you desire most.

Seven of Cups

No 'visions of sugarplums' here! Symbols of wealth and victory are mixed with those of jealousy and temptation. Are they for real, harbingers of the future, or merely exercises in wasted time? No doubt about it - this card is about scattering our energies or just spreading ourselves too thin. It actually evolves from a good start; after all, wishing for something better and trying to obtain it is what makes people learn, create, or invent. There is nothing wrong with having dreams, but this card hints that you spend far too much time in the dreaming and *not* in the pursuit of the goal it can represent. This card deals in your lack of focus because too many things are calling for your attention, sapping your energy, or wasting your time. You cannot be a cowboy, a NASA astronaut, and a ship's captain all at once. It can indicate that you drop one project to start another without ever completing any of them. As soon as something new beckons in the distance, you've forgotten what you are doing and run after it. This card is calling on you to sort out the possible from the impossible, the doable from the merely ridiculous, and focus on what is a priority and what is not. Although this card usually indicates success in the arts (a fertile imagination that results in creative ideas) in business and many professions that deal in practicality you need to be well grounded.

Inherent in this card is also an understanding that these Cups reflect your self-interests and that you spend a lot of time away from others, sometimes even excluding them. You might even disagree, stating that you are *not* scattered and *very* focused - on yourself. Everyone needs a time for privacy, their own space, and a desire to watch a game uninterrupted. If you have a family and yet have the time for your own needs programmed 24/7 for sports, athletics, etc., you definitely have your head in the clouds - the second layer of symbolism in this card. This card deals with illusions - and with delusions, and the sometimes very fine line between the two. Many a man who had mistakenly thought that he 'had it all,' has woken up one fine day to find his partner of many years has just instantly moved out, citing 'incompatibility' or 'irreconcilable differences.' This card may indicate destructive, compulsive behaviors.

This exclusion, intentional or otherwise, may have the slick veneer of being something beneficial for the common good, i.e. buying a cabin in the mountains so you can take the family away for vacations when the reality is you bought it to go on long weekend hunting trips - alone. Everything has a double meaning hidden within it, sort of like when Jeff Foxworthy talks about buying someone earrings that can double as fishing lures. You spend a lot of time dreaming - and scheming - of ways the actions you take will hide the fact that you are doing things for your own benefit. I know that sounds a lot more sinister than it is intended to be, but many men do things only with their own best interests at heart.

Perhaps you are being driven to distraction by a fantasy relationship that only exists in your head, and is taking the place of having a real love affair. Perhaps you are experiencing wild sexual fantasies and are not sure how your partner would react to the suggestion, so it is safer to keep them in your head than try to consummate them. It may be that the person you desire is involved with someone else, or that you can't decide between two or three possible lovers. When dealing with this card and presented with two or more possible outcomes, be sure to study the ramifications of each choice.

Worst Case Scenario: manipulation. In the pursuit of your self-interests you see others only as a stepping stone to your final goals. Your eye is always on the prize, *your* prize, and you will manipulate events, others, time, and space as necessary. It will not matter if the goals are sound or unfounded. Sometimes the pursuit of the successful conclusion of a plan blinds people to the path chosen to obtain it. Rather than being unfocused, you are too focused or have tunnel vision. Once again, you are being called upon to prioritize for the good of the many, not the good of the one.

Reversed:

In reversal those 'pie-in-the-sky' ideals come quickly crashing down, indicating that either a great reality has hit which snaps you out of your reverie, or that you have finally reached the ground and reconnected with what is important. This realization may come calmly and quietly - the light bulb has suddenly come on - or may be more dramatic - you realize (or are told) you may need to seek counseling. When the overblown monster of ego and self-importance no longer is in any control, you can realize how much you had disassociated yourself from others and must learn to reconnect. It is a time for healing, a time for sharing of yourself. Perhaps it will also indicate that you have learned to take that step back and reassess what has gone before and modify and/or adjust the priorities. Learning to open up and share your goals, desires, and fears can bring you to a new sense of interdependence that you suddenly realize has been lacking in your life. You are learning to focus on mutual goals, not exclusively private ones.

Seven of Swords

Through the ages there have been many diverse interpretations for this card, the most obvious being a caution against thievery. The thief sneaks away undetected after what appears to be the successful heist of swords - in broad daylight. The admonition is *'Don't* let this happen to you!' What happens if you are not the victim- but the *thief*? Where does *that* leave you?

This is a card about a lack of integrity, involving misplaced or displaced values. It can indicate a person who says one thing while their actions speak otherwise. They are usually quite skilled at temporarily diverting your attention elsewhere while they scramble for the best office position, the boss's ear, or getting the choice weekends off for their vacations. Sometimes they are very obvious - you know trouble is brewing ... somewhere - but most times they are experts at camouflaging their true intent. They can be convincing human chameleons, particularly when pressed for information. When you are new to a job, these are usually the first people you get warned about - the office sneaks.

People who get to this state have usually made a series of personal compromises that at first seemed minor, even to them. After all, you do learn what to kiss and when to stay alive in a corporate world. But you see these people don't care about what happens to *you*, they only care about what they can gain from it. Having now left seven people defenseless, they will sneak away, hide the evidence, and then act as though they were unaware of the circumstances - even deny they had any involvement. These behaviors did not happen overnight. As their misplaced values seem to bear compensations and their personal compromises lose their impact, the manner and intensity of these occurrences starts to escalate. Have you ever had to deal with someone who was a complete pathological liar? I went to school with one. No matter when you had done over the weekend, they had done more, played more, read more, seen more, etc. We used to make up lies just to see what superlatives they could come up with. 'That's just child's talk,' you are saying. Although children grow up eventually, their ingrained patterns of behaviors do not change; once they learn how to charm the gullible, they just hone those behaviors right through college into adulthood. When you run across one as an adult, they already have a lifetime of experience in the matter.

Perhaps you suspect your lover is, in fact - a dirty, rotten scoundrel, or that you or your lover is being less than honest, or even having an affair. Possibly you or your partner is holding back, feeling embarrassed to discuss certain needs or desires, for fear of rejection or disapproval. Your relationship will suffer if you only continue to sidestep honest discussion.

Then again, this card may merely indicate that you are thinking about changing jobs but are not telling anyone until you clinch the interview; the swords represent your job skills, something your employer cannot take back from you. A second (and positive) interpretation for this card is that you are good at creating and applying fresh though unconventional thinking against long term problems. This uncanny ability of yours helps you to get the 'jump' on your competitors who have fallen asleep at the wheel, proving once more that the early bird catches the worm.

Worst Case Scenario: (In your mind) you've sized up the potential loser and have made plans to support the side you expect is going to win. However, you are fighting the wrong battle. What appears as something so simple that a child could figure it out is in actuality a far more deeply complex situation than what appears on the surface. The figure in the card is handling those swords with his bare hands ...hmmm.

You may be expecting to obtain a significant gain and/or an easy victory at the expense of others. As you smile to yourself while you look over your shoulder seeing no one pursuing you, remember not to drop the swords on your foot as they put the handcuffs on you.

Reversed:

In reversal, the thief drops the stolen swords and is either caught, confesses to his crime, or the stolen goods are returned - in traditional imagery. What we have here is an application of strong personal values. My Grandfather (if I haven't quoted him already) had a pet phrase that went something like 'Money sticks in the hands of saints - and I don't see any saints here!' Sometimes what we see as an 'opportunity' is in reality 'gaining from someone else's loss.' As sure as hell if I find a $50 bill on a New York City street I am not going to wave it in the air and shout, "I just found a $50 bill - who does it belong to?" We are talking about a sense of pride in knowing what belongs to us and what belongs to others. We do not take from others merely because they are gullible or may be acting foolishly. We have a sense of honesty and we try to do 'what feels right' as often as we can, others feel our sense of integrity and respect us for it. That is not to say that some money won't stick in your saintly hands but that will be the exception, not the rule.

Seven of Pentacles

The Seven of Pentacles is a card about anticipation of the outcome from plans already put into place. It deals with an awareness of the 'process' but appreciating each moment every step of the way. The farmer pauses mid-hoe to look at the growing Pentacles aware they are starting to mature but still are not ready to pick. It may only be days or weeks until the expected harvest. Underlying that contented smile is also the knowledge that other factors can affect the harvest- insects, draught, violent storms - but he knows that they are part of the process, too. The Pentacles represent material things such as investments of money, but can represent projects for the home, goals for a job, or courses needed to complete an education. Or maybe you just like to grow tomatoes in your backyard.

O.K. - you're not the gardening type, but you do want a flagstone patio. The helpful guy at Home Depot explained all about tamping the base soil down, layering soft sand, then placing the stone and filling in around it. About halfway through this project you start wishing you had shelled out the bucks to have someone else install it for you, but you plug away at it, getting a good suntan, and learning more about yourself in the process. Yes, you sweat and curse and your back hurts but you start to notice the small details about the stones and patterns in rock. Maybe you even learn something about clouds as you hope that sudden storm does not come up and then wash away all the work you did this weekend. You have the plans, you start the process, and you have the goal in sight. Soon, (hopefully) all the ends will meet in the middle and you will throw a barbecue to christen your patio and your biceps and tan will be the envy of your friends.

Appreciating the moment is more than noticing the details that you might normally have missed or learning the subtle differences different yeasts have on your homemade wine. Such statements make it sound like a ponderous or eternal process. You don't have to grow flowers to appreciate their beauty of internal structure or the symmetry of each flower head. It can be a totally spontaneous thing you realize one day when you go to a flower or garden show. Part of your awareness has to do with *not* consciously looking for things; sometimes it means you have to have little diversions to keep your mind from growing stagnant. Some days it's saying 'I'm not working on that damn patio today - I'm going to the beach!' Did you ever notice how things sink into beach sand, how footprints are different as you get closer to the surf? Suddenly you realize why you have to have at least an inch of soft sand for the patio stones to rest on. BINGO! A little diversion, a little fun and suddenly the goals seem a lot closer than they were.

Reversed:

You cannot 'speed up' the process. In today's world where instant gratification has become the rule, the idea of 'having to wait and see' is a foreign concept to many. The Bible speaks of 'A Time for Everything,' and everything happens at its own pace and time, which may not be yours. In reversal this card speaks of impatience that something is not happening fast enough or - God forbid - isn't happening *exactly* the way you had planned it out. Sometimes the best-laid plans get abandoned as hopeless when all they needed was a period of rest.

People in this mode tend to be inattentive or even disinterested because they feel it is a waste of their time to pause and wait. It's like the parable about who sees the growing plant as flowers and who sees them as weeds. Maybe you should listen to the words to "The 59th Street Bridge Song" (Ooh- showing my age here!) Perhaps (like a certain home decorating matron) you take credit for designing or planning or building great projects. In reality you have a large staff of underpaid lackeys who do all the work, figure all the fussy details, troubleshoot all the piddle-y problems, and get their hands dirty for you. Maybe you are one of those bosses who just cancel things if they don't show great profit or potential right away, particularly if there are lots of small but annoying problems at the beginning.

Worst Case Scenario: you are one of those unhappy people whom 'want it all yesterday.' You expect people to have things done and ready for you without reasonable notice, that others have nothing else do to except wait on you. There is an early scene in the original *Swept Away* where the rich bitch wants coffee, and when the deckhand brings her some demands to know if it is reheated or fresh because 'she only drinks fresh coffee.' Why would *anyone* expect her to drink reheated coffee? This puts a great distance between you and others as they scramble to make the situation right when in truth it is you who are wrong. It also brings a source of confusion, as they have to second-guess what whim of yours they will have to deal with next. This behavior is barely acceptable when you are four, and it becomes quite tiresome when you reach your forties.

THE EIGHTS

Eight indicates a positive change of mind or status because the beneficial qualities of the number Eight (2 times 4, the number of manifestation) are rarely diluted. Eight is the number of justice, judgment, material progress, and health.

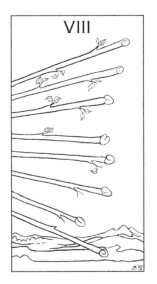

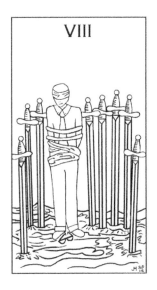

Eight of Wands

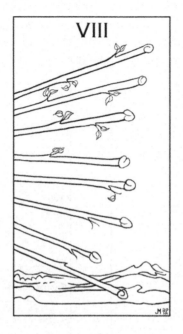

If the Sevens deal with solitude or introspection, the Eights indicate a *positive* change of mind or of status. This may be because Fours are cards of stability and Eights are two times Four and thus twice as stable?

The problem with the design of this card is that you never quite get the concept of *movement.* Things are moving out, moving forward, and are moving towards their eventual conclusion. In the Rider deck the Wands slant from up left to down right as they move back down towards the earth nearing the end of their flight. In another deck they move through the cosmos, but in most card deck representations they look like they are merely floating, not flying. These flying Wands can represent projects to try, goals yet to be accomplished, places to go on vacation, and people to see. They can represent a barrage of letters (or emails) of introduction, resumes, job applications, or term papers. What they definitely represent is *action.* If you were to grab a handful of arrows and shoot them towards the same target in rapid succession, some would fall short, some will hit in different places, and some may even overshoot their mark. Which ones will perform which action may be impossible to know until they finally come to a stop.

We never shoot these arrows only once in a lifetime; we shoot them periodically as we go. Think of the firing of every volley as an expansion process - an expansion of our personal adaptability; after all, we are unsure of the conclusion we will achieve. We allow ourselves to open up to the possibilities we have created. Perhaps a job opportunity will require that we move across the state or across state lines. Perhaps you may receive multiple offers, all with varying specific pros and cons; some might even be ambiguous. Now - you might be asking what the difference is between this card of multiple possibilities and the pipe dreams of the Seven of Cups, or why the Seven of Cups is made to sound negative whereas I've characterized this card as so positive. After all, the pipe dreams could become a reality as quickly as the barrage of Wands could end in dismal failure. The difference is *stagnation versus participation*. In the Cups card you do not try to see any of the larger picture, only the immediate anticipated outcome. You may not actually see that your dreams actually conflict with or antagonize each other. In the Wands card, you have opened yourself up to a myriad of possibilities and made certain decisions about how the path will be reached and what deviations can be allowed if necessary. You might be required to juggle a few multiple roles as you develop your plan, but you participate and then you just adapt as you go, staying flexible and open. Changing a dream is easy when it is only a dream - there is nothing tangible to deal with. Adaptability is a whole different world- even if it's only because you opened your briefcase in a meeting to find your son stuck your catcher's mitt in it - a subtle request you come home from work and toss some balls. We do not close ourselves down to any possibilities while some are still up in the air; that would be foolish and diminish our potentials. This is a time to practice "Go with the flow."

Reversed:

In reversal, the Wands come clattering down and fall into a heap as their forward movement is arrested. Major unseen forces came into play and not only have your plans been put on hold, they've been canceled mid-course and will not be resurrected. This will come as a major shock because it knocks your legs out from under you. Before you completely panic you must assess the threat before you start to access the damages. Was this a 'wild card' action that no one could have foreseen such as a tornado destroying your home? Recovery will be more important than future plans. Was this disaster caused by the actions of others - your company announces Friday afternoon that they will not be operating the following Monday? Has this problem been caused by our own neglect (spreading ourselves too thin) or did we deceive ourselves to ineffective sections of our plan - and the IRS is now waiting outside our door?

With such a major potential for disaster hanging over your head (be sure to duck those falling Wands), you are being warned to *simplify.* Maybe you are trying too hard (overshooting), wasting your energies (undershooting), or simply have scattered your energies with too broad a range. Remember- firing a salvo off has a low potential for actually hitting the target except by chance. Perhaps you are being warned to *focus* down rather than spread out. Conversely, it may be telling you that you have restricted yourself and are focused on the <u>wrong thing</u> or by going about it in the entirely wrong manner. Since those Wands are now lying in a heap at your feet, pick each one up separately and take the time to reassess what it represented and why it missed its mark.

<u>Worst Case Scenario</u>: disintegration. Perhaps this last volley was a last-ditch effort on your part and you had no expectations that it was going to work - ever - but carried on, deceiving others to the caliper of disaster awaiting them. Rather than be truthful and up-front, you are just waiting for the failure so you can say 'I <u>knew</u> it was *never* going to work.' Even worse, you will then make no efforts to correct the situation and will not be there to help someone else pick up the pieces.

Eight of Cups

For some unknown reason the man has neatly stacked the eight Cups and is walking away from them towards mountains that represent abstract thought; also understanding or wisdom. We do not know if the Cups are empty and he seeks fulfillment, or if they are full and no longer hold his interest. There are two schools of thought about this card. The first says the upright image is someone looking for enlightenment; in reversal you seek only base earthly pleasures. The second says while upright the meaning is one of being overly cerebral (although that is not necessarily negative) about things and in reversal you have grounded yourself out and are more focused. We will lean towards the latter; upright will be your coming to terms in the understanding of your own emotional and physical needs and reversal will deal with how you share or demonstrate this knowledge to others.

Many men fall into the 'Tale of the Unfulfilled Prince or Hero' category sometime in their lives. They search about tirelessly for something better without knowing what it is they are looking for. Consequently, they don't know if they ever found it; all they know is that the gnawing feeling in their gut has finally gone away and they accept this as 'the sign' that they have found their answer to the great mystery of life and they stop searching. It's like trying to find something in a dark room with a flashlight with very weak batteries; you say 'Some light is better than no light at all,' but you really are left to feel your way around rather than see what you need to see. Perhaps you are walking away because you have a superficial understanding of the problem and believe that it is not a problem at all. Perhaps you are failing to perceive that you can change things and alleviate the problem so you are trying to get away before it grows and sucks you in. Maybe you say 'Hey- those Cups are filled so my job is done,' and don't perceive there ever was a problem to begin with. Perhaps this is the prelude to the Hermit card; the individual who says "I'm mad as hell and I can't take it anymore!" or "There's gotta be something better than *this*!" Possibly you are really just being overwhelmed and need to get away - which brings me to the image of the double moon. The Moon is pictured in both Full and Last Quarter phases. Depending on the position of the real moon at the time of the reading, this condition will begin or end during that phase of the moon. [In reversal it's the first Quarter and Full Moon.] Thus this action can happen anywhere within one to three weeks of the reading.

Worst Case Scenario: enlightenment has nothing to do with it. You are so preoccupied with mundane concerns that you didn't even notice the Cups when you passed them, much less stopped to inspect them. They could have been full of opportunities or possibilities, but you only seek the exact thing you are searching for and accept no substitutes. Are you one of those men who are constantly buying another tool because 'you don't have the right tool for the job?' When you have your blinders on, is there no one who can get you to change your mind?

Reversed:

You have taken the time to reconnect, or at least understand that you still have to reconnect the disparate parts of your life. You have started doing things that expand your awareness, small things like taking a class in photography. Learning to see through a camera lens helps you focus on what is important and what to crop out. Perhaps these steps are a little more exotic, such as taking an 'Iron John Weekend' to reconnect to lost male values. Maybe you just said 'If I can't carry it on my back, then it isn't necessary' and hiked off into the mountains, the desert, or the Serengeti of your mind. Perhaps you joined a man's drumming circle and learned what 'marching to your own drummer' really means.

Regardless of the route you have taken, you cannot come back home from such a journey without having some kind of amplification of your senses. In when upright you closed them out, here you welcome every experience and look forward to each new sensation. The opening of your closed eyes brings with it an understanding that there are new lessons to learn, not knowledge merely to be filed away somewhere like historical dates in a boring history class you couldn't stand taking. ["What year *was* the Magna Charta signed?"] This brain expansion also brings with it a desire for investigation of the world around us. Maybe you have found that those eight Cups were indeed empty; however, now you look into their value and offer them for sale on eBay! Don't think of this idea of 'becoming grounded' to mean that you have to haul out the easy chair, slippers, pipe, and smoking jacket; it can be a very dynamic experience. Don't think about 'rusting out' - think about *moving out*. Remember - it's a *positive* change of mind!

Eight of Swords

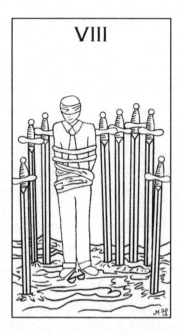

In traditional imagery, the figure in this card is bound, helpless to aide themselves, and their vision is obscured. Swords block their path and the ground looks shaky. How are they ever to cope? Where's Superman when you really need him? This concept also supports the idea that this all was done *to* you and that *they* have locked you up in a prison cell. It's easy to see yourself as the victim to someone else's actions.

What if this is not the case at all? What if you yourself have specifically created this situation, and even planned the details? What if what we see here is actually some internalized kind of disharmony being shown as a physical manifestation? Rather than only being unable to help yourself, you make yourself unavailable to others, or you make it difficult for them to reach you by putting obstacles in their way. You are hoping that their weakness will get the better of them and render them useless to before they try to come to you.

The blindfold says you tend to be uncompromising; it says you will not look at a situation because you do not wish to see the situation. Oh, you hear everything going on around you, but you are blinded against taking action. You have bound your hands up so that you will be unable to lend a hand or lift a finger to come to anyone else's rescue. "Look at me - what do you expect me to do about it?" You are resistant to input from others; the ground is shaky and uneven and with your blindfold on you just might trip and fall. We wouldn't want *that* to happen, would we? That might require getting another person or their viewpoint involved.

This card possibly may scream 'I'm sexually frustrated' at you because you are lacking a sexual partner or outlet, or because the physical relationship you now have is unsatisfactory. You may feel trapped by those wants and desires particularly if you are alone, a mate is ill or absent, or if you are unhappy or bored in your current relationship.

Worst Case Scenario: lack of cooperation. You have very carefully placed those eight swords around you – all the sharp edges pointing out - as a deterrent to keep others away. You really wish that others would stop bothering you and leave you alone. You will deal with your own problems as they come but you have no desire to help others with theirs. Remember that the swords' sharp edges facing out also have a sharp edge facing in, too. You can easily trap yourself while putting up your own defenses. Do you recall that episode of the *Twilight Zone* where Burgess Meredith played than man who only wanted to read his books and wished to be left alone? Be careful what you wish for, and make sure you have a spare set of eyeglasses.

Reversed:

Using the same imagery, when the figure is turned on its head, the swords, ropes, and blindfold fall away, leaving the figure unbound and unfettered. Once your senses have been opened there should be an increase in cooperation. No longer is it *I versus Them* but the dawning of mutual understanding bringing mutual good. Have you ever wondered about Robert Frost's poem about good fences making good neighbors and wondered how they are supposed to be a good neighbor to you when they wall you out?

Another form of cooperation is compromise; the ability to give and take along mutually agreed guidelines. A popular horror writer recently admitted that during his writing heyday that he closed the door to his office and did not emerge until he had typed for six hours or had written X thousand words. Writing was his only employment, so it behooved him not to have to get up every five minutes to deal with distractions. When I was about 94% through with writing my first book, the two men I shared a house with changed their schedules. Whereas I used to have an empty, quiet house to write in, I suddenly had to deal with the two of them home all the time. The television was on long before I got up and it was still on when I went to bed at night. With an estimated two weeks to go for my manuscript to be completed, they started to remodel their kitchen! Unfortunately for me, my computer did not fit in my small bedroom, so I was SOL. After all, (to them) when I wasn't at my real job all I did was sit there and type all day, so why should their obnoxious activities bother me? {I later found out their obnoxious activities were an effort to get me to move out of the house without having to ask me to do so- *some* friends, huh?}

Being freed from your restraints allows you to handle what you once saw as weakness in others. As part of your abilities for compromise you now help others to understand what your own limits are, such as explaining to your children that you can help them with their latest math homework but will not do it for them. At work you will deal with true problems that arise, but that you cannot be expected to do the jobs of others because they simply refuse to do them.

Speaking of harmony - we are also talking sexual harmony, too. Whether sensual or sexual - sexuality comes with its own unique, dynamic levels of compromise and cooperation.

Eight of Pentacles

The apprentice sits carving his eighth Pentacle; we do not know how many he has already made or is still required to make. With the understanding that 'practice makes perfect' he plugs away, perfecting what he is doing so that he will be allowed to move up to the next stage or level of development or opportunity. "Apprentice," you're saying, "Does that mean I have to start all over again from the beginning? Have Donald Trump for my boss?" No - but it does ask you to think for a moment. If you recall the master builder in the Three of Pentacles you will remember that he is at the pinnacle of his power in his craft. The apprentice is just beginning but he, too, has a desire to succeed. So, too, should you consider what your *potential* is, what your goals are, and start to prepare for future opportunities that will bring you to your goal. This may also take some physical learning, such as taking night classes or online courses to learn more about your job, get that certificate, or finally earn that degree. A friend of mine has been teaching at a college for over fifteen years, but does not have a 'terminal education' (Ph.D.)

that would raise his salary. It will take two years of work to get it, putting everything on hold to do so, with no guarantee he will still have a job when he is done. He will also be at least 60 if this gets done. With a hopeful retirement age of 62, would the increase of salary for such a short time really benefit him? He originally would have liked to be able retire early, but at the moment he knows he must work right through to his retirement to be able to live comfortably when he does. It's a tough call.

Preparing for the future opportunities might also involve the use of foresight. When you were in high school, was French the 'international language' - now replaced by Spanish? What has four years of French gotten you? Knowing one foreign language may help you in learning another, if languages are a part of your job. {Where I work there's a lot of Asian languages, but many Asians speak French!} As a junior draftsman I learned to do mechanical drafting on the eve of the birth of Computer Aided Drafting. CAD is terrific, but many small companies could not afford to make the technical leap and paid the 'pencil & eraser boys' to do their pencil lead drafting for quite a few years (until the cost came down) after CAD became popular. Of course, the 'boys' knew that someday their skills would be obsolete and learned CAD on the side so they would have jobs when their companies switched over. That was foresight with a time of being an apprentice mixed in, too. Part of that foresight is attention to details that might otherwise be overlooked. There will always be a need for skilled draftsmen to create blueprints, even if someday those blueprints are holographic.

You are possibly wondering why all this fulfillment is all based in the future on an idea of what will be happening later - what about preparing for *now*? The future *is* now, buddy boy! As soon as someone comes up with a product idea it's already out in the marketplace for sale. Do you remember early entertainment uses for computers - playing 'Space Invaders' or animating the movie *Tron*? Some computer exec of the time is quoted as saying 'the personal computer would not have a future.' The idea of a 'web' of computers all over the world connected to each other by a 'net' was only something for the military to consider. Computers were something out of *Star Trek*, the grist for science fiction writers to put in their story mills, not something in the dashboard of your car, your phone, or your watch, Dick Tracy! If you don't grab each opportunity by the balls as it comes you'll lose it. Preparing for the future starts today, not five years from now. Keep a strong mind, a strong body (you'll need one to pedal to work after they ban automobiles), and keep your eyes, ears, and hands open.

Reversed:

The reversed apprentice represents someone who works too hard, too much, or both. More than just a textbook workaholic, he does the same tasks over and over without missing a beat. He is so entrenched in his ways that if someone moves the contents on the top of his desk around it will throw him for a loop. He may have blocked out the drudgery and not realize he is bored out of his mind. He may even be fully aware that he has reached or passed the 'burning out' point but is powerless to do or change anything, possibly out of fear. These individuals can be functioning perfectly but working with them is like being on the set of *'The Night of the Living Dead.'* A friend once told me about the professor who was teaching a course he was taking who had been teaching the same class for years. One night she 'forgot' her teaching notebook, and instead of 'faking it' - having taught the class hundreds of times - she froze up and dismissed the class- could not teach without her notebook in front of her!

This is the card of the person who is being overworked, all too common in this age of 'downsizing' where fewer people are expected to do more work for the same low rate of pay. When I was working for the casino - which operated 24/7 – they were famous for changing your daily schedule at the last minute to accommodate the company for people calling out before the start of the next shift. Some of us knew where we will end up if things got crunched. We also knew that when things got slack that we would be required to work those same areas *alone*.

<u>Worst Case Scenario:</u> You are working at a job/company with no future and have to get your head out of the sand and break free. One can almost say you are disregarding the future - almost deliberately forcing yourself to be stuck where you are by thwarting any efforts to move forward. This effect became known as 'The Peter Principle' - being promoted to the height of your incompetence. It can also be the mature employee who says "I'm gonna retire in three years, so I'm gonna coast along until it's time to leave."

THE NINES

Nines indicate that situations or events are nearing completion or have just been completed, and another plateau waits.

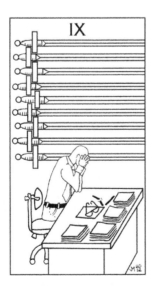

Nine of Wands

Have you ever felt that the whole world is out 'to get a piece of you?' No matter where you go it seems as though someone has to get your attention or pick your brain for the most minor, trivial matters and no one will leave you alone? Look at this poor guy with his head bandaged from a previous assault, warily leaning on his wand, wondering who or what is going to pop up next. Will it ever stop?

We create defenses for various reasons, some valid, some not. Who among us would not want to 'protect our space?' We see an attack coming - we build a defense. We lock doors and windows and put up fences, clearly saying *'This is mine, not yours.'* When you go to bed at night you want to feel safe and secure. However, not all attacks come from land, sea, or air. Although the Internet may claim it's anonymous but it's far from private and all the Spam blocks you put up will not keep your mail box from being filled with unsolicited advertisements. Smart phones - all you have done is make yourself more accessible to more people who can now more easily find you in the men's room. This card says to stand ready and remain vigilant. Nines by their nature indicate that events are nearing the conclusion although there may be a temporary plateau.

Philosophically, the other question that arises is whether the wall keeps 'them' out or does it actually hold you locked within (something we will also see in the Nine of Pentacles card). Perhaps this defense building is not as healthy as it seemed. "Once burned - twice shy." Perhaps you are imagining that people are plotting against you. Suspicions lead to paranoia as you prepare for an enemy that isn't there. Simon & Garfunkel sang about 'being shielded in their armor,' becoming an island unto themselves. Perhaps you don't have stores of food buried in your backyard or a bunker with a spider hole in your basement {when I was a kid it was atomic bomb shelters} but you have begun to think of everyone not aligned with you as being against you. This has started to permeate your personal relationships, also. You start looking for reasons why you do or do not trust close family members and selectively refrain from sharing certain information with them.

O.K. – we are being a little dramatic, perhaps. What we can see in this card is someone who is constantly being interrupted to the point where they have become defensive when anyone approaches them. In one of the casino banks I work in the word of the day is *multitasking*. If you cannot function while doing at least three simultaneous tasks while answering the phone then you will probably never be successful there because you have no other choice. Yes, we *do* yell at the cell phone when it has rung four times while we are still trying to complete one simple task; we have written the correct information down for the wrong patron. The problem is learning to channel the frustrations elsewhere rather than wall you in by creating defenses. In truth I detested this one bank; when I would get assigned there my stomach would tie up in knots. One night it built to such a frustration level that I almost lost my job, so I asked to be removed from it. About ten or so months later I was asked to rethink and retry it and I went back with many reservations and I struggled with it for another 8 - 10 weeks. I finally decided one day to stop taking the problems personally, to stop getting upset when things did not always work correctly, and learned to say 'Where is the problem and how do we correct it?' One fine day I suddenly realized that I wasn't having as many problems or that they didn't seem as monumental. I became the 'bank trainer.'

Worst Case Scenario: You have started to be secretive or guarded about your actions, one eye always on the lookout or over your shoulder to see if you are being observed, waiting for the best (and unseen) moment to do something. You close up like the proverbial clam and become protective at the mere hint of suspicion in the actions of others.

Reversed:

The defenses have fallen down, either by the actions of others or (hopefully) by your own hand. Perhaps you have decided to initiate these changes on your own; perhaps you sought the counsel of others. Once the bandage has fallen off, you can forget about what hurt you and focus on now sharing who you are with others that you once may have been shutting out of your life. Many men discuss what they think but not how they *feel*. {"My son needs a kick in the ass if he thinks he'll get into college with these grades!"} This type of disclosure is not easy for people who have always feared any disclosure, for they feel it shows weakness. This development may be very slow and needs constant and sufficient support to become a reality. Men who fear disclosure may also have problems with open signs of affection {"I bought them a card - what more do they want?"} and reversal may indicate that they are seeking to understand the process but still feeling vulnerable. After all, it is easier to construct something than it sometimes is to knock it down.

If the Wands have fallen away in your cards today it can indicate 'the moment of truth' or clarity of purpose. Perhaps the trees have been obscuring your forest and you suddenly realize the clear way to get something done or see how to alleviate the problem that has been pestering you. With the obstructions removed, move forward from the darkness into the light.

Nine of Cups

Sometimes referred to as the 'party hearty' card, sometimes as the 'wish' card (if you make a wish before your reading and this card pops up, *supposedly* it will come true), this is the card about enjoying all that life has to offer. Whether you accept this image as a celebration, a wedding banquet, or a party with an open bar, the seated man looks very content and his posture says 'Life is Good.' Underlying it all, he may be aware that tomorrow has yet to come and that it may bring sadness and disappointment, but for the next moment life is sweet and the problems that may loom for tomorrow just do not exist. Why take the edge off a good time worrying about stuff that hasn't happened yet? Eat, drink, and be merry, because if we're going to die tomorrow we're going to have one hell of a good time tonight!

This is the card of someone who takes the time to appreciate the beauty in day-to-day living. There's a free lunchtime concert in the park, so he grabs his lunch and finds a spot under a shady tree. It didn't matter if he is dressed in his Brooks Brothers suit or his flannel shirt, faded dungarees, and hardhat - the idea of a short, happy diversion was more appealing than sitting under the florescent lighting in the company cafeteria. This is the person who notices the first crocuses of spring, having learned to value the details that other people take for granted or overlook entirely. These people tend to be robust and energetic, by not allowing themselves to be pulled down at all by minor things or to become upset by major ones. They have learned the give-and-take process and cannot understand why so many people they come into daily contact with cannot see how much fun life could be. Perhaps it is because they learned to 'stop and smell the roses' either by choice or because something happened once in the lives that made them realize that no matter what you do - you will not get out of this life alive.

So, what do these people have going for them that others do not? They set out to enjoy their daily lives, looking for beauty, valuing details, and smelling roses - wherever they may find them. They deal with problems in the same way by taking them in stride and not sweating all the small stuff and not ignoring the big stuff. They share this lust for life with others, knowing that enjoyment shared is enjoyment multiplied. If we were put on this earth to make others happy then these are the people who are life's cheerleaders. They teach that by their example of gently pointing things out to you and not forcing you to think or become like them. Their enthusiasm may never make you want to hunker down and learn how to tie fishing flies but you can still go fishing! Perhaps listening to Bach is on your 'not to be caught dead' list but the mathematical precision of his musical compositions appeals to your sense of order and structure. Learn to enjoy it while it's in your lap and enjoy it for as long as it lasts. Make a 'bucket list.'

Reversed:

When those Cups are upset and spill their contents it is an indicator that you tend to waste time, energy, and emotion without ever enjoying what you are doing. You tend to be unhappy with everything and discontented in your dealing with others. By not attending to the overturned Cups you show that you tend to neglect many things in your everyday life, sometimes accidentally but most often deliberately. No one would tend to think to describe you as a 'happy person,' and it was in this manner an acquaintance was once told that he 'acted and spoke like a commencement speaker.' He is an award-winning journalist, but he carries his problems and stresses around in a briefcase and always looks and acts pissed off, wondering why he can never get anyone to be friendly with him. He would go to the beach with three books and his laptop; was it any wonder people avoided him? He really expected that total strangers would find him not only exciting and intellectual and *attractive*, but he went places alone and he always left from them alone.

Rather than sharing or encouraging others to join you in your journey you tend to have a severe case of single-mindedness. You may take great pride in your own accomplishments but you banish your awards or kudos to a dark basement somewhere. It is as though if you were to share your accomplishments with others that they will somehow rob you of your power, or even worse - inspire them to try to take it from you. You do not praise others for their works for you feel that will put them on equal footing with you, and being the Numero Uno game player means you must always stay at the top. You do not applaud for others at award dinners.

Worst Case Scenario: the reversal of this card speaks of tunnel vision or a myopic pursuit of a set of goals. Like a horse with blinders on you ignore what you cannot see or wish to see, having decided that you will be wasting your time to see the roses, much less to stop and smell them. Men in this category tend to be very opinionated, highly stressed, and perpetual loners.

Nine of Swords

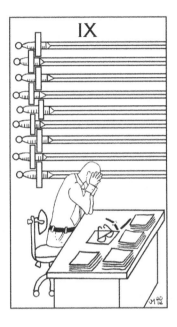

Holy Crap! What's going on here! Our figure (sometimes in a bed) sits bolt upright awakened from unknown dreams and weeps into their hands in despair. The nine Swords (imaginary, not physical) hover over them, signifying mental anguish, self-torment and an unquiet mind. In the Rider-Waite-Smith deck the card has a few clues - the red flowers in the coverlet usually signify willful desires and the carved panel in the bed is a swordsman falling in defeat to another. These desires and temptations spiral through the mind and the desired sleep does not come readily. Do the astrological symbols in the bed quilt indicate that we feel that things are not under our own control? Has Life turned into a real bitch? This is one of those cards that immediately signifies the stresses and strife of the Querent. Mercifully, it will only be a warning in hopes of stopping a situation from developing and not manifest itself as reality.

The next question to come to mind is whether these problems are real or imaginary and if they come from within or without. Is this card telling you that you are ignoring what is necessary - things like routine auto maintenance - and hoping the strange sound or clicking wheel will 'just go away' if you ignore it long enough? Are you deliberately sticking your aching head in the sand, closing your eyes to a situation you do not wish to acknowledge and deal with something by choosing not to deal with it at all? Being labeled a procrastinator is probably the least harmful interpretation for this card; however, crying will not get your taxes done or filed by April 15th. Some people do not understand the difference between illusions and delusions and are typically unprepared to deal with the consequences; they are later discovered standing in the middle of the destruction with a 'deer-in-the-headlights' look meekly asking how this could have happened. Looking back they sit and wail and say 'How did I ever *miss* that one?' Then there are others who spread themselves much too thin, pulling one stunt after another telling fabrication after boldfaced lie and barely able to keep their bases and asses covered. They can become very deft at this and they keep the illusion going for *years* until that one tragic day when everything fails. This is the card of half-hearted efforts and these are the people who lay there in the darkness night after night with their eyes unclosed wondering what they will have to cover up next and when someone will finally see through them, bringing those swords crashing down at last.

Worst Case Scenario: this is the card of loose cannons, those that speak without thinking - people who put their mouth in gear without engaging their brains first; there is no taking back something you have already said. This is the anguish of the person who realizes all too late that they said the wrong thing at the wrong time to the wrong person. Remember my 'Control Freak' coworker? She was eventually fired. Outspoken and opinionated, she said one hostile thing too many to too many people and received what is unofficially known as a 'bitch final' - meaning that if she created a hostile work environment *again* within a twelve-month period she would be unequivocally fired. Knowing this, wouldn't you *try* to be a little more careful for a year? One night she got into an escalating argument with another coworker and *in front of witnesses* she threatened to have the other taken out in a body bag. Had she gotten this card as a warning that day, would she have taken the hint that problems were brewing for her?

Reversed:

The swords of torment fall away and the troubled mind is allowed to rest. Delusions get replaced by discipline and discipline means taking the necessary steps to bring changes that will dissolve or absolve you from being so out-of-control again. *Watching* all the exercise videos will not help you lose weight unless you get out there and break a sweat. Unfortunately, many men ignore their bodies, health, and diet until they suddenly wake up one day in the Coronary Care Unit and find out they almost died. In the 1970s there was a great made-for-TV movie called 'My Father's House' where Cliff Robertson played a man in his forties who gets waylaid by a surprise heart attack. During his recovery he starts recalling his own father (played by Robert Preston) and his father's lessons about life and living and makes an effort to come to terms with a lifestyle/work style that almost killed him. {Life never looks as good as it does in a flashback}.

Instead of agonizing 'Oh, woe is me!" and playing the victim of outrageous fortune we stand up and take action against it, prioritizing what already exists and creating new priorities when necessary. Have you ever grown grapes? Every autumn you have to prune the year's growth back to the main vines because grapes only come from new growth. So, too, you have to prune away the dead wood of illusions and delusions in your life and settle into a plan with established goals while continuing to establish new ones when it becomes necessary.

Nine of Pentacles

When I set out to reinterpret the Tarot for men I knew I was going to hit a few thorny sections. Making the protagonist of this card a male bought a few issues to a head. The implied elegance of the usual woman in this card carries a few ironic downsides including 'seeking the material' and the Taurus in me asked 'What's *wrong* with seeking the material?' Still, there are many overlooked positive aspects to this upright card, so I decided to follow the 'plateau before the conclusion' concept rather than use the 'your undeserved wealth makes you feel insecure' or 'a rich widow or a kept woman' idea.

Our figure walks through a well-tended garden of grapes and Pentacles and a large manor house looms in the distance. The hooded falcon represents having both good luck and controlled thoughts and the snail is an omen of happiness to those to work diligently. We have reached a stage in our development where we worked to have things to enjoy and now have the time or ability to enjoy them. (Yes, you can interpret that as a happy retirement, but why stop there?) You have come this far and attained this end because you have endured and overcame obstacles placed in your path. Once our basic needs of food, money, and a place to live is fulfilled we can move on to the next plateau which is working on our spirituality. Some may argue that this card concept is backwards; you should seek a higher understanding first and ignore the material like the Hermit does, living a Spartan life. [Have you remembered that the Hermit is also another 'Nine' card?] I remember Wayne Newton (who worked himself into a great fortune) talking about an interviewer once asking him if he wasn't happier living poor in the old farmhouse he grew up in, and the printable part of his response was "Are you *out* of your mind?" We all have different paths to tread. Perhaps you enjoy long trail hikes through woodlands, identifying plant and bird life as you go, finding the most solitary section that puts you at peace with the world. Perhaps you like to climb mountains because you like seeing the spectacular views from the top. Perhaps you like gardening because you like watching things grow and seeing all the cycles of nature up close and personal. Spirituality is much more than kneeling to pray, sitting to learn, and standing to praise. Anything that strengthens your faith or belief is spiritual. Now you are being given the opportunity to try and make the connections. The falcon and the snail also indicate that we can overcome obstacles placed in our path by controlling ourselves when necessary and working towards our goals. The falcon may fly swiftly and the snail may plod tenaciously but they still accomplish what they set out to do.

Before this card gets too highfalutin for its own good, we should talk about the 'higher understanding' part of the card. This higher understanding comes from within oneself, influenced by the teachings of others, but those teachings act only as the catalyst for our search, not the end result. For many years people involved in organized religions just sat there and they believed whatever they were told to believe and thought whatever they were told to think, not questioning the where and why because they were told not to ask questions. "Just Do It" sure works well for future Olympians, but somehow cannot answer the questions of the soul. This created a lot of Hermits out there seeking to find their own answers to their own questions. When you remove the hood from the falcon it can do two things: one is flying away and return; the second is to fly away and not come back. You have faith that it will come back but you cannot control what will happen. Are you the falcon or the falconer? Will you be the bird of prey that swoops down and prepares the attack, or the bird that flies into the void seeking answers and touches the face of God, returning forever changed as a spiritual messenger? If you find yourself on a plateau, this is the lesson you must learn; if you have passed this plateau you are on your way to the next step.

<u>Reversed:</u>

Instead of having a plan for your future you follow uninspired pursuits, going with a flow that leads nowhere, forgetting that fluid seeks the lowest level. Perhaps you have been sucked in by someone else's misplaced values believing that if those values worked for them they will work for you - perhaps you were even manipulated by them into thinking so. If so, this card says push your head up through the surface and take a good look around.

Perhaps you are feeling that you work constantly to get somewhere and no one person even notices and that makes you feel undervalued. Possibly it is time to reassess what prompts and inspires you. According to job interviewers, the first thing you say at your interview should *not* be "I want this job for the insurance." As men we have always been told we should selflessly provide for our families, that we are their sole means of support. There is nothing wrong with wanting to better our families or ourselves but instead of moving towards an eventual conclusion we have come to a living dead end. Instead of looking forward with anticipation we have locked ourselves up with the trivial and the mundane.

Worst Case Scenario: wasting time. Instead of trying to overcome obstacles or to defeat them, you allow them to block you from further expansion possibilities. You may even be erecting them yourself under the guise of 'let's wait and see,' that wonderful delaying tactic your parents used on you as a child. The catch is you both knew it meant 'no' and that is what you are doing - saying 'no' to yourself.

THE TENS

The Tens can be read the same as the Aces (10: 1 + 0 = 1); however Tens signify the cyclical re-beginning, and a time when you must come to terms with something you may have avoided in the past. The Tens show the ultimate quintessence of each suit. The Cups and Pentacles show the heights of bliss; the Swords and Wands show the depths of tribulation.

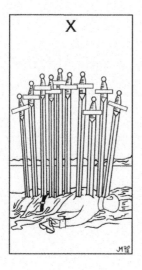

Ten of Wands

In the Tens we come full circle; Tens are at once the 'reaching of the end' and the epitome of the nature of their suit, but they also represent the end becoming a new beginning once more. [10 = 1 + 0 = 1] Here we find the height of tribulation or the depth of despair and once we reach those ends move forward into the next cycle.

It is very easy to characterize this card as 'struggling under the burdens we bear,' hinting that one small intervention will make or break us so close to our goal. It would be very easy to describe the workaholic blahblahblah, but since Wands deal with 'what we do,' I did not feel that 'taking on too much' - an accepted interpretation for this card - should be the defining limit. After all, in the distance there is a large building or the outskirts of a city which indicates to me that even though it was a real bitch to get there it is close enough to taste. Perhaps this isn't your job at all but your retirement planning and those are your golf clubs and condo in Florida!

Why do men work? We work to give ourselves a sense of purpose, a sense of satisfaction, and a sense of achievement. Perhaps the Wands Guy struggles at times because he found out the same trick that I did long ago: don't take your work/job home with you - leave your job problems at work. What we also share is that 'what we do' and 'what we do when we're not doing *that*' have no connection to each other. I have jokingly described my casino job as doing banking in the middle of a nightclub during the Carnival in Rio. I am writing this book in total silence without even background music playing.

So, where does this card go? It goes to what happens when you finally put the Wands down (notice: I did not say trip, fall, or drop them). Once you do this you can realize the essence of yourself, realizing self-expression as the antidote or release valve. You may remember Col. Potter of *M*A*S*H* up to his elbows in human guts who would then go out and paint imaginary peaceful sunsets. Perhaps the antithesis of your struggle is to 'find the real you' and unlock your creative genius. This can take many different forms from imagining you are going to be the next undiscovered Picasso, leaping out of planes to indulge yourself in skydiving, or quietly banging away at a word processor hoping someday someone will read what you wrote late one dark and stormy night. Throughout this book I have written many times that the Wands cards represent 'that which we do,' and that is not confined or restricted to the company that issues your paycheck. Perhaps the Wands Guy *is* struggling a bit today, not from being overburdened by stress but because he is seeking perfection of art, knowing that he will get the perfect snapshot of the morning dew on his prize roses if he patiently waits for the sunrise one more time. If the end result is worth the struggle, is the struggle really so bad? If the end result is exactly what you wanted (maybe you paint houses instead of canvases), was it really a struggle at all? The point is that you have your vision and you have your goal and to settle for anything less or to leave it unfinished is totally unacceptable. Don't drop those wands, and sign that canvas large enough for future generations to read your name.

Reversed:

Butterfingers! Instead of working at it a little more, you've decided to throw everything to the floor and stomp your feet as you walk away, dejected. Instead of looking for the essence or keeping your eyes on the prize you have decided to settle for less, not more. So close to the finish line and you have let the baton drop! 'I didn't start this!" you start to whine "Someone else dropped it on me when they decided to dump it and I got stuck with it!" You have started to develop a defeatist attitude; settling for less has brought you down and you next lowered your aspirations. When you were younger and your parents argued with you that you needed to bring your grades up, did you say "What's wrong with a 'C' - it's *still* a passing grade!" You have lowered your expectations and your standards and no matter what those architects of the 1960s said - less is still less. Being an underachiever may have made Bart Simpson famous - but he's just a cartoon personality. Reach down and pick up those wands and try to carry them across the finish line.

Worst Case Scenario: leaving things perpetually unfinished. No one said that life was going to be fair, a bed of roses, or a chair full of bowlies. Is your life a filled storehouse of broken dates, unfinished business, and not-completed projects? Do you paint a room but not clean the brushes afterwards allowing them to harden and become worthless? Do you check for all the materials before you start a project so you don't have to stop in the middle to go and buy something, which becomes your excuse not to get restarted again? Do your weekend projects take two seasons to complete? When you settle for less, it's no wonder.

Ten of Cups

Think of every cliché Hollywood ending there is (no- you don't have to watch *Steel Magnolias*!) and double it. The ecstatic couple sees a rainbow with Ten Cups appear in the sky over their modest home, but their home it is. Their children dance and play nearby, happy and contented. This family may be mortgaged up the butt to have this home, but it is theirs and no one will be taking it or their joy from them anytime soon. The Ten of Cups card has appeared in your spread today to tell you that which you seek the most is within your grasp. Tomorrow a new cycle will start but for the present the view from the top of your world is magnificent.

This is a card about support - having the support of others and freely lending support to others. Everyone has dreams and aspirations and sometimes they need a little kick, sometimes spiritually or financially. The couple in the card did not have a split-second decision to buy this house. Much time and planning and worrying went into it, too.

But by receiving encouragement from others they sought out and eventually fulfilled their dream. Encouragement is a strange thing. When I was younger I did a lot of theatre and the one thing I *hated* the most was after the performance when your friends would be at the stage door and gush like ninnies about how good this, that, the other thing, and *you* were. I preferred those that took you aside and shook your hand and said 'Good Job!' - plain and simple. To me *that* was real encouragement and all the rest of it was just mushy gushing. Somewhere in 'couples therapy' is the notion that you both have to have things you do together but both need hobbies you don't share for when you 'need your space.' You may think running is a dumb sport and your partner is an endurance runner. Wouldn't you still want to be at the finish of the big race to greet them with a bucket of ice water - even if only to dump over their head? Sometimes I am amazed at how little couples actually encourage each other. Helping others to grow and achieve is inherent in this card.

Support implies teamwork and teamwork is not accomplished with a team of one. You may insist that only you know how to put the strings of lights on a Christmas tree but others will decorate it and the rest of the house. Many large community projects such as building children's playgrounds need people not only to work them but also to run them. It can take a lot of cajoling to get a local business to donate materials for a community project, and you are right up front with your crew showing all your abilities and determination. Teamwork means working together.

Support and teamwork go hand in hand with stimulating and developing those ideas that everyone can participate in and feel the same sense of accomplishment at its conclusion. We all hope that shining rainbow shows the fulfillment of our dreams. The Nine of Cups card told us that the end was in sight and now it is! Enjoy it! Your financial outlook improves dramatically with the backing and encouragement of family and friends, perhaps even leading to an exciting new business venture. Contacts bring in new customers, clients, and *capital* that can lead to new opportunities.

<u>Reversed:</u>

Uh-oh! That many overturned Cups tell us something just short of a
disaster is brewing. It will have a large emotional impact upon you and
will involve the emotions of several others. Having reversed Tens signify
the end of the cycle, and in this particular case, it ends in waste. It could
be that the plans or the execution of those plans were wrong; it doesn't
matter now because it's over, it's done, and dead. It there is anything
positive that could be said of this card, it is that tomorrow the new cycle
will start and possibly you will be able to pick up some pieces and
rethink and restart again.

Where once you sought out others for support you now avoid any
particle of involvement with them. They may or may not have
contributed to this dilemma - in fact it might be because you do not
want others involved - but you now have some macho idea that you can
do it all alone and don't need anybody to help you.

This lack of involvement spills over into your personal life, too. This
looming emotional devastation affects your ability to perform and a lack
of intimacy makes the void seem larger than it is. Rather than seek the
closeness of loved ones you push them away. This is a big hurt to all and
may require the intervention of an outside party.

<u>Worst Case Scenario</u>: separateness. This is the card of the unhappy
divorce, the coming home to find the locks changed and your stuff out
on the lawn. At this moment all your lines of communication are down
and the emotional distancing seems worse than ever. This is the pink
slip you never expected, the bills that cannot be paid, the need to file
for personal bankruptcy. If you were worried about hitting the rock
bottom, its time is here.

Ten of Swords

It is impossible to soft pedal this image - a figure lying in a pool of blood with Ten Swords protruding from its back! This image is so potent that its sudden appearance does not require any kind of explanation, and the Querent is usually quick to react. In its defense, it is usually only a warning and not an event in itself - but it needs to get your attention as quickly as possible and it must be dealt with in the same vein (pun intended).

Many readers talk of 'hidden enemies you don't know about' or 'watching your back,' and similar circumstances that indicate the violence connected to this event come from the external and that you must be wary and watchful. This theory, although it is quite plausible and entirely acceptable denies the concept that you *yourself* have set yourself up, stabbed *yourself* in the back, or have put yourself so close into the danger zone that you cannot see it. Many medical sources will tell you that the warning signs of an impending heart attack appear two weeks or more before the attack, and are usually ignored by the patient until the ambulance brings them to the emergency room. Have you recently made some radical decisions that go against your better judgement or are diametrically opposed to the 'normal' way that you do things? Are you ignoring the warnings of others when they say 'a change has come over you'? Have you decided that these 'desperate times bring desperate measures' and are about to do something desperate and equally dangerous?

Whatever the dark circumstances are being hinted at in this card, they are not usually long-standing ones; if they were you would probably have gotten warnings about them long ago. (Then again - maybe you did - and ignored them.) This situation has a strong sense of immediacy attached to it and the immediate reaction is what becomes potentially dangerous because it now catches us off-guard and unprepared. Historians say that if the Titanic had hit the iceberg head-on it probably would not have sunk (but oceanic research has not been able to prove the 'gash below the water line' theory, either, even 100 years later). The Ten Swords imply that rather than watching and waiting for plans to unfold of their own accord that you have decided to ignore the warnings to the contrary and kick the engine into overdrive to make something happen faster. This exploitation of the moment - things that have turned ordinary men into heroes throughout history - is ripe for *disaster*, not victory. This card says you have disregarded or discarded your dreams and are now about to abandon those carefully made plans to achieve a quick end. Rather than try to Carpe your Diem, you are being warned to try to avert your plans that can only end in complete ruin.

Worst Case Scenario: being unconcerned with the future. We all take chances every single day. Usually, as we make the choice to take that chance we automatically run through the alternatives and decide which choices are least likely to give us problems. This extreme case says 'I don't care, and why should I, anyway?' It shows a lack of regard for the self and for others, the human time bomb that can explode at any moment and not care whom gets hurt in the process. If this card has elicited no reactions from you or you feel that it 'must have come up in error,' it is time to re-examine what we want from our future and how we intend to achieve that end. Some person is going to be vastly disappointed to find his or her cardboard rainbow ends in a broken chamber pot. Or perhaps you simply refuse to see the truth?

Reversed:

Can the reversal of this card improve its nature? When the Swords fall out, a time of healing can begin to take place. Where once the pain and anguish caused you to disregard your dreams, this turnabout in time and viewpoint brings us to a time of paying attention to our dreams. Our new dreams may now show us our potentials, not our shortcomings. Remembering that the Swords may be gone but have left their scars, some permanently, helps us to see the lessons in what we endured. Perhaps the situation that brought this card to the fore was necessary to get our attention and so detrimental that it had to be stopped - cold. Instead of just exploiting the moment we start to study shaping our futures instead of merely forcing things to happen, the way a greenhouse forces bulbs to sprout in the midst of winter.

Perhaps having been 'stopped cold' causes us to review our impact on the lives of others the way this event impacted us. Even in reversal, the Ten is still the beginning and end of a cycle and being 'stopped cold' gives us the new slate to write on. Possibly this is the time for planting trees both literal and literary, nurturing things that will outlive us but ultimately will serve a future generation in our memory. For unexplainable reasons, there is a Connecticut resident who has decided that he wants to create a generation of one million ukulele players and donates used ukuleles to school music departments at his own expense. Whatever his reasons are for doing this, school children are learning music playing a child-sized instrument - and loving it. To quote Stephen Sondheim: "A vision's just a vision if it's only in your head." Take this time of starting over to try to correct the mistakes of the past by learning from them. Change those nightmares into visions for the future.

Ten of Pentacles

In the culmination/rebirthing of the Tens we come to this very comforting image of a multi-generational family safe and happy within the walls of their ample home. Family interpersonal relationships are shown - even the family pets are all included. This is a card about connections and connecting - reconnecting, if necessary, recalling that concept that 'no man is an island.' Isn't safety and peace of mind for our families and us exactly what we all want in the back of our minds? The Patriarch sits contentedly, dressed in finery that his wealth affords surrounded by his adult children and a grandchild playfully pulling a dog's tail. How can anything negative intrude here and spoil this scene? It can try but it will not get very far.

Here is a card about connection. Its happy ending does not reach the overt Disneyesque proportions of the Ten of Cups, but its effects are similar. In this technological world that gives us instant access into other people's lives yet forces us farther and farther apart by the impersonal nature of its machines, we no longer take or make the time to connect. Do we really 'know' anything about the people we work with - other than their cell, pager, and home phone numbers? Do we take the time to share our life's experiences with anyone? Do we take the time to learn from other people's experiences? Do we even *seek out* the company of others?

There is probably some hint of oral traditions and family history inherent in this card, too. Have you ever done a family genealogy search or tried to run down the last three or four generations to see who is related to who - or tried to create a family reunion? My parents have lived to see Lindbergh fly the Atlantic and to watch men walk on the moon. Now cell phones have cameras built right in - how 'Dick Tracey' can you get? As I approached fifty years of age in this early twenty-first century I wondered how many wonderful family stories are being lost forever as the older generation leaves us.

In this card of connections and sharing we come to be a social person, not a stray loner. Sometime in our lives we learned a really hard lesson a really hard way, and time has given us the advantage of seeing the humor in the learning process. We may have heard Uncle Joe tell the story of how he shot himself in the ass in World War II one time too many, but maybe it's time to write it down for the next generation to read about. Maybe he does not wish to revisit the horrors he saw and this painful but humorous incident seems like the only thing he talks about. Perhaps it is time to sit down with him and ask him about what he remembers about it all. Sharing one's real life experience should happen in an air of confidence, cooperation, and meaningful participation in all experiences that are available in life. Isn't that what 'family' is all about?

Linked to this card are also a love of nature (the grapes on the Patriarch's robe in the RWS) and a love for animals. There are few animals depicted in Tarot cards and these dogs speak of loyalty, trust, and *belonging*. We may never have the palatial home (material wealth) or coats of arms (social stature) this fictional family has or even spear-carrying security forces to protect us! But - we do have our family and its support.

Reversed:

Forget the loving kindness, the loyal brethren, and of the warm fuzzy sweaters. Think instead of *Deliverance* or *The Texas Chain Saw Massacre* type of family relationships. All right, maybe not *quite* that bad, but sometimes you wonder how your motley crew of relatives even qualifies to be called a family. No sharing band of lively, warm personalities willing to help each other out in a jam, but rather a bunch of cutthroats and thieves who don't even wait for the body to be cold. They are in stripping the bed and checking the drawers for hidden loot the deceased didn't tell them about, looking for the will. You think I'm kidding?

You tend to become meditative, but not reflective, dwelling on what is wrong, what went wrong, or who wronged you. You only come to a family gathering to complain about all your shortcomings, whine about your problems, or bitch about what someone else in the family did to you. You are unhappy most of the time, consumed with petty family quarrels. Rather than being connected to family you are feeling unconnected to the whole process.

Perhaps you feel beleaguered by your annoying family who never seems to leave you a moment's peace. You are trying to seek out your own livable life and the phone constantly rings call after call from someone who 'wants' and wants you to buy, fetch, carry, or work for them without any regard for how inconvenient it will be for you. Sometimes family ties are the biggest bitches of all. Perhaps *disconnected* is what you are becoming or would like to be.

Worst Case Scenario: being alone by circumstance or by choice - usually choice. You avoid groups of people whenever possible, do not visit large public places such as shopping malls, and do not speak to others, especially strangers. Unlike the Hermit who is seeking knowledge, you are becoming a reclusive soul whose minimalist contact with others deals with survival, not socialization.

3 – THE COURT CARDS

We now enter into the feared and enigmatic world of the Court Cards, with shades of meaning oftentimes difficult to pinpoint and considered by many to be the worst group of cards to understand. The Court cards work on several planes simultaneously: they can represent someone else, a situation brewing, what you are doing, or the way you are acting!

On top of this, the Court Cards fall under the whim of the deck's creator and as I mentioned earlier there can be anywhere from twelve to twenty Court cards, all with different names. In a standard deck there are (in ascending order) Pages, Knights, Queens, and Kings, one for each suit. In one feminist deck, the Pages (generally considered female) and the Queens ranked higher than the Knights and Kings (always seen as male.) In another New Age deck the creators eliminated the Kings entirely, but gave their attributes to the Knights, which they ranked higher than the Queens. One deck calls them the Girl, the Boy, the Woman, and the Man; another has Princesses, Princes, Queens, and Kings!

All these confusions frazzle the beginner who wants answers, not philosophical wrangling. For our male understanding of the Court, the Kings are at the top of the food chain and the Pages (regardless of their gender) are at the bottom. From my experience and from countless discussions with other readers, every one of us worked with the Court cards until we found a 'system' that worked for us, no matter what books may tell us.

THE PAGES

Pages may represent both boys and girls from a young age up until adolescence. The Page can represent the Querent or someone the Querent knows, but this character is usually the message (or the messenger) bringing some news or information to the Querent. The different Pages bring different types of messages.

PAGE OF WANDS

PAGE OF CUPS

PAGE OF SWORDS

PAGE OF PENTACLES

The Page of Wands

PAGE OF WANDS

Pages usually represent the arrival of news you may or may not be expecting, or may not want to hear at this time. The Page of Wands brings very important news - he is about to bang the end of his wand on the ground to get your attention. If that doesn't work he will swing that wand around and smash it into your skull - so listen up!

Firstly, this news is not trivial. For good news it can be something important such as the birth of a child, a job promotion, or the receiving of the ownership papers after paying off your car. Although - upright he can still bring unexpected news, such as the death of a family member, an IRS audit, or legal papers from your ex's attorney. Whenever I get a Page (or Knight, for that matter) in a reading, I usually wait until I have dealt all of the cards needed to complete the spread. I then go back and flip over the top card from the pack onto the Page or Knight and see it that helps clarify the matter. This is known as using a Clarifier card.

Secondly, the Page can represent _you._ It can represent you going to the boss or in HR, pounding your fist on someone's desk demanding attention for correction of a perceived wrong. It may represent your need to seek legal counsel in some important matter or petitioning a court. Ultimately, it can represent a person with no one else to turn to, and reaching that last resort of believers and non-believers alike: prayer. You petition for your needs as though your life and livelihood depends on it.

Lightening this conversation up a bit, The Page of Wands also represents spontaneous expression and liberation of the self, that slapping yourself upside the head and asking 'How did I miss that?' Suddenly the light bulb goes on and you are off and running. Things that were once permanently set in place now get discarded because you 'had the breakthrough' and nothing is going to hold you back. Where once you were petitioning for your needs, you now are clarifying them, streamlining them, and honing them in a better way to achieve a better result. Perhaps this clarification makes its presence known in other ways and you see what was keeping you from reaching goals and it helps you set better goals. Perhaps getting whacked over head by the Page's wand was the best thing that could have happened to you. The point I have tried making many times to people is that it is not the _news_ that is good or bad- it is how _you react_ to the news that makes the situation good or bad. Remember, for every person who jumped out a nearby window when Wall Street crashed, someone else stuck around and recouped their losses or later made a fortune. Lastly - in a somewhat contradictory statement - I am the first person to state that man has Free Will to make the decisions he needs to make about what will be best for him. I do not believe that we are predestined to some particular or sad fate set in stone and our lives are merely ourselves reacting to a preset stimulus. No matter how random you might accept the Universe to be, I accept it to be _ordered_ in an elaborate code we do not yet understand. No matter how good your skills with Tarot for prediction may become, sometimes there is nothing we can do except trust to Providence, and that, too, is part of the petition process.

Reversed:

In general terms, <u>any</u> reversed Page represents that there is no news is forthcoming, or news will be delayed. Also, the news may contain misinformation, or the message received is not the answer that you sought.

In reversal the Page of Wands can also represent not so much misinformation but rather an unclear expectation on your part. If we only can reap what we have sown, perhaps your plans seemed sound at the time but were flawed to begin with. Without a clear path or goal it is hard to get a clear or definitive answer, and having an unclear goal most certainly will not have a clear answer. It should be of little surprise that the answer you received is not the one you anticipated.

Perhaps you gave up too early or decided that something was taking far too long to be completed and walked away from it. Perhaps there was a loss of faith in others or even within yourself. Rather than wait for the end to play itself out, you shot yourself in the foot and short-circuited the process, effectively destroying it.

Worst Case Scenario: despair and discouragement. After all, we were once waiting for something of importance, and now the information we seek is dubious or the lack of news delays or halts our abilities to move forward. What others may perceive only as a mere minor setback represents a major obstacle for you. The Page smashed his wand into your crotch and flipped you on your back and it is a situation you do not enjoy. Like a prone fighter on the canvas, you must wonder how you will gather the strength to lift yourself up before the referee finishes counting to ten. Some men stand up and fight, some men give up and flee. As I have already said - how you react will determine everything.

Page of Cups

PAGE OF CUPS

The Page of Cups deals with the world on an emotional or gut level. The undulating seas behind him are not completely placid, but they do not churn in emotional upheaval. So much discussion has been written about 'the fish in the cup;' just what exactly does it represent? Both the traditional Pages of Cups and Pentacles wear a circular hat with a drape which represents their use of the mind (not force) to deal with problems and solutions, usually hinting at some use of psychic capabilities. The fish (sometimes one with wings) represents the Page's imagination although sometimes that imagination borders on being overactive. While the Page of Wands is very serious, the Page of Cups is light hearted and has an artistic temperament to match his artistic talents, usually art and music. What types of news does this Page bring? Usually something equally light hearted, such as thank-you notes, valentines, or wedding invitations. By being able to balance his emotions and his imagination, The Page of Cups can use his emotional objectivity to find solutions to difficulties. You are possibly wondering what kinds of difficulties this Cups character might actually have, being Mr. Goody Two-shoes, after all. The Page of Cups gets involved with issues that have an impact on his world, where making a difference - such as acts of civil disobedience - become necessary.

The Page of Cups is about getting involved and being an active participant in Life. All too often people dismiss the really important issues with an attitude of 'you can't fight City Hall,' or 'what difference will we make, anyway?' Being a product of the 1960s myself, we watched as whole neighborhoods of homes, shops, and lives got bulldozed and destroyed under the catchall phrase of 'Urban Renewal.' Those small ethnic neighborhoods disappeared to create glass-and-steel office buildings that were considered the epitome of high technology, with little regard for the displacing and disrupting of the lives of the people who once lived there. In the neighborhood I grew up in, whole city block areas were destroyed for the building of a new interstate highway system; some of those flattened lots were still vacant twenty years later. Does a phrase about 'paving paradise' spring to mind?

The Page of Cups warns us that it is time to make changes in our lives, and become aware of changes that are being made to our lives by others. I have a friend who literally did chain himself to trees to protest the destruction of a park to build a municipal building. He was arrested, but it was reported in the papers, so when the building was built anyway, the city did turn one of the vacant lots into a small park in the center of town. The Page of Cups fights with his head, not his fists. When he gets into 'head games' it is with a clear purpose and an express outcome in mind - the balance of his emotions and imagination. The Page does not jump from one cause to another similar to belonging to a 'jelly of the month' club. He knows that to make a lasting impact that a significant action may have to be taken, and perhaps, like my friend, be taken away in handcuffs if necessary. As I wrote this, the state of Vermont had placed its entire state on an endangered list to try to stop a major retailer from building multiple new mega-sized 'big box' superstores which it fears will destroy the rural nature characteristic to

Vermont. It is an attempt by some Vermonters to make all Vermonters realize that the impending urbanization of their state (which is home to the largest known independent freethinking society in the USA and Ben & Jerry's Ice Cream) will change their laid-back lifestyles forever should Mr. Big Box go unchecked. If this idea catches fire, will they be chaining themselves to trees? Yes, and all their cows, too, if necessary. (Vermonters are an obstinate bunch!) Remember - this is a card about *impact* and making a difference. Sometimes your fertile imagination may run away with you ("They're going to turn our green state into one big parking lot!"), but that may be the way to get things moving.

Reversed:

The fish in the cup (similar to the talking fish in a Dr. Seuss story) may have popped up from time to time to try to tell you something important. Those little flashes of appearance were good to stimulate your thinking. In reversal, he is a fish out of water flopping about on the floor, so desperately trying to stay alive and get back in his fishbowl. Rather than focus on what is most significant, you waste your time in trivial pursuits going after whatever is topical or momentary, and what is superficial in regards to the big picture. You have become one of those 'Cause of the Month' supporters who whole-heartedly throws yourself into something only to be bored a short time later and almost as quickly picks up the next cause to advocate.

Rather than deal with how the pieces fit into your personal puzzle you experience living as a series of unending daily dramas with peaks and valleys coming at you almost hourly. For you everything is 'big stuff' and it sucks up your time and drains your energies and you find the most insignificant things anger you. People around you constantly tell you that you need to find relief for your stress.

Worst Case Scenario: being absorbed with insignificant issues. Everyone finds varying degrees of importance in the same situation but of late it seems that the more important some issue is the less you are interested in it or concerned by it. In fact, this intense interest in minutiae may be your way of not dealing with the important issues. It is similar to never doing some auto maintenance on your car's exterior but you are enraged when a bird craps on your windshield. Your emotional objectivity no longer exists.

Page of Swords

PAGE OF SWORDS

The Page of Swords stands on a mountaintop surrounded by activity in the motion of the birds, clouds and trees. Although at a standstill, this Page is about to charge, his right foot showing that he is about to pivot or even change directions and when he does he'll be off and running, sword in hand. Traditionally, this Page carries news that brings distress - bad news or news that was unnecessary to have at this time. (This Page is charging down a hill towards you with a bared sword - you think that this is good news?) Whatever it is, it may catch you off guard and you'd better think fast to recover - you won't get a second chance to do so.

This Page represents practical thinking - the ability to think things through quickly, find the truth in the situation, and size up the actions needed to support or deflect it. The movement of air refers to higher brain functions, so combining thought processes with practicality and speed indicates this Page is a catalyst for getting things moving and getting things done. Once this Page sets his energies in motion there is no telling what he might be capable of. However, his sword is two-edged and he must be careful not to swing it too wildly in his furor, for he may undo the good he is trying to achieve. (Always remember those damn double-edged swords!)

So, where does all this bubbling energy get us? Hopefully, the energy radiating forth from the Page serves to put him in a leadership position where he can use his energies to inspire others to follow him. Being aware of his ability to rally others, he is in the perfect position for instigating changes, particularly social changes. This is the man you see leading the banner that says 'World Peace Now,' carrying signs in a protest march, or leading a union picket line. His double-edged sword reminds him that he can be arrested for his actions no matter how noble they might be, but that is worth the price to him. For this Page there is a difference between being a radical thinker and just being a rabble-rouser for the sake of protest. When Rachel Carson wrote *Silent Spring* in 1962 many people within the scientific community said she was being an "alarmist" and they denounced her for being a crackpot, her theories too far-fetched to ever become real. I remember the first 'Earth Day' celebration back in the early 1970s when this concept that modern man was poisoning the earth was a *radical* concept. After all, weren't there enough clean air and water to go around? The world is a big place to live with infinite resources, so we all thought. Of course, it was twenty years before there was a second Earth Day, but now it has become a yearly activity, and globally, too. Did Rachel Carson swing that sword around? Perhaps more subtly than she wanted to, but good thing she did; now they teach ecology to grade school students.

This Page announces that important beginnings are about to happen, so look out when he starts running at you. These changes may be important, but that does not mean that you shall embrace them with open arms, initially anyway. You may find yourself very resistant to the news he brings, perhaps even defiant to them. Remember the phrase in *The Battle Hymn of the Republic* "He has loosed the fateful lightning of his terrible swift sword"? That can refer to another failure of a peace agreement, an incredible natural disaster, or another historic rise in gasoline prices.

Reversed:

The reversed Page has stumbled in his stride and tripped and fallen on his sword; this does not make him happy. It is an over-simplification to say that he brings only bad news for he can also represent a misinterpretation of the news, or even a deliberate distortion of the news by another party. Whatever he tells you - you are not going to like it.

The least upsetting interpretation I can give you is that he has tripped over a series of obstructions that suddenly appeared in his way, obstructions that could not be foreseen since this Page does not pause for reflection or to take a long look around. It foretells plans being made too quickly without thinking the entire process through, or that you are moving too fast to see the obvious warning indicators in front of you.

No longer able to run, this Page foretells of a stalling of the process that you do not need to have hindered. If you were looking or hoping for a swift conclusion to a series of events (good or bad) they will now become delayed for an uncertain period. The swift sword barer now uses that sword for a walking cane or a crutch. If you were planning to instigate some kind of change, those changes are now inhibited, and like the wounded animal who finds a convenient cave to crawl into to lick and nurse his wounds (or die), those plans could never see daylight again.

Worst Case Scenario: meddling in the affairs of others. The reversed Page can look and even act the same as the upright Page, but instead of having a purpose in mind, he randomly sticks his sword into places it is not necessary nor wanted. Rather than working for a cause, he lives to cause trouble, and pissing you off becomes his true intent. This is the relative who has to argue politics at the family dinners, the coworker who has to discuss religion in the employee cafeteria, or the person who sends you unwanted propaganda emails about causes that are not yours. Whatever they are, you will have to learn to say you have no interest in their petty games, refuse to participate in circular arguments, and if necessary report them as a spammer or block their emails. Get yourself as far away from this Page as possible.

Page of Pentacles

PAGE OF PENTACLES

The Page of Pentacles stands contemplating the pentacle that seems to float above his fingertips, a serene meditative state on his face. Considered the card of the psychic (the drape on his hat – here modernized into a hoodie - similar to one on the Page of Cups) this Page absorbs knowledge wherever he can find it on both the material and spiritual planes. Traditionally this Pentacles Page is someone with a boundless thirst for knowledge, the guy who reads any periodical that comes into his hands. He tends to study every conceivable angle before making a decision and is goal-oriented. This is your classmate who never once raised his hand because he always had the correct answer anyway when called upon; however, he was far from being the class nerd.

The news this Page brings comes in the form of or a response to his gut reactions. Due to the manner of his intense mental facilities he is aware of things not considered by others and he adjusts himself accordingly. He will always choose the 'best' response even if it is not what the others are expecting or would consider the correct response. You may wonder why someone with all that brainpower listens to his viscera instead. This Brainiac knows that mere cognitive thinking is not always going to be his answer, for he can produce something new entirely by his own creativity. A friend of mine says that he knows when something is going to be good or right because his 'balls buzz,' so the next time your balls start buzzing, maybe you should pay more attention to why they are trying to tell you something.

So, what does this Page deal with? He deals with answers - obtaining them, sometimes from the past - and learning from the answers that he finds or receives. In truth there are easily hundreds of self-help books out there, aimed at every human idiosyncrasy imaginable. Some of them are pure garbage; duplicated endlessly in an attempt to cover all topics hacked out by a greedy publisher somewhere. All they do is substitute one condition for another one and present it to the gullible public as a 'new' book. They are meant to be stepping stones - not a be-all and end-all. Many men find that the best way to achieve self-improvement is similar to home improvement - do it yourself. One of the best things you can do for yourself is to keep a written journal about something, either writing it in a blank book or using electronic storage, as I do. Learning to write about what you do, think, and feel is the best way to see if there are patterns in your life that hold you back, or if there are cycles that need to be broken. In this way you may be obtaining answers from your past. Self-analysis can be a difficult thing, particularly if you are not one who can accept the truth about yourself. Perhaps you will discover (as I did) that you have always dealt with major problems by not dealing with them at all - burning bridges and walking away as quickly as possible. It is time to find out why.

Parts of your answers may come from existing knowledge that you may not be aware of. A good self-help book points you in the right direction; it does not provide you with cookie-cutter answers that are supposed to apply to every person who buys the book. Sometimes those proverbial light bulbs do indeed light up over our heads, shedding light on the fact that darkness was hiding the correct answers all along, similar to the lantern the Hermit carries. Several occult theories state (more or less) that we carry all of our answers within us if only we would shut up long enough to listen to what is being said. I have always said that our bodies are a lot smarter than we are. Sometimes it gives us subtle hints like vomiting our guts up because we drank too much; sometimes it's the heart attack that makes us know that we have not been taking care of ourselves. When you are not listening it is hard to hear an answer. Are your balls buzzing yet?

Reversed:

The Page's head is no longer in the clouds but on the ground, effectively 'grounding out' all higher functioning, returning him to the basest of levels. In this instance the Page repeats and repeats the same cycles and errors because he indeed 'never learns his lesson.' For example - people who have a hard time with relationships that do not see that they tend to fall for the same personality type every time, no matter how many times it happens, and bemoan the fact that 'everyone takes advantage of them,' or whatever their favorite peeve is. Wouldn't you expect that if your relationships break up for all the same reasons, or you get fired from jobs for all the same reasons, or that you continually indulge in abusive activities that leave you without any money, family, or friends that *something* needs to be changed? The reversed Page doesn't see it at all, and if perchance he does, he blames someone else for it happening. He doesn't look for answers because he doesn't want to face the questions.

Is it possible to repress knowledge, as in the form of 'convenient or selective' memory loss? Is it possible to deliberately *not* seek answers when an answer is needed? The reversed Page is a moody sonofabitch who cannot seem to 'follow through' on anything, and he resents the implication that he is lazy, and possibly has an addictive personality-each one is problematic singly and lethal in combination. The drape over his face hides the truth he does not want to see, and it blinds him to what is true and what is false.

Worst Case Scenario: complete denial. In a famous movie exchange, Jack Nicholson snarled "TRUTH? You can't *handle* the truth!" And so it is - refuse to seek answers to problems, deny there *is* a problem, avoid making a decision that might serve to make you admit you created the problem, and you are ripe to become a classic denial case. It is almost impossible to deal with this person because they refuse to see that which they do not wish to acknowledge.

THE KNIGHTS

Before we even start to discuss the Knights, take them out and look at them placed in this order (left to right)–Knight of Pentacles, Knight of Cups, Knight of Wands, Knight of Swords. Look at their horses and what the horses are doing:

KNIGHT OF PENTACLES   KNIGHT OF CUPS

The Knight of Pentacles: his horse is standing completely still.

The Knight of Cups: his horse is starting to walk or walking.

KNIGHT OF WANDS   KNIGHT OF SWORDS

The Knight of Wands: his horse is about to trot or canter.

The Knight of Swords: his horse is charging at full gallop.

Knights, too, can bring messages and news, similar to the Pages. The appearance of a Knight or Knights in a reading usually indicates a long-term condition or life process that is about to change for the better or the worse--or end—and the horses indicate the speed of that process.

Here we see the full spectrum of possibilities from a complete standstill with slow or no progress to a change happening so fast that it will possibly overpower or run roughshod over the Querent! These are the time indicators for the Knights.

As with all the Court cards, the Knights can also represent people and their personalities, and have both upright and reversed aspects. When reversed, consider that the Knight has fallen from his steed; all forward progress for better or worse is halted, and the Knight is very angry!

Knight of Wands

KNIGHT OF WANDS

In general, Knights deal with changes going and coming into your life, the speed of which can be judged by the position of the Knight's horse. The Knight of Wands' horse has reared up and lifted its front legs off the ground; we don't know if he is going to charge or merely walk, but he *is* about to move, which means that this change is about to start or just starting. What type of male personality does this Knight have? He is one of those guys who are always doing something, zipping back and forth across the countryside in constant motion. He gives the impression of being scattered (or totally lost) but in reality he just likes to keep himself moving and he keeps things moving right along. Sometimes he goes off without having all the information he needs so he makes repeated trips. It is part of his endearing charm. The Knight of Wands easily represents inspired creativity, and sometimes that means working without a plan (or a net), seeing where the journey takes him rather than sticking to an organized plan. He knows it will all come out right at the end. So, where does this assurance get us? This assurance gives us belief in our own potential, helping us rise to challenges we have determined to be important challenges, but not necessarily life-threatening ones. (It's one thing to try hang gliding, but you might not want to try white-water kayaking.) Others - or ourselves - may have set these challenges but we decide we will take them in stride, even if they initially leave us perplexed about the best way to tackle them. Of course, the better we are at accomplishing the goals or the sooner we can get through them, the more positive we become at self-appraisal, a quality many men lack. We are all keenly aware of the blowhards who puff up their personal accomplishments and stuff them down our throats at any opportunity. We are aware of men like 'The Donald' who have built and control such large financial empires who don't get fazed by anything. However, most of us don't have a clue about how well or how deficient we are because we rely only on the input of others to act as our measuring stick. I believe it was Woody Allen who said that he didn't read reviews of his plays or movies because if you believe the critics whenever they say you are good then you would have no choice but to believe them when they say you suck. Learn to have confidence in your capabilities, and faith in your ability. Jump on your horse's back, grab your saddle horn, and see where the journey takes you.

One thing - you have to learn how to *accept compliments*. There are many people who have a strange notion that it is unmanly to accept compliments, other than the usual 'Good Job!' stuff that we normally get for anything we do. {"Oh! You took your feet off the coffee table- Good Job!"} Some people have a high modesty level and shun any kind of compliment, using self-deprecating statements to 'neutralize' the praise they are given. Listen to your ego-driven author: when someone pays you a compliment, no matter how large, small, or backhanded - say 'Thank you, very much!' Having others believe in you is another step towards positive self-appraisal and a belief in your own potential.

Reversed:

When a Knight is reversed, think that any forward motion is delayed or stopped completely. This condition does nothing to improve the personality of the Knight, so expect a few sparks to fly.

Reversal moves us from positive appraisal to blatant self-questioning, usually with negative results adding insult to injury. It is one thing to truthfully say 'Oops! I really screwed that up!' and look for correcting the situation; it is quite another to develop self-destructive tendencies where minor errors or fluctuations are treated as though they were committed with criminal intent. We can be very harsh judges of ourselves when judge and jury are one. This is why you need to accept or involve the opinions of others. It would be comparable to sneaking into your own art show and smashing your own statuary, declaring that if the art didn't please you then it should please no one. We will always find fault with our own work: one thing to find it casually and another to go out looking for it with a microscope.

Another effect of reversing this Knight is the creation of unrealistic beliefs both pro and con. We can brick ourselves into a wall believing that everything is too challenging for us, or that others are deliberately doing this to us to prove how worthless we are. This can manifest as obsessive or compulsive behaviors. It can also make us go out and do dangerous or foolhardy things believing that we have to show the world that we are invincible and can rise to almost any challenge - similar to people who go on 'reality shows'. People disregard pure logic and reason to accept a prize usually inversely proportional to the hardships they faced. Personally - who would endure six weeks of eating bugs and other grotesque requirements for a *mere* one million dollars - *ten million* might make me consider it.

<u>Worst Case Scenario</u>: pride affecting judgement. Falling or being tossed off a horse is a source of embarrassment and this Knight whose Pride has been hurt lashes out at others, denying he has made any mistakes and questioning the judgements made by others against him. In return, he will find fault with everyone else, and if he is in any kind of power position will make those people's lives miserable. If he cannot do so (the judges are his superiors) he will strike out on a lateral course, bullying others until he feels he has caused as much pain for others as

he judges he has received. All Wands Court cards have a fiery temperament, so be careful not to add fuel to his fire.

Knight of Cups

KNIGHT OF CUPS

Here is one of the cards that are the reason I decided to write this book! In female-oriented Tarot books, this Knight is oftentimes described as (are you ready?) *"A romantic dreamer … if the Querent is a woman, she may be falling in love with such a young man…"* GAG ME WITH A SPOON! "He may be bearing a token of his affection for you." BARF-A-RONI! Do real women really still believe this shit about a white knight that is going to come out of nowhere and sweep them off to Camelot? Nowhere do these books mention anything if the Querent is a male … that is where I come in.

The horse of the Knight of Cups is walking; indicating that the change he brings to you has already begun. The wings on the Knight represent his imagination and his change and cup will bring about an emotional change in your life. Here is a card dealing with *charisma*, the inner ability to attract positive energy or others to you, not wimping around waiting for the absolute best thing to happen of its own accord without your input. Having charisma is more than simply an ability to attract the opposite or your own sex to you. At work, one of my coworkers would frequently comment that she loves watching me walk because ' I walk so proudly.' We both know she's staring at my butt, but I gave her this piece of advice: "Just remember - I don't lead the parade- I *AM* the parade!"

Confident people attract other confident people - and the wannabes - but you can spot the genuine article a mile away. Think of this Knight not as 'seeking you out', but rather that you attract him to you. What makes people confident? They make wise choices. You must learn the best way to get yourself into where you wish to go, then do what you wish to accomplish by being there, how to get out, and having an extra escape plan - just in case. Think early James Bond movies - did Sean Connery ever sweat?

Another effective habit of charismatic people is to learn to use the positive influences in their lives - accepting advice when necessary, learning from the successes of others, and trying to develop similar strategies. This is done without malice or jealousy. The flip side is that highly charismatic people learn to be a positive influence upon the lives of others, too, either indirectly by example or by direct contact. They also accomplish this by being outgoing and friendly, not withdrawn or enigmatic. If you have all the wealth, power and best advice in the world but you cannot convey it to others you will never attract another to you.

Although this card may speak of emotional longing as an undercurrent, it is also a card about the finding of and the using of complimentary energies. When someone tells you that clichéd 'opposites attract,' remember Felix & Oscar - is that what you want for a relationship? Although Jack Klugman and Tony Randall had a wonderful screen charisma together, it was only a television show - not real life. My late partner and I had a successful ten-year relationship even though he was Aries and I was Taurus - which lie next to each other in astrology - and supposedly are not the best combination of stars. It was bumpy at times, but I was told by many that we complimented each other well - filling in the gaps and supporting each other unconditionally. Learn to find and ultimately develop those complimentary energies without become a *user*. Unless you set up a few road signs along their way to help point you out, they may - as Dionne Warwick once sang - "Walk On By." Learn to attract what you want by projecting the best image you can and living that image.

Reversed:

Somebody dumped you, literally and figuratively, and you sit watching the stars spin around your head. What happened? This image is the best example I can think of for 'looking for love in all the wrong places.' When you want something or someone in the worst possible way - that is usually how you get them. You have played too fast and too loose and instead of attracting some positive energy you have attracted adversity instead. The proverb (and witty movie of the same title) states: 'when you lie down with dogs you will end up with fleas.' Rather than blame the poor dogs take a good look at yourself - too many parties, too much booze, and too much anonymous sex? Has your emphasis become finding someone new to bone every weekend?

The deadly seeds of negativity have crept their way in like vines growing under a fence. When you have few positive experiences to help, you hold large areas of doubt in your mind- of your abilities and of others. Doubt finds its voice in criticism, and self-criticism can evolve into self-loathing. Your criticism of others becomes louder and more prevalent, so instead of your attracting others to you they now avoid you whenever they can. As the cup has spilled you spill your guts, and once you get started ... there seems to be no stopping. Once you start crying in your beer, it's time for the bartender to shut you off; you must learn how to become your own bartender and seek counseling, if necessary. When my partner of 10 years died the event left me emotionally screwed, a group of friends finally convinced me to get grief counseling. Although I was medicated for about six months, I eventually came out of the spiral and off the meds.

Worst Case Scenario: negative expectations. I knew a couple that *thrived* on negativity, so much so that my partner and I made a conscious effort to avoid them for a period of almost three years. They bickered, moaned, and complained about everything and anything minor that even riding in a car with them was unpleasant. One of them looked for and found the negative in any situation, and finding it practically guaranteed it would happen as though they were casting a spell to make it happen. "If I'm not having a good time, neither shall you" is the mantra of these kinds of people. Avoid them!

Knight of Swords

KNIGHT OF SWORDS

Another figure with a sword is charging somewhere – and so there is a reason to be concerned. Traditional imagery says this Knight brings sudden and fast changes - as swift as lightning and that same tradition also holds that they will cause dismay or be really unwanted and unpleasant. This Knight is abrupt and disruptive in all that he does, even when his change actually destroys something that would have been bad for you to begin with. He is rarely viewed with any positive connotations, and if you are the person to bring about this change for someone else, you will be viewed as the harbinger of doom.

If the Page of Swords deals with practical thinking, the Knight of Swords deals with creative or intuitive thinking. We have all used the phrase 'shit, or get off the pot,' and this guy is definitely 'off the pot.' There are several ways in which this intuitive thinking outburst can manifest itself. Sometimes it happens quickly in a highly flexible fun situation such as a group of comics getting together on a television show and being given a 'motivation' and having to create the actions and results, usually in the most humorous way possible. These manifestations are short-lived but still burn up a lot of energy.

This creativity can happen in a slightly slower mode, also. Carol Channing, who in the 1960s played over 1,000 performances of *'Hello, Dolly!'* seized creative moments to keep her nightly performance lively and fresh. She found that when she had a particular thought while saying a line - which produced the anticipated laugh - she had the stage manager make a note or two in his master script so that she could deliver the line *exactly* the same way every time. You may be wondering how <u>that</u> is creative instead of static. When you are in a long-running hit show, every performance has people seeing the show for the first and only time, and they still expect to see that same great opening night performance the star gave three years ago. Being able to keep a performance from going stale takes more work than the original rehearsals!

Sometimes these creative moments come from the synthesis of one's experience, where years of work give you an edge - and an overview - of what is or isn't happening, or why that 'thing' is or isn't working the way it should be. During the 1940s Gertrude Lawrence was contracted to play the lead in *Lady in the Dark*, and disliked the show, the music, and the songs - even flatly refusing to rehearse one of them - 'The Saga of Jennie.' Opening night came and newcomer Danny Kaye stopped the show and received multiple encores for his big comedy song. Realizing he needed to get the show moving again, he politely refused to do one more encore and turned to the audience and said ' Miss Gertrude Lawrence' and gave her the stage - to sing her next song - the dreaded, unrehearsed 'Saga of Jennie.' Miss Lawrence, every inch the star, pulled out a performance that stopped the show again - proving that 'once a star - always a star.' Such are the moments that become Broadway legends.

O.K. - you're possibly never going to become a Broadway star or legend. You may not feel that your life, job, or sexuality has any creative moments to seize upon. Perhaps that is why this Knight is coming charging into your life - to tell you to get into the flow of things, to get off that pot and stop shitting your life away. The appearance of this Knight means that contentment is over, dull is plain old dull and must be dispensed with, and your beige little world needs a big splash of bright color. You are going to be made unhappy by some of these changes and those around you are going to be shocked as you are. May you get the support you need to keep the necessary momentum going!

Reversed:

SCREECH! That steed suddenly plants his feet and the Knight goes sailing ass-over-teakettle to the hard ground, whacking his head and knocking the creative and intuitive capabilities out as the Knight is knocked out cold. As he slowly regains consciousness, his first thought is "WHAT JUST HAPPENED?" followed by "Am I still in one piece?" What happened is probably a major loss of self-confidence in your abilities and capabilities, and without that self-created safety net you fall and hit hard. Perhaps others are (successfully) undermining you and it is time to access the weak spots in your armor. It is one thing to go down and quite another to be brought down. It this is your past, you have quite a bit of damage control to take care of to ensure that this will not happen again. If this is in your future you are being warned that your enemies are going to hit hard; if you are caught unawares there is no coming back, so maintain your defenses carefully.

Reversal tells of ill-timed plans becoming totally self-defeating. Sometimes Life deals us immediate choices and any decision seems like a bad one; sometimes the decision is taken totally out of our hands and the choice being made for us is not to our liking. You may well be asking yourself how you will ever recover from such catastrophic actions. Your answer comes back: not well, and very slowly on top of it. This card may speak of unused and therefore wasted available opportunities that waved their placards at you and you were too busy or too confident or too proud to listen.

  Worst Case Scenario: missed opportunities. Perhaps you didn't see them as opportunities at the time, but they were, and once over have now evaporated. Early after the release of my first book I went to a book signing that two other Tarot authors were having, hoping to meet them and buy a signed copy of their newly-released book. I also took six copies of my own book along with me 'just in case.' Upon arriving at the store, I very quickly discovered that neither the store nor the authors had *any* copies of their book to be signed - each one was expecting that the other was to provide them! {PS – if you become an author, the STORE is supposed to provide copies for your book signing – not you.} I gave the authors a signed copy of my book (with a promise from them to extend the same courtesy to me) and signed and sold two copies of *my own book* to the public gathered there! Did it take balls to crash someone else's book signing? Yes, it did! But I'll never travel without at least six copies of my book with me no matter where I go! With God as my witness, I'll never miss a sales opportunity again!

Knight of Pentacles

KNIGHT OF PENTACLES

A heavy man sits on a heavy horse in the middle of a freshly plowed field. Tradition says that since his horse is not moving at all that the change he brings hasn't even begun and when (or if) it does it will be slow in coming. Unlike the Knight of Swords who charges about erratically, this Knight's movement is ponderous and methodical, and he will never be considered a mover or a shaker. If you are looking for excitement or sexual combustibility, look elsewhere. Unions signified by this card will develop slowly over a long period of time; however, he is deeply kindhearted and also warmly sensual and will bring to his partnership a solid foundation and a strong sense of reality.

In our revisionist view of Tarot, we must learn to look through his eyes and learn why he acts this way. Far from being lazy, this Knight is practical; rather than fighting his way against the current or attempting to cross the swollen river, he learns how to align himself with the many energies around him, accept them for what they are, and to 'go with the flow.' You may consider this 'taking the easy way out,' but in truth this Knight knows what is a waste of his energy and time and rather than work against himself, this Knight has decided the best course is to try to harmonize with his environment. After all, why would you trample a field that has been prepared for planting? Why would you actively choose to undo the labor that has been invested? You can be sure this Knight will walk his horse very carefully through the soft earth so as not to destroy the furrows or plantings.

Part of this acceptance and flow comes from the realizing and accepting of limitations, and then respecting the limitations of others or ourselves. In my employment there are three different types of banks, and as a banker we are expected to understand, balance, and run each one of them. Some people excel in one or two but rarely all three. The assumption that if you run one well then you should run all of them equally well … just doesn't hold true, even though the company mistakenly seems to think so. Luckily, the shift managers can alter the daily computer generated schedule and assign whom they consider the best people into their toughest positions, particularly on holiday weekends. There are times I didn't even check my assignments because I knew I'll get bumped before I start my shift! Such is the nature of having the complete trust of your superiors and being able to adapt accordingly. Have you ever gone out hiking on the most beautiful day with the most beautiful weather report, only to find yourself in a sudden downpour without your most beautiful rain poncho? Your choices are to find shelter and sit the storm out or to keep hiking since you are not going to get any drier. Being caught unprepared for the storm the possibilities have now forced a series of limitations upon you - how will you deal with them?

Sometimes we are blessed with being able to see the larger picture; sometimes this only comes with experience. The reality of the Knights of Wands and Swords is that they are moving so rapidly that they never stop to take a good look behind them and see where they are coming from. Standing almost completely still our Knight can do a

360-degree turn, size things up, and make a decision accordingly. Now, you're probably wondering why our Material Boy can just sit and wait, particularly if his changes involve his finances or his creature comforts. If his changes will involve entering new worlds, why doesn't he move his ass? Our boy understands that instant gratification is fleeting and is in no hurry to get through a moment to be savored. Good wine and cheese only improve with age, so grab a good friend and sit on your deck, watching the sun set over the lake. Sometimes you have to understand that living in the beauty of a moment - such as the setting of the sun - has to be allowed to happen at its own pace. Boldly charging ahead just guarantees you'll miss it, not participate in it.

Reversed:

If this Knight isn't moving to begin with, how does falling off his horse affect him? Contrary to the movies, suits of armor are heavy, cumbersome things, and without the possibility of his horse carrying him elsewhere, this Knight is staying put. Putting his own comfort (or lack thereof) first and foremost, he creates for himself an air of self-importance, denying the possibilities for any changes to others until his own needs are met. Tradition says that any hope for future changes have been stalled indefinitely, which translates into: Forget it! They ain't happenin'! Whereas the upright Knight still had the possibility for a slow saunter forward, until someone arrives with a crane to hoist this Knight back in his saddle, he's just going to stand there and rust until someone else does something.

Self- importance turns to ego, and once an egocentric perspective enters the picture, the personality of the Knight undergoes an abrupt change. There is no savoring of moments, only demands for things to happen faster and faster. Believing that their situation cannot be changed, and not lifting a finger to try to acquire any changes, they seek to maintain the status quo so that the situation cannot deteriorate - for them, at least, since they have no concern for others or the problems that they are causing. They quickly learn to play the role of 'victim' quite well and can sometimes carry this illusion off for years.

Worst Case Scenario: control by coercion. Without the grace or style to endear others to him, the reversed Knight bullies others into doing his bidding- after all - are you going to argue with a man in a metal suit? Going with the flow now means: do what I tell you to do, the way I told you to do it, and don't argue. Limitations in others are handled with intimidation. His view of the larger picture puts himself in the direct center with everything else as the background.

THE QUEENS AND KINGS

As with the Pages and Knights, the Queens and Kings also work on multiple levels, sometimes simultaneously.

The Queens and Kings usually represent people, either the Querent or some aspect of the Querent's personality, or someone entering or affecting the Querent's life at the moment. They can be parents, bosses, relations, or even total strangers that the Querent hasn't met (yet). They can also represent people the Querent looks to as counselors or confidants. As with other Court cards, the Queens and Kings have extremely differing and strong personalities, even within the same suit.

Queens and Kings also can represent situations, the way the Pages represent news and the Knights represent changes. When Court cards appear in a reading and their meaning is not readily apparent, I usually find it best to describe the personality type to the Querent. In that way, we see if they are someone the Querent knows, or whether their personality in some way reflects the Querent's current frame of mind. The Querent may be unaware that he or she is acting in such a way that is different from normal, particularly if it is contrary to their usual pattern of behavior. In this case it may be a reflection of how others see them or are interacting with them.

These situations usually encourage the Querent to pursue a particular endeavor or they caution against it. Sometimes these conditions are easy to decipher; at other times they can only be arrived at after some discussion with the Querent.

(At this point I'd like to note that there is nothing wrong with the reader asking questions of the Querent. Some people disagree with this, as though the reader were the "all-seeing, all-knowing" infallible oracle. Wouldn't you want to stay on the right track, rather than venture off in a totally wrong direction and ultimately confuse the Querent and the reading?)

Once again, although these cards may seem gender-specific, they do not have to be. When applied to the Querent, they can represent masculine or feminine qualities.

THE QUEENS

QUEEN OF WANDS

QUEEN OF CUPS

QUEEN OF SWORDS

QUEEN OF PENTACLES

Queen of Wands

QUEEN OF WANDS

Along traditional lines, when choosing a card to represent someone, the Queen of Wands is listed as "A married woman, yada-yada-yada." If you were to only accept that Queens can represent only females then you will be misreading the card, for that is too narrow a focus. All of us carry male and female attributes within us, regardless of our gender. To complicate things, as I have stated earlier - all the Court cards can represent ourselves, someone else, a character trend or flaw that is dominating the present, or a situation. It is little wonder the Queens and Kings get especially confusing! I once did a reading for a man who turned up all four Queens. Since four Queens in a spread can represent a great debate going on, it took us quite a while to sort out who was who, and if they were female. When gay men get Queens in their readings, it's really anything goes!

As a situation, the Queen of Wands can represent a good time to be moving forward in a business venture. As a personality type, she is cordial, enthusiastic, aggressive, motivated, and outgoing, the sunflower representing a very sunny disposition. However, all Wands cards represent the element of Fire (the lions represent Leo- also a Fire sign), so there can be little flashes of temperament even when she is in a good mood! As you the Querent, she represents the qualities you now have or that you will need to cultivate to succeed. Everyone will prosper soon when this Queen channels her inner energy and outward independence into something, whether it's business or the arts - particularly if it is a venture that requires or demands courage, a competitive spirit, strong foresight, and particularly - confidence.

The ability to succeed will come from your developing strong bonds through interactions with others especially those actions that help build energy together. There are times you may have to learn to squelch a little ego; there is a need to create mutual encouragement here, not the need to find a group leader. These mutual situations can be from something as simple as finding a jogging buddy with whom you can enter into friendly competition with, or something much elaborate, such as finding a person to go into business with. The most important thing will be having open communications so that all partners are aware of what the common goals of the group are and will be going forward, which will also help keep those flashes of ego in check. It goes without saying that in order to have those common goals that a sharing of mutual trust is also a key ingredient. If there is suspicion or skepticism on the part of one person, then the energy flow will stop. This is not to say that such an arrangement will be devoid of a flash point or two. The Queen of Wands deals with self-knowledge and it will be important to convey that knowledge at times in ways that might be viewed as 'forceful.' Hopefully, the intellectual give-and-take will keep these situations from turning nasty. Unions that fall under the effect of this Queen are also blessed with equality and strike a rare balance between devotion and independence.

Reversed:

When this Queen is reversed, the black cat usually present on the card is suddenly put into prime focus. The cat represents several 'sinister' aspects to be wary of including deceptive behavior, petty jealousies, evil intentions, or infidelity. These contraindications are a warning that someone is talking a good game to cover other activity. Among the least of the problems you might soon encounter are frictions - things that were working smoothly suddenly get really bumpy without apparent reason. This can be expected even when the card is upright, but bears some very close watching when it is reversed since it indicates business problems or to at least be careful in all business dealings.

In reversal what may have started out as a 'friendly rivalry' changes complexion and that rivalry starts becoming unfriendly competition. Disagreements start developing where they are least expected and suddenly you begin to question the motives of others. An uncomfortable feeling enters the back of your brain and you start noticing that you have more questions than there are answers. At this point you must try to reopen communications and this action may in turn close them down. Perhaps you are overreacting, but perhaps not. The dark energy side of this Queen is the belief that only you are perpetually right and everyone else is always perpetually wrong.

Worst Case Scenario: uncooperative conflict. When any Queen or King is off his or her throne, they get nasty, or as Peter O'Toole once bellowed in *The Lion in Winter*: "When the King is off his ass, nobody sleeps!" The cordial aspects of this personality are gone and the aggressive Leo/lion aspects, such as roaring, become all too obvious. These may begin simply as small rumblings in the distance, but very quickly they will become out-and-out verbal warfare. They will reject any and all pleas for understanding and refuse to see anything other than what they wish to see, or only if you agree to do things their way. It is an uncomfortable position especially when both partners involved are strong personalities and neither one can dominate the proceedings. The conflict can get destructive. It may take the intervention of a third party to resolve the conflict, should it get to such extremes.

Queen of Cups

QUEEN OF CUPS

I have always considered the Queen of Cups to be cerebral to totally spaced-out. She possesses the only covered Cup in the deck (which represents her desires and dreams, which she keeps to herself) and I have always felt that she is shallow emotionally. Although she is warm and can be wonderful with her family and close circle of friends, she can be quite aloof to outsiders. Her calm inner oceans match her calm exterior (compare her to the King of Cups, who handles his emotions differently.) Once again - 'she' refers to the figure on the card - but a Queen can also easily represent either gender. A situation represented by this Queen usually deals in with creativity or creative endeavors.

So, where will all that 'vision' get us if we keep it bottled up inside ourselves? It will get us nowhere. It is time to crack open the lid and allow our visions to develop into inspirations, ones that will allow us to follow our dreams. What have you once felt inspired to do, but ignored as being too silly, outrageous, or plain impossible? It's time to get past that; they laughed at the Wright Brothers and Robert Goddard. Someone probably told Picasso, the father of Cubism, to forget about being an artist because his ideas were considered too radical for the straight-laced normal art world to grasp. Open that cup and toss the lid aside – or even better still - make it impossible to reclose.

"WHOA!" you're saying - "I always wished to go climb Mt. Everest - but *that's* just impossible!" Maybe *that* is impossible- you don't even walk to the corner store to buy some milk without getting in your car first. Maybe you do enjoy hiking, but lack the knowledge to become a climber of mountains. Many cities have organizations that teach orienteering classes that provide challenges for those who like to combine a challenge with their love of walking in woods. Many health facilities now have those moving 'rock climbing walls' where you can practice and hone some skills. Perhaps you may never climb sheer rock faces with your bare hands, but you have given yourself a clarified goal, something within your grasp with a possibility of challenge, and explored an old vision that's been rattling around in your brain. Perhaps it's the time to clean off some of those dusty goals and take a good look at them.

Maybe you do have flashes of inspiration - but you still have muddled goals about what to do with all those stimulating thoughts you have. George Bernard Shaw wrote: ' Those who can - do; those who cannot- teach.' (To which Woody Allen added: 'Those who cannot teach - teach gym') Perhaps you can try sharing your vision with others by motivating others to try, to do, and to expand. There is a great responsibility in this - promoting vision in others - because you can't know where it will lead - for them. Edison was partially deaf but he invented a machine to record speech. Perhaps someday someone will ultimately develop the technology to lift the old sound recordings off of those fragile original wax cylinders, and that someone could well be inspired by your input.

If the Knight of Cups deals with emotional longing, then the Queen of Cups embodies emotional integrity. If you seek to motivate others, stimulate their thoughts, and promote their visions, you have to believe in yourself and what you stand for. Actions do speak louder than words, and what you do will last longer than what you say to people. Since Edison is no longer here to record your words, have the guts to make a lasting and indelible impression on the minds of others. Heroes never die; they continue to inspire long after they are dead. What person is your favorite American hero? Why?

Reversed:

The Queen tumbles off her throne and loses her grasp on her Cup of desires and dreams. All of her worst character flaws come to the surface and the Queen who inspired others becomes the Queen of the Cynics. She begins to question the sincerity and goodness of other people's actions or even the value of living. Previously I said that she is shallow; now she doesn't even bother to polish her veneer and her true colors as a sniping, suspicious, gossipmonger start to show.

Rather than being a take-charge person, the Queen now starts to delegate authority to more and more of her minions and subordinates. This action is twofold: first, she is divesting herself of any responsibility where she might have to make some decision or even worse - make a choice. The second step of this process is that it allows her to blame others for the decisions that *they* made and this feeds into her cycle of cynicism: aren't subordinates a disgusting, obnoxious lot? Forget about integrity - you will barely get out of her presence before she starts complaining to someone else about you. The only thing she will inspire you to do is get your resume updated and to look for another job.

Worst Case Scenario: self-focus. Do you remember actor Rex Harrison as 'Professor Higgins' in *My Fair Lady*? He is so focused on making Eliza Doolittle into the perfectly speaking and acting woman that when she finally achieves this effect at the climax of the story he is so busy congratulating himself for his achievement that he doesn't even consider that he should thank Eliza for what she accomplished. He is totally confounded by her actions when not only does she *not* thank him for *his* work but even walks out on him - the useless baggage! Her insult is so much to bear that he imagines (in song) how she will not be able to survive without his help and how he will spite her if she returns! Are these the actions of someone who hopes to inspire others to achieve their own greatness?

Queen of Swords

QUEEN OF SWORDS

The Queen of Swords has always been characterized as the uptight, unfeeling bitch - always ready to condemn and if she doesn't slash you with her sword, then her tongue will work equally as well and maybe even quicker. She is gesturing for you to rise, proving to both of you that she is the Queen and that you are not, and there should be no mistake about it on your part. In her defense, she is used to having to use clear, objective thinking as part of her survival, having to size up people and problems in small amounts of time. The storm clouds gathering behind her warn her of problems brewing, and lone the bird overhead speaks of use of higher intellectual functioning. As a situation, she usually represents an emotionally devastating experience.

Whew! What do I do with this Queen whom you've already sized up as being your bitchy boss, landlord, or the teller at the bank you cannot stand? As you might have noticed with the other two Queens, I have tried to shift the emphasis from the "Them Doing This to You" –

type mentality to more of a "what is the lesson I should learn from this card?" We have had Queens of Interaction, Inspiration, and this is the Queen of Making a Sacrifice.

Sacrifice - the forgoing of something of value to obtain something else of greater value or having a more pressing claim. {Webster's Universal Unabridged Dictionary} In the 'Me Me ME 1990s' the emphasis on whom or what is important changed from others to ourselves, and the concept of 'If I can get it I will take it all - regardless' was born. At the start of the Twenty-first Century, you would think that with all the wealth available in the world that hunger, illness, and poverty would have been eradicated long ago; instead, the chasm between the Haves and the Have Nots is getting more vast. No one wants to lose anything, no matter how worthless, and yet everyone still wishes to obtain everything, no matter how valueless. That 'me Me ME' mantra is a hard mental conditioning to turn off. I don't know about you, but I'm now 60 years old, and when I was a child in the 1960s and my birthday came around, I was lucky that I had a cake and some gifts from my siblings to open, maybe a cousin or two who came over to celebrate. Now it seems that no child's birthday is 'correct' unless twelve to fifteen children are invited and they *all* get a plastic 'take-home' bag of loot that includes plastic novelties, gizmos, and cheap toys. It's similar to giving a wedding gift that is equal in value to the cost per wedding guest's dinner, I suppose. So, you *get* gifts for bringing one to someone *else's* birthday party? Is it any wonder that greedy children grow up to become greedy adults? This Queen says that sometimes you will have to learn to surrender even if you feel it is not in your nature, or even if you do not believe it is your 'turn' to do so. Such is the nature of surrendering to a higher power.

Being able to accept the surrender terms can be an equally challenging to formidable task, for it entails the understanding that there are going to be temporary setbacks, something those driven by instant gratification cannot fathom. Sacrifice will mean compromise, and the foreign concept of losing something to gain something will be a harder thing to accept than the actual loss. Not accepting setbacks sounds great when you are the Captain in *Das Boot*, but we have to realize the extent of our own limitations and plan accordingly, making adjustments as we go. Sometimes those adjustments will not make us happy - sometimes there is no other way.

There are usually butterflies on the throne of this Queen, the symbol of transformation or transformative energy. It is said this Queen has seen deep sorrow such as the loss of a loved one. You must learn to transform your energies from one that does not serve you into one that does. Sometimes when you have no choice but to play by someone else's rules, you find what the rules' weakness is and *exploit* those rules, commonly referred to as a 'Catch-22.' In my casino job I was under the constant scrutiny of surveillance cameras, but in some assignments I finished with my work by seven p.m. and still had to work until midnight. Since we could not bring in any books, magazines, or crossword puzzles to do on *company* time, when I found myself in these situations I would write a portion of my current writing project out by hand on the backs of blank pages, right under the cameras! Since I *was* being paid to sit there, and <u>nothing</u> to say I *could not* write - I did - sometimes three pages a night. Make you want to read Joseph Heller again, doesn't it?

Reversed:

The Queen with the sharp sword has fallen and cut herself - now there is hell to pay. Just like a wounded animal striking out, she whips that sword around her cutting a swath in all directions in an effort to create some cushion of self-protection, effectively keeping everyone at a distance. Since being dethroned makes her equal to everyone else and being unaccustomed to this condition makes her angry with everyone and even more so with herself. She wants to be in charge and make all the decisions and being deprived of that privilege brings out her worst side. Compromise? *No way in Hell!*

<u>Worst Case Scenario</u>: selfish concerns cloud objective thinking. Instead of looking for the best and probably long term solution for all, we seek the soonest even if only temporary solution for ourselves. The needs of the many outweigh the need of the One, but they don't see it in that way; their need to be in control or in the spotlight means that everyone else should do without so that they don't have to. There is a reported story of an opera diva that was in California riding in a limousine that she felt was too cold for her vocal chords. Instead of requesting to the driver to turn the a/c down, she used the limo's phone to call her agent in New York to tell *him* to call the livery company, which then called the driver to tell him to turn the a/c down. What - couldn't use the intercom because she doesn't talk to people who work for her? A true Queen of Swords!

Queen of Pentacles

QUEEN of PENTACLES

This Queen with dark eyes and dark hair sits on a heavy throne surrounded by lush symbols of a plentiful harvest. These in turn represent her bountiful nature, seeking the good in herself or in others, and the prudent use of wealth. She is charitable and giving, but is very contemplative and people often mistake this for being melancholy. Although not readily apparent to us, there is an industrious work ethic connected with her. As a situation, the Queen represents the harvest after much planning and labor; remember, a Pentacle represents material wealth, not just financial security.

So where does this final Queen lead us men, and what is the lesson connected to her? The Queen of Swords dealt with compromise and sacrifice, but the Queen of Pentacles deals with collaboration. How can one Queen be so bountiful, caring, and charitable - all alone? She isn't - she forms such strong alliances with other people, blending creativity and practical care, looking for and developing the best in others. She controls by leading, not by demanding. She is the team captain when there is no official team, for she understands the mind of the 'group' and what the group goals should be, looking for ways to move the group forward. The team also trusts in her leadership, and believes the good of the many outweighs the needs of the One. Have you ever been on a team comprised of individuals? In the 1980s I found myself sitting on the board of one of the oldest continuously running community theatres in the country, and quickly began wondering how it ever lasted so long. The board was made up of many truly creative theatre personalities - but no businessmen, merchants, or anyone with a grounded business sense who knew how to raise and handle money. One thing these people knew was how to *spend* money! Everyone wanted their particular theatre department to have the highest production values, but no one could ever make it work in some financial way. About this time many major national theatre companies with separate financial and artistic boards started having money crunches, and the little guys were faring no better. As theatre production costs soared there was no practical way out except to close the doors, which they reluctantly did. To paraphrase *Pogo*: "We had met the enemy, and it was us."

The Queen of Pentacles deals with building and supporting cooperation. The 1970s were good for the development of food cooperatives, or 'Co-ops', as they were known. Many groups of individuals got together to extend their food-buying power by buying foodstuffs in bulk quantities and then having the co-op individuals themselves repackage or distribute it, doing the work in exchange for saving money. Properly handled, some of these co-ops became small markets able to sell to non-members. The fragile nature of such businesses depends on the individuals who comprise it, so when interest lagged, some of these groups disappeared. In her capacity as the Earth Mother (similarities abound between the Empress and the Queen of Pentacles), this Queen seeks the best that an individual has to offer, bypassing their many weaknesses and concentrating on their many great strengths. She knows that by blending people's skills and then balancing all their skills, all will find strength.

Reversed:

The crown falls off, the Pentacle rolls away, and the harvest goes to seed. With so many things going wrong at once, it is hard to know the next best thing to do while you are waiting to exhale. Unfortunately, you are going to find that you are unsupported in this instance, so the waiting for someone to come along and help you will be futile. If this also finds you in a group situation, there is no one who will step up to the podium and lead the group out of the quagmire. A lot of creative work and energy is getting wasted because there is no one to know it exists, or cares that it exists. Did you ever find out that something really cool already happened and you didn't know about it until it was over? The same theatre organization mentioned above produced a children's theatre production that I took part in, a small musical that was very creative and entertaining. The two performances one weekend had less than fifty people attend (in a thousand-seat auditorium) because there was no publicity to be seen, much to the cast's consternation. The publicity person (who was a board member) apologized to the cast and crew afterwards; his excuse was - *are you ready?* - 'He was busy.'

On the other hand, you may possibly be *avoiding* support, something men are famous for doing, their machismo and testosterone feeding their pride in 'doing it all themselves.' Are you famous for turning down help? Will another couple of hammers help you get the garage roofed a little faster? Do you expect to gather in your entire harvest unassisted?

Worst Case Scenario: the maverick. Lack of caring or support on the part of others or of himself has created alienation, and alienation usually leads to mistrust. The maverick would never join a group, much less become a member of a team since they hold no trust in teamwork. If he has no choice but to work in a group, he will not support others and become the least effective member, even if he has something valuable to contribute.

THE KINGS

KING of WANDS

KING of CUPS

KING of SWORDS

KING of PENTACLES

King of Wands

KING OF WANDS

The card for the King of Wands includes clues to his personality that his Queen card does not. His throne is in a desert; his crown has flames, and his throne and cape contain salamanders - all symbols of the element of Fire. [Why a salamander that lives on the damp forest floor is always historically the symbol for fire has never been satisfactorily explained to me.] This King is very intelligent, upstanding, and a good leader. He is prone to instant flashes of temperament, but they do not override his personality; when he raises his voice it is to make a point, not to intimidate. He can be strongly opinionated at times but can get his ideas across without browbeating others. The most important thing to remember about him is that he *burns* with this inner fire and he seeks outlets for the fire's release - which gives him the impetus to keep moving and keep doing. As a situation, this King tells of good fortune - possibly from a very unexpected source - coming your way.

This is a card about vitality, stability, and empowerment. Other

Kings might sit around contentedly on their Kingly thrones enjoying being the Lord of all they survey, getting a royal kick out of deciding which peasant should get a cow - not the King of Wands! He understands ceremony and knows the rules that must be followed, but he can't wait to get off that throne and do some white water kayaking! He is in possession of some great physical reserves of strength and power that he can call on in moments of need. He strengthens his kingdom by strengthening himself. In 1961 when JFK became president after years of dusty old men occupying the White House, it was a breath of fresh air for such a young man to be the leader of our nation. When he said we would put a man on the moon and then we would return him safely to the earth - something taken right out of science fiction - we all believed him and worked to make it happen as he had predicted. Did FDR ever inspire others to take daily five-mile walks? This King believes in setting the example for others to follow.

One way to achieve empowerment is to avoid negativity. This does not mean surrounding yourself with 'yes-men' to fawn and fall all over you. You must seek the truth and seek to find all those supporters in whom you can place your trust. Being a King means that you must learn to size other men up quickly and effectively and then remove those who are detrimental to the process, not merely those who oppose your ideas. Control brings stability and stability supports control. Think of Grima Wormtongue sapping the strength of King Theoden in *The Lord of the Rings* and resolve ever letting negative people that gain control over you by letting them feed your fears. Do not let others hold you back.

Knowledge is power; you must become master of yourself before you can be a leader of others, and you will not achieve this by burying your head in the sand. You must learn or relearn to challenge yourself to discover where your own strengths and weaknesses lie. Rising to a self-challenge leads the way to your standing strong against the challenges from others. Knowledge is obtainable from many sources, so do not limit yourself in any regard. Strengthen your mind and body and meet your challengers head-on.

<u>Reversed:</u>

Being knocked headfirst into hot, dry sand is a rude awakening for anyone, and when this King's temperature starts to rise, he loses control of his mannered way to speaking and thinking. Soon embarrassed by his facedown situation he does not think about composure or formulating a game plan - he starts swinging that wand around at anyone who comes close enough to him, seeking to knock them to the ground. He will waste a lot of time trying to beat others into submission, most often overpowering them by surprise, or just knocking them out cold. This hard stance drains him of his strengths, and he realizes it, too. However, rather than try to conserve or rebuild his strengths he allows himself to become more drained by the attack process.

With his head in the sand, the little voices of the salamanders reach his ears and fill his head with negative influences. These naysayers sap his strength and invade his reason and he starts listening to those he once would not have trusted to give him the correct time of day. At last insecurity starts to build and the more untruths he is told the more he starts to believe them. What this King needs to do is shake the sand from his ears and eyes and pick himself up, dust himself off, and regain his throne. His advisors tell him otherwise.

The reversal of this card can also indicate that situations are not as stable as they were once considered, or that the bases of stability were not as strong as they were surmised to be. This card can appear as a warning that the status quo has become too complacent and there could be an unexpected shakeup could be in the works, externally or internally. Once again, knowing this ahead of time can lead you to research and rethink or at least make you aware that no detail is too small to be ignored. Even when you have hand-assembled the best team you can, it does not mean you can sit back and relax without checking things on your own from time to time.

<u>Worst Case Scenario</u>: not challenging the self. Being a leader is always tough job because someday, somewhere, someone is going to challenge you and you have to be prepared to defend yourself or your beliefs, sometimes more than once. Some men thrive on this; many do not. The ones that do are usually military tacticians; the ones who do not are usually couch potatoes. It is time to stop being another armchair warrior and to stop living vicariously through the lives of others. Get up - get out - go do! If you can be content by living life in your living room, playing bingo once a week, or get most of your activity by paying your rent, then someone needs to come in and kick your butt.

King of Cups

KING OF CUPS

The King of Cups deals with Intuition (his Queen deals with Inspiration.) His throne has been depicted as being by the water, but in reality his throne is floating calmly upon a turbulent sea indicating a troubled subconscious. In spite of the churning seas about him, he is in fact serenely bobbing along wherever the tide takes him - in fact, he almost looks as though he is out enjoying himself. He is following his feelings - or not fighting them - and letting things either work out or waiting until the situation wears itself out. After all, you can't make plans about what to do when you hit dry land when there's no dry land in sight! At times, many current events sweep you up and carry you along whether or not you wished to participate in them; the important thing is to be swept along but not become part of the aftermath.

Another aspect of his personality is that deep inside he could be very frightened about the situation he finds himself in, but he very good at not letting his emotions show- like an old poker player hiding how good his hand is. His intuition guides him along and he makes many decisions based solely on his intuition. He is a man of 'first impressions,' so make sure you always put your best foot forward. If you try to con him or deceive him, he will see right through you since he is an expert at reading body language - he's an expert at controlling his! If you are a King of Cups, you listen to that inner voice of yours quite a lot, whether it's telling you which is route to take home, or which horse to bet on in the third race!

The King of Cups deals with emotional loyalty and devotion; if a loved one upsets him one day, he knows that everyone is prone to peaks and valleys and does not let one spike ruin everything. Calmly floating around on the ever-churning sea is better than capsizing the boat - and his inner voice tells him that, too. It should not be mistaken that he is somehow blind or deaf to the proceedings or is ignoring things in hopes that they will 'go away' - blind he is not! His Cup indicates the King has full emotional involvement in the situation. His inner voice tells him when he should get involved and when it is time to come forward to aid in a situation. He is not aloof - like the King of Swords - he is very much a part of what is ongoing. He is the hero who swoops in at just the right moment and rescues you from your problems. Did you think he would just leave you dangling? Not him - he has too much emotional time invested to let it go to waste.

A situation represented by this King indicates that the given situation will be received favorably at this time, particularly if it is artistic in nature. There may be a few bumps getting it there, but do not let any setbacks deter you from moving forward.

Reversed:

OOOPS! The seas get too choppy, spilling you off your throne into the drink. Rather than rising above your emotions you have been immersed into them and you don't like what you find. Your throne kept you safe from all those suppressed emotions and repressed feelings and now that you find yourself one-on-one with them you see that you were deceiving yourself - and there's really no easy way out as you scan the horizon desperately looking for a rescue ship. All those fears you have, all those lies you told to cover your back, all those vicious things you said when you had a bug up your ass - all come back to haunt you. Your intuition deserts you and it is now the rescuer that must get rescued.

What could have led you to this sorry demise? The King of Cups is not ignorant, but in reversal his powers of reasoning are compromised. Even calm people have troubles picking away at them for which they learn the best ways to improve a bad situation. This reversal may indicate that instead of doing the homework and finding out the best way to deal with projected outcomes that you might have chosen to mask your thoughts. This may have been done to 'save face,' to hide a deception you have perpetrated on others (which they just figured out, despite your best efforts), or because telling a boldface lie was easier that revealing an ugly truth. Masking your thoughts (and emotions) was an act of treason against yourself, and that great white shark sneaks up to bite you in two.

<u>Worst Case Scenario:</u> total disregard of your insights. It has been said that the American voter does not vote to support a candidate but that they vote for the lesser of two evils. Every party has its rabid supporters in whose eyes their candidate can do no wrong. The candidate you elected changes his platform once when he gets into office. {When Batista was overthrown, many of Fidel Castro's supporters were shocked to find out they were becoming Communists - he never told them *that*.} Did you not see these things ahead of time? My father had a favorite election saying: "Re-elect Nobody." Once someone has served a term of office it's time to move him or her along. My hometown sent two sitting mayors to prison in ten years - both of them in their second or third term. Can someone in such a public seat of power be so stupid? Oh - our governor resigned that year, too. I guess that taking bribes is against the law - isn't it? When all the indicators tell

you not to sail your luxury liner through an ice field it is not the time to gun your engines. That warning klaxon, red flag waving, or feeling that fist in your guts are real clues that something is very wrong somewhere and you should be paying more attention, no matter what the picture on the surface shows you.

King of Swords

KING OF SWORDS

This somber King is drawn with a rather vacant stare. In some decks he is stern with a furrowed brow, but he never looks you directly in the eye. Somewhere in his mind big wheels are turning, wars are being won, and answers are being sought. This King is not absent-minded; he is deep in thought and it may take a bit on your part to remove him from his reverie. This is probably his most frustrating feature. Many people get angry with him for they see him as unfeeling as a marble statue, a poor communicator, or even someone who just doesn't give a damn. Emotional outbursts from you get you nowhere and he keeps looking right through you while you rant.

The saving grace of this King is that you are far from the truth in your assumptions. The King of Swords is a careful and calculating thinker, very analytical in what he does and is very detailed in how he goes about it. The mind beneath that crown is whizzing along at computer speed running calculations, scenarios, and probable outcomes. He wishes to give you only the best and most qualified answer that he can, and he is unwilling to give you bad advice. So, rather than speaking his mind and giving you false hope or an incomplete answer, he doesn't say *anything.* This personality quirk drives most people to distraction. This is the King of purposeful but impassioned thinking, and as a situation he represents a time for clear thinking without haste.

But what happens if this card represents <u>you</u>? You are possibly being asked to become more analytical about what you do or are anticipating doing. Many times throughout this book you've heard me talk about 'doing your homework' and quite realistically most people are very superficial about researching something. We make millions of split-second decisions every day, some without even realizing them. We buy a car by its price, styling, and color after driving it once around the block. How does it handle packed with adults? How many people have bought an SUV to find it doesn't fit in their garage? The King of Swords tells you to take enough time to look at your past mistakes and to avoid them. Slow down! Stop rushing through big decisions as though you get 'extra credit' for speed. More than simply avoiding past mistakes, he tells us to pay some more attention to the anticipation of the future. There is a Native American saying about considering the effect of our actions upon the next seven generations. One of past my supervisors (who is less than half my age) once told me about his future plans for he and his girlfriend to whom he was pre-engaged. It was amazingly detailed from where they will work to what they anticipate making to when to get married and what kind of house they wanted and how long they would have to work to pay it off. Each of these planned steps included how many years that it would take. There were even new cars and a child included in these plans, and when they could retire. When he was finished, I said that the plans were fantastic, but he forgot to factor in *living* into his plans. What would a long term illness do to these plans – or a house fire – or another recession? Perhaps John Lennon was right when he said: "Life happens while you are making other plans." Learn to make other plans.

Prediction - is that possible? {It must be or you wouldn't be reading this book!} Prediction is actually a part of a cycle - not a separate entity. This cycle includes anticipating the future, taking charge of the present, and creating the future. Using Tarot cards can show you many possibilities for what is ahead. You can accept them as they lay, anticipate those which please you, and change those that don't fit into your plans or that you simply find unacceptable. Sometimes you just don't blab your every move to the world at large. Sometimes you have to learn to keep that big mouth shut.

Reversed:

The statue has been pulled from his pedestal, lying on his side like an ancient temple soon to be buried by the sands of time. The truly comatose do not react to changes in their environment, and instead of anticipating you merely drift aimlessly along like a leaf on the surface of the water going wherever the current does or doesn't take you. You make no efforts to move independently or think for yourself. If you were incommunicado before the fall, you are worse after it. Reversal sometimes does not improve a bad situation - it just exacerbates it.

The other side of the reversal coin is that you have been put into a situation where you feel powerless against the will of others. You have decisions and opinions that you cannot make heard or are being ignored by those around you. Try as you might, you are continually stifled and eventually your resolve deserts you and you become another faceless worker in *Metropolis*.

Worst Case Scenario: not anticipating. Certainly Life has a deck of unpleasant surprises for which there is no immunity, but remember that you will never make it out of this Life alive. By the time you've reached forty years of age, you know that you have to accept what Life hands you and try to make the best of it. {Sounds like *Fiddler on the Roof*!} However problematic the things are out there in the jungle are, some people develop this Pollyanna fixation that Voltaire wrote about in *Candide* - that since this is the *only* possible world that it follows that this must be the *best* of all possible worlds. Candide and his hapless companions tumble through the story facing ravaging hoards, flogging at the hands of the Spanish Inquisition, rags and riches - and believe that no matter how bad it gets that everything happens for the best possible reason! At his wittiest, Voltaire was being comically sarcastic. Drifting unscripted through life is the shortest route to disaster.

The King of Pentacles

KING OF PENTACLES

The King of Pentacles sits on a throne containing symbols of the Taurus bull (his ruling sign), grapes showing a bountiful harvest, a stone wall indicating physical security and his Pentacle indicating financial security. Time has obscured the details of the original RWS drawing {what's his foot resting on? An armadillo? I turned it into a pile of books.} But there is usually it armor similar to the Emperor's that he wears under his robes to show the World that contentment comes from vigilance and is not happenstance. This is a card about prosperity. If you were to combine the Emperor and the Ten of Pentacles cards, they would produce this card - situation-wise. There are many notable similarities between the Emperor and the King of Pentacles and sometimes in a reading they are interchangeable.

The prosperity of this card comes not from knowing what you desire, but from knowing what you have, counting your blessings, and appreciating each one. Although financial security seems to be what we most desire, recall that the Pentacles also deal in non-material wealth as well. Some men are always looking to be the first to acquire the newest this, the biggest that, as though possessions count for everything (also a Taurus characteristic - materialism) and he who dies with the most toys wins. Remember - he who dies with the most toys - dies anyway. For some men, their wealth is measured in the quality of life that they can or have provided for their loved ones; after all - you can't take it with you. There are few big emotional displays this King; he will buy a gift or perform a service to show you the things he does not express in words.

One reason for this prosperity has to do with pursuing reasonable expectations and goals, keeping your eyes on the prize and keeping your feet on the ground. This King is a careful and methodical thinker, so rather than blindly seeking vertical achievements, this King tends each asset, spends them wisely, and provides them a space in which to grow. He is the King of pragmatic understanding and pleasures; however, the Taurus influences of being a fixed Earth sign keep him grounded and close to home. Taurus also prevents him from taking big chances or making hurried or unnecessary changes. There will be times when money does burn a hole in his pocket, but what he buys are objects of beauty or ones that will enhance his surroundings and give joy to others and to him. Yes, he can be a real homebody most of the time, but when you have your cherished family around you why go jetting off to Majorca or Rome?

Most importantly, this King deals with acceptance of limitations imposed by himself or situations. It's great to have a lot of goals, ideas and hopes for the future. After all, what else is there to look forward to except the future? However, a wise man knows that there comes a time when you have to size things up, make a few necessary although possibly unhappy decisions, and move to the next step. Sometimes that step may be a plateau and accepting that plateau may be part of the great scheme of things. Mr. Taurus says "O.K. - since I am going to be here for a while, what can I do to best spend the time?" Do not mistake that complacency for being lazy!

As a situation, the appearance of this King in your spread can represent success in some worldly enterprise. Playing your cards right (no pun intended) can help you to reach this lofty pinnacle. Perhaps it is time to seek a raise or to start one's own business. This King can represent a banker or a lending institution, so perhaps it is time to seek a loan, or receive approval for one. Every man's castle acquires a little dragon-damage now and then, so this may be the time to take 'care of your house.'

Reversed:

Does the analogy of a bull in a china shop spring into your mind? Reversal brings sudden awareness of discontentment and disillusionment and Mr. Taurus goes charging around ready to gore anyone that gets in his way. He wants more, he wants it now, and no excuse will change his mind and no obstacle will hold him or dissuade him from blindly vacillating hither and yon in search of that something that he doesn't know what it is yet. No plans for the future, no goals to be set, only acquisition of material items that he doesn't want, need, or ever intend to use, like the packed crates in Charles Foster Kane's storehouse. He shows no overt discretion in purchases - buying both extravagant objects d'art and the cheapest tchotchkes you'll ever see - only to grow quickly tired of them and throw them out, replacing them with his next newest fixation.

Another imbalance caused by this reversal is the replacement of reasonable expectations with the meeting of demands. You can only expect someone to produce a reasonable amount of work or stretch a dollar only so far. This imbalance turns a supervisor into a tyrant or a boss into an ogre. His interpersonal relationships suffer as he refuses to pay his own way or provide his fair share of the expenses. He grows impatient with others and demands they toe his line or are replaced with others who will. His throne turns him into a couch potato, as he becomes more and more inactive.

Worst Case Scenario: the loss of perspective. The King was once thoughtful, congenial, and kind. He always looked for the best in others, and nurtured those around him, keeping the Big Picture in mind. After all, as King he is responsible for the wellbeing of others, the 'good of the whole,' as it were. Now he no longer knows what he has; in fact, he doesn't even know what's missing at this point, and what's more - he doesn't even give a damn about it.

4 – STUDYING THE CARDS

"Revisionist Tarot"

I shied away from openly using the term 'revisionist'; what mental picture does this term create? Some asked 'why I was out to destroy Tarot.' I am not out to destroy Tarot - I am out to *expand* it. Many Tarot traditionalists (and I include myself in that term) use terms such as 'universal' when they speak about Tarot symbolism. Most of what is accepted as traditional Tarot meanings and symbols are one hundred to five hundred years old, most of it the former. I learned most of these ideals and ideas when I started to study Tarot; now I see how stymied and stifling they can become. I felt it was time for Tarot to see the light of the twenty-first century, to blow away the accumulated dust of five hundred years, and have Tarot touch base in the real world.

This is not an easy journey, nor do I feel the journey is complete. No matter how universal Tarot is supposed to be, I felt that it was not *keeping up* with the times. There are a great many Tarot decks out there all with their creator's unique vision of Tarot interpretation in artistic areas. However, when I read the little accompanying booklets these artsy or gutsy decks have included in them, I see the lasting tried-and-true one hundred year-old thought patterns are still there. Why are we still stereotyping ourselves? Why do we drape heavy tapestries over airy scenes and obscure them? This is a tactic from Arthur Waite's time where only initiates were shown the path 'to the truth' and blinds were to be set up to confound the uninitiated. Does this sound like something out of the late Victorian era? It sure is, and Waite, and a few other occult writers who were alive and writing at that time let such ideas permeate their work and perpetuate the same idea: confuse them and only the truly interested will stick it out long enough to learn what they came seeking. {Waite was a member of one of the most secretive yet influential occult societies ever created - The Hermetic Order of the Golden Dawn.}

When I started to study Tarot at the end of the twentieth century, even with the plethora of books, shops, decks, online availability and occult practitioners around me I found it was a 'stumble and search' type of learning atmosphere. I stumbled and searched and eventually I developed my theories and personal understandings and was able to transform them into realty by teaching classes and writing and publishing a book about it. During that process I started to realize that something was boiling under the surface. Most Tarot books are written by heterosexual women for other heterosexual women, and most of the theory is based on a heterosexual context of living and loving. About this time I was starting to develop an enlarging client base of gay men (and women) and everything the books said - no matter how universal it was intended to be - just didn't apply to my gay clients. It would take a chance meeting with another Tarot author who had similar concepts to bring this into focus - What does traditional Tarot card interpretation tell gay men about their relationships and lives? - Nothing.

How do we rectify this problem? We revise Tarot with a definite plan in mind, deciding on parameters and working within the system. This is why I feel my book is vastly different - and *better* - than other authors who decided, for example, to show how males dominate society so their vision is to remove *all* male symbolism from their deck and replace it with 'more appropriate' symbolism. {In one feminist deck where the creators could not replace the Hierophant card - a card they saw as male domination and an image they needed to keep - they added female breasts to him instead - I don't get it}. I wanted to create a basis for what I wrote and I wanted it to be based on experience - not theory. It is easy to destroy something; that doesn't take talent or time. It is even easier to create a parody of something. It is quite another thing to work on trying to develop concepts and ideas and then working through them, taking notes and then making adjustments as you go. This book is written from my experience, by my using the system in readings, talking with my clients, and a lot of sweat!

I also knew that when I created my revisionist interpretations for the cards that I would have to develop a new way of using them. The standard Celtic Cross layout (included in this book for those interested in trying to use it) is just too many cards to read using my revisionist methods. Less is more! A lot less! That is why in the section on card spreads I found that you need limit yourself to five or six at the most.

So, how does this revisionist Tarot fit in (or not fit in) for the traditional Tarot user? If you are versed in Tarot already, my revisionist ideas will definitely make you stop, think, and hopefully *rethink* what you know. Many readers read with blinders on - they give the same cold reading of the meaning of the card no matter where it is in the spread, what the question is, or who they are reading for. These people are liable to be traumatized by a book like mine. Mae West once remarked that she thought that people who are shocked easily needed to be shocked more often. I couldn't agree more.

There are those with a casual but earnest interest in Tarot and Tarot card reading. These new concepts pose no threat to these readers for they are open enough or creative enough to see that having only one way of looking at things is stifled and detrimental to the process. Perhaps they will learn that they have to learn to see beyond the borders of the card (and Waite's strong influences) and see that any experience shared by two people is still a different experience for each of them. These men and women will be amused by what I write here but will not deny that it is time that someone dared to think differently and write about it.

But what about the person with no Tarot background or understanding to back them up? Won't they be confused to learn 'my system' if they decide that they would like to know more traditional methods? On the contrary, any man gay or straight that picks up this book will start relating to it immediately and will definitely want to also learn more about what traditional Tarot is all about. My concern is that once they see how stifled and/or confusing the 'traditional way' is that they will decide to add the traditional to the revisionist, not vice versa. I seek to help men use Tarot to understand themselves and their world. Once inspired - there will be no stopping them, similar to 'If you build it, they will come.'

*The complete quotation from Doreen Valiente's *The Charge of the Goddess* is:

"And if thou thinkest to seek for me, know thy seeking and yearning shall avail thee not unless thou knowest the mystery; that if that which thou seekest thou findest not within thee, thou wilt never find it without thee."

So, how does all this 'work'?

I am not psychic nor do I pretend to be. People are intrigued when I say this, for they are expecting that I have to morph into Lon Chaney or will start speaking in a fake Jamaican accent in order to do a reading. When people ask me 'how this works' they are usually expecting me to give them some complicated answer involving incomprehensible esoteric principles, having had long studies in a cave with mystic gurus, coming in contact with high voltage wiring, or by my surviving an industrial accident. The truth is - I don't know and neither does anyone else. My favorite theory/explanation concerns the human aura where anything you handle is within your human electromagnetic field and magnetic traces linger on the object. Some people are very good at picking up on this energy - you've seen psychometric stuff done on many television shows with someone's watch or ring. The people who can do this are truly psychic - or are good fakers. In my theory, the person learning the cards leaves his psychic imprint upon them. As he is studying and learning each card he is holding it, saying 'this is a card about X.' Then as he goes through the deck he leaves different but definite imprints on each of the cards. The Querent (the person being read) comes along and seeks a reading, shuffles the cards, and asks a question about X and -Voila! The cards about X get shuffled to the top of the pack to be turned over. [I can also refute this theory because I can take a sealed, unused deck off the shelf, have you shuffle them, and still give you an accurate reading.]

Tarot is based in archetypes {pronounced 'arch-a-types' or 'ark-types'} defined as the original from which everything else is a copy. Psychologists such as Carl Jung believe that we are all born carrying symbols from our cultural past within us. We already have them, understand them, and when we see them in real life we instantly recognize them. Unlike the character of Roy Neary chasing the elusive shape of Devil's Tower in *Close Encounters of the Third Kind,* these symbols cross gender, time, and space. The symbols of an old lady in a tattered cape, the conquering hero on horseback, or the blushing bride all resonate within us whether we live in an ultra-modern city or a Stone Age hut. When we see the symbols flash before us, our memory seeks out what we already understand.

The problem that developed - and one of the other reasons this book came about - is that I started to discover that the 'universal archetype' supposedly inherent in Tarot cards is not as universal as the purists would have us believe. I started finding loopholes and red herrings where others said that they didn't exist. The first time I explored the possibility that men's readings were almost consistently different from women's readings I was 'pooh-poohed' by an "expert." They flatly stated that 'energy is energy; it is not male or female,' by which they were declaring that no one is allowed to think that Tarot is *not* universal. I also discovered that Tarot cards are gender-biased and somewhat racially-biased; the former concerns this book and me. I suddenly found a theory that had me searching for a new set of 'male archetypes' and the searching them out and writing about them would consume the next two years. So, I very carefully but deliberately had to toss those long-held and long-learned ideas aside, forget what I knew and search for female-to-male replacement archetypes. Then I had to make sure that they worked in the real world.

As we work through the sections of the book I provide ideas and stories on which you should think, build upon, and elaborate or personalize. These explanations are based on my own experiences and those of the men for whom I read. So if there are times when you feel that you are still missing something to relate to or I'm stretching a point a little too far, I apologize. You have found a plethora of Broadway show tunes or old movies being referred to in here; if I found something I felt could something better explain or be more articulate than I am, I used it. It's tough to be a pioneer!

BTW – The term 'Querent' – used extensively throughout this book – means 'The One who Queries", or the person that is seeking an answer from the Tarot.

-Illustrator John Mangiapane

5 – SHUFFLING THE CARDS

Before we get into anything else let us talk about the most basic aspect of Tarot cards - shuffling them. Every guy knows how to shuffle cards – right? *Wrong!*

People who are used to shuffling standard playing cards each have their own variation–some lay them out flat on the table and move them around like in "Go Fish." Some do the "casino shuffle," where they split the pack in half and riffle the long edges or two corners together and mix the cards. Some flex the two halves and snap the short edges of the cards together. All of these techniques *do* shuffle the cards together. The most-heard comment from Querents when I ask them to shuffle is "Wow! These cards are *big*!" I tell them to shuffle in whatever way is most comfortable to them.

Used to standard playing cards that have no upright or reversed position, people unwittingly flip part of the deck around—and this is where reversals come from. [Actually, if you take a close look at any card deck they *do* have uprights and reversals built right in to the design- but the Ace of Spades is the Ace of Spades, regardless.] Some readers lay out the cards and then flip the reversals so that the cards are all upright. I get no reversed cards with my particular shuffling technique, but since Querents do, it is best to understand reversed meanings. This is my technique to get no reversed cards:

Go through your whole deck and make sure the cards are all upright. Place the deck in front of you so that the tops of the cards are away from you. Pick up the deck with your left hand so that the tops are at your index finger and the bottoms are at your thumb. Lay the deck on its left long edge.

With your right hand take approximately half the deck and separate that half by sliding the cards along the table – similar to closing a sliding door; the tops of this half of the deck will be at your right thumb and the bottoms at your right index finger. Do not spin this half of the deck around! [You would be surprised how many people do]. Flex the deck, and riffle the "thumb" ends together. Push the two halves of the deck together. Congratulations! You now have shuffled the deck without turning half the deck over to be reversed! Do this as many times as feels comfortable. No matter how many times you do it, the tops are at your left index finger and the bottoms will be at your left thumb. When you are through, place the deck in front of you.

This is where the next mistake is usually made--card orientation. Do you flip the cards over side-to-side as though you are turning pages in a book, or do you flip them over top-to-bottom? When you shuffle my way, *always* turn the cards over side-to-side to preserve their upright positions. If you flip them over end-to-end, you will reverse all the cards. In fact, try this both ways right now and see what happens.

Think about this: if you are reading for someone and the Querent hands you back the deck and you flip them end to end, you are reversing all the cards *including* the reversed ones: is this what you want to do? Reason says do whatever you have been doing all along, since it is what works for you. That may be true if you are reading for yourself-- the cards will give you the answer you need. However, since the shuffling of Querents can vary widely, you may be better off telling them "hand me the cards with what you consider the top to be facing me." This way you will have the deck in correct orientation. You may or may not cut the deck; it is a personal preference. If you do, tradition suggests you cut the deck with your left hand to the left; the number of piles is irrelevant. You or the Querent can take the piles to reassemble the deck.

Now you are ready to do a spread and conduct a reading!

6 – USING TAROT SPREADS

This book is decidedly different from other Tarot books you may have seen or read before. If you are familiar with a Tarot deck, the illustrations I have chosen are very normal; only the interpretations of the cards are vastly different in this book. All you will really need to do is shift your regular way of thinking to incorporate what I have written here. You can still use any spread you are familiar with and still enjoy yourself without any major problems.

We are all familiar with the stereotyped image of a card reader using piles of cards and flipping them over, reading them on the fly. Some spreads use 10 or more cards, some use the entire deck in a single reading! Quite truthfully, the more cards you use the more information you can gain, but sometimes these large spreads overwhelm you with too much information, particularly when you are just starting out. To utilize the interpretations in this book we will have to modify how we use the cards: bear with me while I sidetrack -

I read Tarot cards in some way, shape, or form <u>every single day</u> - and that is a lot of cards. If I were to do a seventy-eight card reading for myself every morning or any time I had a question, there would be little time left to do anything else. Every day we meet many challenges, but not every one of these challenges needs the Encyclopedia Britannica to get the necessary information needed to answer a question, resolve a problem, or clarify a situation. Quite truthfully, since the card interpretations in this book do not follow traditional pathways, to use them in traditional spread situations such as a ten-card Celtic Cross Spread simply may not work! These cards are being reinterpreted for men and a man's point of view and do not conform to such 'tried-and-true' outmoded ways of using them. These cards break with tradition and the spreads that use them should do likewise. Let us start at the beginning with a single card.

A single card? What can a single card do for you? Sometimes you do not need a roadmap but only a correct direction signal. Many people use a single card upon waking up or retiring for the night. Many of these same people ask the same question in some form every day, such as "What do I need to know about this day?" "What challenge will I face this day?" or "Answer my thoughts about today." They shuffle the cards and cut, and then turn over their single card to reflect on. Some people merely leave it on their dresser (or desk) where they can glance at it when necessary; one student placed theirs in a Lucite frame, another liked to carry the card with them in a pocket all day. Someone suggested those small metal place card stands like they use in restaurants to hold their card up; do whatever works best for you.

Other people perform this ritual shortly before they retire, usually asking something such as "What is the lesson I learned today?" or "How did I meet today's challenge?" Regardless of which method, what time of day, or what question you ask - write the card and its meaning in a journal! Keeping a journal will help you to keep track of patterns passing through your life.

Back to the single card --

You have innocently asked the cards to tell you about the day ahead of you, and you turn over something 'drastic' such as the Tower card. Does this mean that today is going to be a total disaster? That you are going to get fired from your job today? Is someone is going to scratch the paint on your new car at the shopping mall? Settle yourself down and take a good look at this card. Contrary to incorrect popular belief, these 'drastic' cards DO NOT and CANNOT cause these things to happen, nor can they pave the way for nasty things to come into your life. Tarot cards are paper, some colored ink, and a light coating of plastic: they do not have magical powers. A card such as the Tower popping up is to give you a warning that things today may not be hunky-dory. If you are being warned to be careful, will you not proceed with caution as you go about your day? Hiding under your bed with your balls tucked between your legs is not the way to go either. Warnings are usually just that - warnings, and nothing else. Perhaps having the foreknowledge that the road may not flow smoothly will help you adjust to the smaller problems that crop up or even to help you ignore the minor inconveniences.

Or-

Today really *sucked* and you had pulled a 'goodness-and-light' card, such as the World. How do you reconcile a situation like this? This card may have appeared to help you keep your spirits up in the face of distress. What about the converse situation: your picture-perfect day is summed up in a seemingly negative card such as the Seven of Swords. Does this signify a probable bad ending to your otherwise perfect day? No- it is a statement that you should look back over your day and review it. Perhaps you were so caught up in yourself that you missed the opportunity to help someone else out of his or her problem.

Using one card a day is also a good way to learn the individual cards. You can study this card, learn about it, write about it in your journal, and see how you can apply it to yourself. Soon, however, once you get a hang of the cards you will find a need to expand yourself into two-card or three-card readings. The easiest two-card reading uses the first card upright (or reversed) and the second card lying across the first on its side. This is known as a 'Cover and Cross' spread. The types of questions best answered by this spread deal in wanting to know 'a tad more' about the depth of something. An example would be "Tell me how my day will go today and what challenge (or obstacle) I will face."

You shuffle and cut the deck and lay out the two cards, the first (upright) being the situation, and the second (crossing it) being the challenge to face or obstacle to be overcome.

For example, the two cards you chose today turn out to be #1 - the Fool crossed by #2 - the Emperor. The Fool card tells us that the day should run fairly smoothly and present many opportunities, some not looked for. The Emperor crossing the Fool tells us to be aware of others, particularly those in positions over us. The reading says that while it may be a great day - don't forget to perform your duties, particularly when the boss is hanging around! Once again- forewarned is forearmed.

Two-card readings turn into three-card readings rather easily. My daily personal reading is a three-card reading and it gives me a lot of leeway about what the position of each card could represent. Most people see a three-card reading as an easy 'Past, Present, Future' (or PPF) spread. It gives us enough information to feel satisfied that the question was answered without overwhelming us with a ton of additional cards. It is an easy spread to use when using your cards to read for a group of people - such as a party - when you don't want to weigh yourself (or others) down with a lot of extraneous baggage.

Readings are easy and fun! Shuffle and cut the cards and spread the top three out Left to Right; left being the Past, center is Present, right being the Future.

A second variation of the PPF spread is referred to as a situation-action-outcome spread. Shuffled and laid out in exactly the same pattern, the first card will represent the Querent's current life situation. The second card is the action the Querent could possibly take (or is thinking about taking). The third card is the result or the consequence of taking that action. Some readers use both of these three-card spreads in tandem, particularly if the PPF spread has a questionable ending or the Querent is unhappy with what is revealed. Used in this manner, it might be possible to see where an unhappy outcome can be avoided by changing a future action.

My personal favorite is three cards in the shape of a pyramid, #1 and #3 the base and having #2 as the peak.

Diagram 1

Card #2 **Peak**

Card #1 – **Beginning**   Card #3 - **Ending**

These can be read as #1 - the Beginning of your day, or what to concentrate on in the morning, #2 the Peak of your day, or the main theme for your day, and #3 the Ending of the day, or the type of closure. Having worked with this spread for years, it turns out that in <u>my</u> daily reading the first card pertains to my day before I arrive for work (I work swing shift - 3:30 to midnight). Peak card #2 tells me what I can expect when I arrive to work, or what the major component of my day is going to run like. Card #3 usually refers to the end of my day, though not necessarily referring to when I clock out at the office. I have found this spread to treat my day very accurately. Sometimes I may not agree with what card #3 tells me, but Peak #2 (what <u>awaits</u> me at work) is *unfailingly* accurate! I have passed this information on to coworkers even though it really only does pertain to me. {PS - some people will find it *and you* very annoying if you constantly walk in and tell them how their workday is going to run- particularly when you are accurate! Only volunteer this information if asked!}

Remember how the single card turned into a two-card Cover and Cross Spread? The next step up for the three-card PPF is the six-card Cover & Cross spread that follows the development of a situation. Shuffle and ask the question; lay the first three cards upright left to right #1, #2, and #3, as shown below. Lay card #4 across #1, card #5 across #2 and card #6 across #3. Interpret this spread as:

#1 the past

#4 as the recent past

#2 as the present

#5 as the challenge you are facing

#3 as what you will do

#6 as the result or outcome

Diagram 2

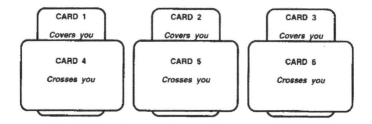

Surprise! Almost all spreads are variations on some version of these!

Creating Your Own Spreads

There is nothing to stop you from creating your own spreads off the top of your head. Start with a purpose: what kind of question do you have and how many cards do you feel it will it take to give you an answer? Let us say you want to know how things are going, but you want to know how the past, present, and future are influencing each other. The present and the outcome make two cards, so what else would you like to know? What influences may be coming in and leaving the picture? What about unknown interference? That makes five cards.

Next, you could lay them out in a straight line, but that's boring! Life is circular, so maybe a circle is the best layout. You might come up with something like this:

Diagram 3

#1 the current situation

#4 the emerging
influence

#5 synthesis of the
previous four cards

#2 the waning
influence

#3 the hidden influence

From *Power Tarot* by MacGregor and Vega, this is called the Wheel Spread, and my clients and my students find it very useful because it gives sufficient information without overpowering them. Interpreting the final card as a synthesis of the previous four can be tricky, but we all found it very accurate.

But why or how does creating a new spread *work?* It will work because you have made the decision about how many cards to use, and what each one will tell you in its placement; you are going into the shuffling with this thought in mind. The answers you seek will fall into place; this is why it's a good idea to record such observations in a journal. You may become so adept at using your own spreads that you might never use any of the other hundreds of recognized spreads out there. No one universal spread is appropriate for all occasions.

With some questions, there can be two options and/or two outcomes. People who are unsure of which way to proceed usually ask these types of questions. The Horseshoe layout can help in such situations, and it's also another spread that uses only six cards. A typical question that uses this spread is: "Should I stay with my present employer *or* should I look for a new job?" Here, the Querent wants to find out about the future with the present employer, and also whether changing jobs will be a good choice or a mistake. Shuffle, ask the question, and then lay out six cards in this order:

The Horseshoe Layout

Diagram 4

| **Future** | Card #5 | Card #6 |

| **Present** | Card #3 | Card #4 |

| **Past** | Card #1 | Card #2 |

Although you lay the cards out #1-6, you read up each arm separately, # 1, 3, and 5 being the first side of the question (staying with current employer in the above question), and #2, 4, and 6 being the alternative (what can be expected if a new job is taken). Of course, in this question I doubt if the new employment can really have a "past," but it probably could be read as the "past" the Querent brings along to the new job.

Using more cards: **The Celtic Cross Spread**

Here is the great-granddaddy of all Tarot spreads and the one even non-Tarot people may be familiar with through movies and television. Time has brought many revisions; some variations have 9 to12 cards, but we are going to stick with the basic 10. As I have said earlier - this spread gives a helluva lot of information and is not suitable for everyone to use for every question. I do not feel it is in the best interest for new readers to try to use it until they have an established working knowledge of the cards.

First off, there is the question of the need for a Significator card chosen to personify the person being read for by matching physical or other characteristics of the Querent to the character in the card illustration. I seldom use a Significator card for I feel that to remove any card from the deck could be detrimental to the reading. Since the Significator card is not read, what if that card represents something the Querent should know, and you're now removing it? Phyllis Vega's (*Power Tarot*) slant is that you choose a Significator to represent the Querent or something in their life and *return* it to the pack, then shuffle and deal as normal. If it appears in the spread, you will know that it relates to the person or situation in the question. If that statement confuses you - you are in good company. Do you now understand why I don't bother with a Significator?

In the Celtic Cross Spread, the Significator is placed in the center of the table, and card #1 is placed over it; this is why many books call the first card the "Cover" card, since it is what covers you. The second card is placed sideways over the first (what "crosses" you). In the traditional layout, cards 3, 4, 5, and 6 are usually laid out so that the spread looks like this:

Diagram 5

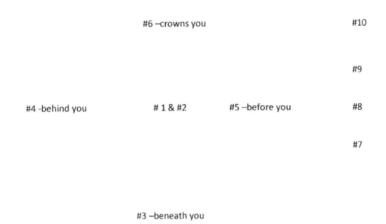

Card #3 is what is beneath you, or the basis of the question—in other words the entire past.

Card #4 is what is behind you—the recent past.

Card #5 is what is before you— either the present or the very near future.

Card #6 is above the Significator and is what "crowns" you—the future.

Cards 7-10 are placed up one side of the reading with #7 at the base and #10 at the top. These are sometimes called the Scepter or the Wand.

I have my own variation of the Celtic Cross based on the readings I do for the public. I find that most readers sit opposite the Querent, so the Querent sees the reading upside-down. I seat the Querent next to me. The placement of cards #3-6 tended to confuse the Querent, so I simplify it and run the Scepter up the side closest to the Querent. I found that running the cards in this style made it simpler for the Querent to understand or remember what I was reading and saying.

Diagram 6

#3- the first conclusion

#10

#6 –the future and
second conclusion

#1 & #2

#4 –the past

#9

#8

#5 – the present

#7

In my Celtic Cross variation:

Card #1 is the *question* or what the question is all about. I never ask Querents their question ahead of time; I feel that would influence my interpretation of their answer. I say to them, "The first card deals with _____." At the conclusion of the reading I ask them if the reading had anything to do with their question. I have found that 90 per cent of the time this card reveals what they were asking about, even though they may deny it at first. {When you peg the question dead-on with their first card, it sometimes unsettles people who are expecting you to give them bullshit.}

Card #2 - the Crossed card. Here we find an influence, challenge, or obstacle, and it might be positive *or* negative; after all, this card is *sideways,* neither upright nor reversed. It has a direct effect on card #1, and the combination of these two cards leads us directly to card #3.

Card #3 - the First Conclusion card. I feel that the Celtic Cross has three distinct conclusions: sometimes all point in the same direction, and sometimes they seem to be in disharmony with each other. This first conclusion is about to happen or is currently happening.

Card #4 - the Past card. Time in Tarot is relative. The past is anything that led up to the previous moment, not necessarily something that goes back to early childhood. The past could be everything up to the time the Querent came to you for a reading!

Card #5 - the Present card. The present could be both here and now or in the immediate future, since time moves forward. This card tells you what is going on in the Querent's life in regard to the question.

Card #6 - the Future or Second Conclusion card. The first conclusion card dealt with the outcome or the future on a short-term basis. Now that you know the past and present, this second conclusion card reveals the next step—how these events impact each other and what result can be expected. Querents may not like what is being revealed! It is important to remember that the cards are showing the future if events are not altered in some way and the situation allowed proceeding unaided or unhindered. Carl Jung wrote that Tarot is of the moment; it reveals what is and what will happen if the situation remains unchanged.

As for the final four cards: I have always felt that Cards 7 and 8 need to be read in tandem with each other since they reveal two sides of the same coin.

Card #7 - the Internal, or how the Querent perceives the situation—not their hopes and fears (that's card #9)--but rather how the situation is impacting them. To understand this further, let's go to card #8 and read them together.

Card #8 - the External, or how others around the Querent see the situation. These two cards can be shockingly opposed. The Querent may be in a bad relationship and feel unloved (internal), but the face put on to the world (external) may be a true Oscar-winning performance. Also, card #8 reveals only what the world *sees,* and it could very well be getting it wrong. Many interesting revelations come from these two cards together. What you say and do --and how it gets interpreted--are two different things.

Card #9 - the Hopes and Fears card. Regardless of how the Querent feels (card #7), this card describes the Querent's projection of the final outcome, realistic or not. Generally, a positive card is a Hope and a negative card is a Fear; however, the important thing to remember is that this card is usually an illusion. Perhaps all the cards so far have been supportive or positive and this one is a "clinker." For example, the card reveals he is afraid the mortgage request will not be approved. The Hopes and Fears card is transitory at best. It is the stepping stone to the Final Outcome.

Card #10 – the Final Outcome card. Herein lays the answer, if nothing is done to alter the events that lead to it. Regardless of the two prior conclusions, this one gives you the answer to the question, the final outcome.

What if conclusions #3 and #6 were great and #10 comes up The Tower card? How do you handle the situation? What if *all* the cards in the reading are clear sailing and the final card blows them out of the water? It can happen. Regardless of the spin you put on the other cards, a lousy final outcome may still be waiting--you may not be able to sidestep it. If this happens (and it has), I truthfully tell the Querent that while the situation in the present *seems* to give them what they want, perhaps they are overlooking something and in the long run it may not produce the results they expect. To get such a drastic "slam" is a wake-up call to review the present situation more carefully.

ASKING THE QUESTION

I keep talking about 'asking the question' but have not addressed the fact that the correctly worded question is a very important part of conducting a reading. What? You just grab your deck, think of a question, shuffle, lay out the cards, and *BADA BING!* read your answer... don't you? It looks that way, but it is not quite that simple. The way you ask the question and its specific wording are very important. The clearer your question is the better chances you will have of getting a clear answer. Much of it will depend on the situation that brings a Querent to a reading, but also the environment in which the reading is being done.

When people make contact for a reading, they probably come with a question in mind; this is true of most one-on-one readings. However, I do a lot of 'public' or group readings such as a party. In a group situation many of the people I read for give me a quizzical look when I ask them if they have a question and say, "I can't think of one!" This is *not* a good basis for starting a reading. Then again, some people are surprised that they have to touch the cards at all--don't you as the reader have 'all the answers'? Some people simply blank out when put on the spot. A one-on-one reading is a serious matter; a "cattle-call" generally results in less important matters. I usually guide the clueless into a general question that has a time limit, such as, "Tell me about my life for the next twelve months," or "Give me an overview of my job for the next fiscal quarter." People in a group may be interested in some information, but are mostly looking to be entertained.

But what happens when you're reading for yourself? What type of questions should you ask? Although the sky is the limit, I find that Tarot has certain limitations and does not deal well with the following:

Yes/No questions--If you can answer the question with only a yes or a no, flip a coin instead. Tarot deals with the past, present, and future, and Yes/No doesn't work based on any background information. If you find you tend to ask this type of question: Should I quit this job --Y/N?, think about wording it differently. For example: Will my job conditions improve or modify in the coming two months? This will allow the Tarot to speak about past, present, and future conditions necessary to answer the question.

Frivolous questions--Most people don't know if they are supposed to believe you or not, if you actually have some psychic connection, or are merely making things up. In a party situation you will always find someone who will be skeptical, obnoxious, rude, or try to make you come off as a fool. Do not degrade yourself by wasting your time or knowledge on such people. Be serious, be professional—give them a quick 3-card reading and get them away from you. When you start getting asked questions such as, "Should I dye my hair purple?" -- pack up your cards and take a break.

Open-ended questions--Beware the open-ended question! Be specific! Ask a question with a specific time frame: "Will we have enough money in two years to be able to move from this house?" not "Will I ever have a million dollars?" The future is not written in stone (you'll hear a reader say this many times); you affect your future constantly. No one can give you an accurate prediction about 20 years or more from now – there are too many variables in such a time span. (Incidentally, the question "Am I going to die?" is an open-ended question, but the answer is "Yes. We all must die sometime.")

Run-on questions--This is a variation on the open-ended question: "Will I meet the person of my dreams and get a married and live in a house with 2 dogs with a white picket fence and what will their names be and am I getting laid this weekend?" What is the real question here?

Tarot deals best with questions concerning situations, challenges, improvements, and of course, outcomes. These are questions that ask **who, what, where, when, why, how** and also **Will I, Can I, and Am I.**

Who can help me overcome my financial problems?

What would be the benefit of _____ at this time?

Where will I be in _____months?

When will my ship come in? **Am I** prepared for it?

Why am I dreaming about tropical climates?

How does _____ feel about us/me?

Will it help me to apply for a job with a rival company?

Will I be able to handle this job effectively?

Can I afford to buy such a large house, or at this time?

Am I going to be successful with this business partner?

Is there a reason that I cannot get ahead? **How can I** change this pattern?

How do I get out of this mess? {*Not* '<u>Will</u> I get out of this mess?'}

7 - LIFE CARDS

It is often discovered - while consulting the cards - that we ourselves stand in the way of our achieving our needs and wants but we are not aware that we are doing it. Reading the Tarot invariably points us toward awareness, spiritual growth and understanding. Another way to use the Tarot is to determine our Life cards-- our soul, personality, and shadow cards—and study and reflect on them. Many seekers find that by working with these cards, they discover invaluable information about themselves.

I have said that Tarot is "of the moment," meaning the moment you shuffled the cards for a particular reading. The next time you ask a question, the cards will be about that particular moment. Since your birth date is an exact moment-- the start of your life-- your Life cards reflect the essence of you-- in this lifetime. You can find them by combining a bit of numerology with the Tarot. Just reduce your birth date to a single digit. Your soul card is the corresponding card from the Major Arcana of the Tarot.

Before we go further, I need to explain something. Tarot and numerology are two completely and separately developed systems, although they do overlap. In Tarot, for example, the number Five deals with instability, but in Numerology, Five deals with freedom and expansion. Once you take a set of parameters of one system and impose the limitations of another system over them, quirks appear. Some need to be accepted at face value; there are only 21 positive numbers in the Major Arcana but an infinite number of possible integers. This results in some birth numbers have three cards, some only two.

Tarot developed over the course of centuries, and the people who manipulated Tarot to their own understanding did not necessarily have a background in "what the numbers are supposed to mean." Numbers are constant; you can "bend" the meaning of a Tarot card more easily than you can make a positive number into a negative one! Hopefully, this somewhat confusing sentence will make more sense as you read on, for numerology is a consuming process, just as Tarot can be, and in this chapter I am limiting our discussion to these two techniques.

For an example of the reduction process, my birth date is May 12, 1955. Adding the digits together 5+1+2+1+9+5+5 = 28, 2 + 8 = 10. 1 + 0 = 1, so my soul card is the Magician. If you wish to check your math, add your birth date up again this way:

```
 05
 12
1955
1972     1 + 9 + 7 + 2 = 19; 1 + 9 = 10; 1 + 0 = 1
```

Our Soul card represents those qualities we aspire to—our soul's hopes, desires, goals, and dreams. It also defines us, the way our astrological signs show us our differences. Our Personality card reflects how we appear to the world. As for the Shadow card-- it represents those qualities we most like to ignore--the bits we don't like about ourselves. Far from being perceived as negative, the Shadow Card reminds us to study, meditate, and reflect upon our actions and Life events. For example, the Star as shadow would indicate a tendency to ignore unconscious signals and to refuse to see the bright side. Basically, if we think in terms of the reversed card meanings for our shadow, we won't go too far wrong. As I said, these cards are for us to study, meditate, and reflect upon.

Enjoy discovering the Life number for all your family and friends!

~

If your Life number is 1, your Soul card is 1--The Magician; your Personality card is 10--The Wheel of Fortune; and your Shadow card is 19--The Sun.

If you have the Soul of a Magician you can make whatever it is you need--or desire to have happen in your life--work out the way you would like. This will take a little planning, a little manipulation, and a lot of determination. Your Personality is the Wheel, which does spin, and Chance sometimes does not fall the way you wish it would. Being a Magician, you should be able to deal with the problems as long as you don't seek to control every situation. The Sun as your Shadow says that you need to look for the "silver lining," even during a downpour (which the Wheel can easily bring you). However, as the Magician, you have the ability to make the situation work, adapt to the changes, and deal with the fearful or pessimistic parts of yourself.

~

If your Life number is 2, your Soul card is 2--The High Priestess; your Personality card is 11--Justice (or Strength); and your Shadow card is 20--Judgment.

With the Soul of a High Priestess your intuitive processes influence everything you do, even unconsciously. You know what people have done before they tell you. This complements your personality, where you seek justice, looking for fairness in everything you do, and in how you deal with the world. This can cause you to seem an enigma to some

317

and truly mysterious to others. The Judgment card as your Shadow, however, cautions you to be careful and not to misuse your abilities or to rush to prejudgment.

NOTE: If you are a Tarot enthusiast you know that in some decks the Justice and Strength cards have changed places and a lot of controversy still exists to this day as to which card is #8 or #11. It is generally accepted that The Hermetic Order of the Golden Dawn changed the order of those cards because they gave the cards astrological attributions; since astrologically Leo (Strength) comes before Libra (Justice) the Golden Dawn changed their order to suit their system. If you feel that Strength is a better attribute of your personality – by all means embrace either or both cards!

~

If your Life number is 3, your Soul card is 3--The Empress; your Personality card is 12-- The Hanged Man; and your Shadow card is 21-- The World.

With the Empress as your Soul card, you are the very essence of the Earth Mother--wishing the best and giving the best to everyone; you are very outgoing in nature. Your Personality of the Hanged Man is a further extension of the Empress: you will go to great lengths to find the "little bit of good" in everyone, and even turn your life or beliefs upside down to accommodate others. The World as your Shadow, though, is a reminder that people will disappoint you from time to time. Accept their faults graciously but don't let them take advantage of you.

~

If your Life number is 4, your Soul *and* Personality cards are both 4--The Emperor; your Shadow card is 13--Death.

With the Soul and Personality of an Emperor, you usually look for the best and strongest to help you in caring for "the good of the whole." You tend to be disciplined, grounded, and practical. You are Shadowed by the Death card that brings changes, but most of these may be used as opportunities for growth and development. Don't be blind to the fact that change is good and development is an ongoing process. The Rock Mountain that you have created will be eroded by time, so plan for the future while maintaining the present. What you build may be lasting, but it cannot be eternal.

NOTE: There are those that will argue that if your receive 22 – which is a Prime Number – that you would never reduce it, and that The Fool – designated #0 is, in fact, the 22nd Major Arcana card. With this aberrancy in mind your Soul would still be the Emperor, your Personality - Death, and your Shadow - the Fool.

~

If your Life number is 5, your Soul *and* Personality cards are both 5--The Hierophant; your Shadow card is 14--Temperance.

With the Hierophant, your Soul strives to maintain what already exists. Your Personality seeks to help others, but is usually conservative in nature and response. Sometimes this behavior makes you anxious because you see the need for expansion, but do not want to take risks. The Temperance Shadow kicks you off your throne and tells you to be more original instead of predictable, to become more active and develop a sense of adventure, because you need to balance your restrictive behavior. The key to your development will be to accept small changes as helpful instead of disruptive.

~

If your Life number is 6, your Soul *and* Personality cards are both 6--The Lovers; your Shadow card is 15--The Devil.

Your Lovers Soul says that you surround yourself with harmony, have passionate ideals, and enjoy the equilibrium that sharing brings to your life. You have an instinctive understanding of what makes things "tick." Your devotion to others is probably the first thing that people notice about you. However, the Devil card, a card of excesses and abuses, Shadows you. You are being warned to be careful of those who will seek to take advantage of your good nature, those who try to manipulate you to their ends. It also warns you not to meddle in the affairs of others under the guise of helping them. Everyone needs to find his or her own balance, so enjoy your friends and hobbies, but do not use love to try to control others.

~

If your Life number is 7, your Soul *and* Personality cards are both 7--The Chariot; your Shadow card is 16--The Tower.

You are passionate, responding to the rhythms of life, jumping in with both feet. You maintain a balance between the intellectual, mystical, and philosophical, cramming more activity into a span of time than those around you, which can confuse and confound them. At times you contradict yourself, embracing both ends of the spectrum but not the center. Those who can keep up with you know that life with you will never be complacent or boring. The Tower as your Shadow means you can become moody or even pessimistic, tending to discard those who cannot maintain your speed or work on your level. It tells you to listen to and even occasionally to obey the wishes of others, for they bring lessons for you to learn. Learn to cooperate with others more often instead of running off to do things your way.

~

If your Life number is 8, your Soul *and* Personality cards are both 8--Strength (or Justice); your shadow card is 17--The Star.

You are a pillar of Strength for those seeking strength and you have an air of justice about you. You are always in control of yourself, and are not unsettled by events that may attempt to chip away at your determined facade. You understand that a few setbacks may be necessary to gain a foothold, but those very capable hands of yours are guided by your very capable intellect. However, the Star warns you against aggression, which may blind you into believing that Strength will conquer all. That mindset would make you zealous, develop militant beliefs, or bring you to greed or a materialistic outlook. Authority should be balanced with justice.

NOTE: If you are a Tarot enthusiast you know that in some decks the Justice and Strength cards have changed places and a lot of controversy still exists to this day as to which card is #8 or #11. It is generally accepted that The Hermetic Order of the Golden Dawn changed the order of those cards because they gave the cards astrological attributions; since astrologically Leo (Strength) comes before Libra (Justice) the Golden Dawn changed their order to suit their system. If you feel that Justice is a better attribute of your personality – by all means embrace either or both cards!

~

If your Life number is 9, your Soul *and* Personality cards are both 9--The Hermit; your Shadow card is 18--The Moon.

Your universal awareness coupled with selflessness and courage show you to be a humanitarian. You have sought the answers in an attempt to find your purpose in life, and you seek to teach others to help them understand the enjoyment of silent meditation, the beauty of a long walk in the woods, or the joys of self-discovery. Solitude is everything to you, so you tend to limit your interaction with others to short though intense moments in time. The Shadow of the Moon crosses your path to remind you that everything is a cycle, and you must sometimes move backward in order to move forward. You need to balance your need for deep thoughts with human interaction, sharing what you have learned with others. In that way all can continue to grow.

8 – YEAR CARDS

You can use the same numerological process to determine the kind of year you will have. Figure your year card the same as you would your Life card, but use the year you want to know about instead of your birth year. Your Year card roughly runs from birthday to birthday but can manifest earlier or later. Unlike the example for your birth number, do not reduce any two-digit number unless the number is 22 or higher, since we want to use the full set of 21 Major Arcana cards. Also, in this exercise, add the numbers in columns, not linearly.

The best example I can provide for this is my own experience with the year 2002. Take my birthday for 05-12-2002 and reduce it in this manner:

    05
    12
    2002
    2019 = 2 + 0 + 1 + 9 = 12 - The Year of the Hanged Man

Well! Let me tell you! That twelve-month period between birthdays lived up to every aspect of the Hanged Man that you can imagine! I literally went nowhere that year. In 2002 I tried to sell the manuscript for my first book, and although I met with enthusiasm--there were even a few takers, the manuscript sat in limbo. At one point I even thought about self-publishing it, but was determined to believe in the strength of my writing. There was nothing I could do but hang there--<u>and</u> hang in there--which is why you can read not only that book but also this one today.

Now—an interesting thing happens. To check my math I added the same date in a line and still got a 12 for 2002:

5 + 1 + 2 + 2 + 0 + 0 + 2 = 12

So logic told me that for the next year all I needed to do was add '1' and the next year (2003) would be 13—Death--the card of changes. Selling the book would definitely bring changes in my life, so a 13 for 2003 seemed right. I was explaining this to my spiritual counselor and she corrected me, saying that I should use only the columnar addition process for the Year Card exercise because:

   05
   12
  <u>2003</u>
  2020 = 2 + 0 + 2 + 0 = **4** --The Emperor! Card of male power.

Now, you can probably argue that both of these cards can and will indicate my future, possibly in tandem. Since 13 does reduce to 4, (even though we are not supposed to reduce a number 21 or less), I am going to take my counselor's suggestion and say that to determine your Year card, add the figures in columns and not in a linear way. (People who study numerology are VERY specific as to what math formula is used to determine which number.) It will be interesting to see how both cards will affect your year.

Create a spreadsheet and plot your life for 100 years and see how things cycle for you; you might be amazed!

9 – AFTERTHOUGHTS

In Chapter 4 of this book where I discussed 'revisionist' Tarot, I did not want to get too far off the subject so early in the project. Many people also asked why I 'just didn't design my own tarot deck' to go along with my revisions. The reasons I didn't do this originally are twofold:

First, I am not an artist. Although I have drawing ability the human figure is not one of my best attributes, so a deck comprised of human figures badly drawn would not exactly be very marketable, although someone did redraw the Rider-Waite deck as stick figures and someone redid the deck as cartoon figures with big noses. Both of these recreations have been moderately successful, but why keep redrawing the deck one more time trying to label it original?

I could have had someone do the artwork for me. In fact, my first book was supposed to have a deck created for it, but the artist was drawn away (no pun intended) by another much more lucrative project. Sure, I could have told him "I want this Queen in a long blue dress with a plunging neckline and a large Celtic border in white along the bottom." He could have whipped it up on his computer software in a jiffy, but how the dress draped and how the hands were held would still become *his* vision, not mine. There would have been a lot of compromises I might not have been willing to make.

I also wanted to create a universal interpretation for men to use. If I had started by creating a deck and began eliminating this symbol or changing that character, I would then be writing a book that applied to that deck only. I wanted a book that would resonate with men and men's feelings, and not just be another book that can only be applied to the artwork of one particular deck.

Secondly, it seems everyone and his brother are creating a new 'theme deck' every week, and truthfully, a lot of them are weak. Although many deck creators have some sort of background in Tarot and its subsequent interpretation, many decks are based around a 'theme,' and sometimes these themes get in the way or become too limiting no matter how great they sound at the beginning. "Let's create a Tarot deck based on *junk food*! The Pages could be .... appetizers! The four suits could be the four food groups!" Yeah-- it sounds like fun - for ten or fifteen cards or so. Many theme decks for sale started out with good intentions and lost steam long before the seventy-eighth card was completed. Parallel to this is the creator who is freaked out by the word 'pentacle' and decided that the Pentacles should become something else less threatening - like cafeteria trays, raspberry berets, or laptop computers. Considering that Pentacles/Coins deal in material wealth, substituting cafeteria trays has nothing to do with that traditional concept, so everything they create to go along with their new suit becomes an intellectual exercise.

{Then again - the Ten of Cafeteria Trays might work well in the *Junk Food Tarot...*}

However – in 2012 I had to amend those thoughts when I decided to reprint my book myself and the owner of the copyright to the images wanted too much money – up front and every three years! It became a matter of necessity and I DID take it upon myself to create these images, imperfect as they are. These images are heavily RWS influenced

(Rider-Waite, or Rider Waite Smith as the deck is sometimes called), so anyone who picks up a RWS or RWS Clone deck should have no problem making some of the connections between the cards, particularly when the RWS image may have been female and I changed it to a male if it wasn't gender- necessary to the card. I obviously could NOT change the High Priestess, Empress, Justice, Star, World, or the Queens. For the 'purists' who only use Thoth or Marseilles (TdM) decks... you will have to cope.

I did try to create consistent characters to go with each Suit, rather than the random ones in most RWS decks. You no doubt may have figured out that the handlebar-mustached Fool and man in the Pentacles suit is I. The Wands Man (Mr. Bear), the Timberline-wearing, khaki-cargo shorted, flannel-shirted man is loosely based on a friend. At one point his flannel was going to be a bowling shirt with flames (he is the element of Fire, after all) but that idea changed. The Swords Man (Mr. Buttondown) represents all the 'Type A' personalities out there; in the Court Cards he sports a tie with clouds (the element of Air). The Cups Man was originally 'Mr. Flattop" but I had difficulty with depicting his hair, and also decided I needed another male in long pants. So Mr. Cups transformed into "Mr. Workout' in sweat pants and a muscle shirt with a Water motif. His long hair became a braid and he ended up looking very Native American – which I think works well! (I do not intend any disrespect to Native Americans.)

So, considering I never intended to design a deck – *I HAD TO!*

    -illustrator John Mangiapane

ABOUT THE ILLUSTRATOR

Author/Illustrator JOHN MANGIAPANE launched his book self-publishing career on Friday, July 13, 2012, and never looked back; publishing his first six books in nine weeks. While developing the concept for his Tarot Book for Men, "Every Man's Tarot: Tarot and the Male Experience" he never imagined that down the road he would end up becoming the illustrator for his book as well. Faced with the financial impossibility of paying annual royalties to someone else for image rights, John sat down and drew the 78 images for his book *in thirty days!* In 2013 he turned those illustrations into a stand-alone deck – "The Everyman Tarot", and in 2014 released a completely colorized version. He converted his card images especially for Harry Vederci to create "The Everyman Tarot – The Bear Edition." All three versions of "The Everyman Tarot" are available online from The Game Crafter. All of John's books are available on Amazon and also on Kindle.

John is the Bear model on the cover.

ABOUT THE AUTHOR

HARRY VEDERCHI is the pen name of an author whose identity must be concealed {PS — he writes children's stories!}. Harry realized in his 30s that he was, indeed, a Bear. He is a member of several gay men's organizations, has appeared on Canadian television, marched in Pride parades, ridden on a float here and there, and is generally known for walking around with a Tarot deck, giving readings wherever he goes.

Made in the USA
Coppell, TX
17 October 2021

64225153R00187